SIMPLIFIED ACCOUNTING FOR THE COMPUTER INDUSTRY

Small Business Management Series
Rick Stephan Hayes, Editor

SIMPLIFIED ACCOUNTING FOR THE COMPUTER INDUSTRY

RICK STEPHAN HAYES
C. RICHARD BAKER

A Ronald Press Publication
JOHN WILEY & SONS
New York • Chichester • Brisbane • Toronto

Library of Congress Cataloging in Publication Data:

Hayes, Rick Stephan, 1946-
　　Simplified accounting for the computer industry.

　　(Small business management series, ISSN
0217-6054)
　　"A Ronald Press publication."
　　Includes index.
　　1. Accounting—Data processing.　　I. Baker, C.
Richard, 1946-　　.　II.　Title.　III.　Series.

HF5679.H35　　　657'-.028'54　　　81-1695
ISBN 0-471-05703-7　　　AACR2

Printed in the United States of America

10　9　8　7　6　5　4　3　2　1

Preface

There have been only three significant innovations in accounting in the past 5000 years. The first innovation (if the shift of media from clay and stylus to paper and pen is disregarded) was the introduction of double-entry accounting in A.D. 1340. The second innovation was the shift from Roman to Arabic numerals fully implemented by the late seventeenth century. The latest innovation is the use of computers in accounting.

The double-entry system has been perfected over the last 700 years, but accounting by computer is barely 30 years old. Unlike the other historic accounting developments, computer accounting is not being implemented by accountants, but by computer programmers and engineers. Because programmers are designing the accounting systems and accountants are auditing them and often changing the rules, there is a great deal of confusion.

This book is designed to make accounting clear to computer personnel and make computers clear to accountants. We do this by using the example of a professional accounting programmer, Kimberly Rogers. The book describes how she sets up accounting software and how she simultaneously learns the basics of accounting. Numerous examples, forms, checklists, flow charts, and illustrations are used throughout to make the complex relationship of computers and accounting understandable.

During our research we found that other books about accounting and computers concentrated on large machines, complex systems, theoretical models, and old technology. This book stresses small computers (micro- and minicomputers) and simple, practical systems and approaches. Our emphasis is on practical, real-world applications and, most of all, simplicity of design.

Topanga, California
New York, New York
January 1981

Rick Stephan Hayes
C. Richard Baker

Contents

Chapter One
Accounting Basics

You could feel the sun, but it was not hot. The sky was the blue of lapis lazuli. Kimberly Rogers sat in the garden looking at its reflection in a pool of water. The water was static, unmoving. But the trees that were reflected there seemed to be blown by the wind. The tree branches were bent and released by the birds as they landed and flew away. The trees were constantly in motion.

Kimberly was thinking of accounting.

Not accounting, exactly, but simplicity. The simplicity of *intention* and the simplicity of *action*.

Kimberly Rogers was a tall woman, tall and thin. She was an attractive woman with an unmistakably sophisticated air. She was Black. She had a passion for knowledge, knowledge of all kinds.

It was her passion for knowledge that motivated her to graduate at the top of her class—both at a Western school, where she received a Master of Science in information systems, and at an Eastern school, where she received a Master of Business Administration. And it was that passion for knowledge that drove her to crave simplicity and elegance.

Kimberly Rogers was a computer systems analyst. Her specialty was accounting systems. Her clients were almost exclusively people in the computer industry.

She was an independent consultant. She did not have a secretary or an office, and her phone number was unlisted. She never advertised. The companies for which she set up accounting and financial systems were all recommended by previous customers.

The reason that Kimberly had specialized in computers was that there was so much to learn. Even now, after working with computers and systems for over 10 years, she still didn't understand it all. The more she learned about computers and systems, the more there was to know. On the other hand, she chose accounting as a specialty because of the great demand for accountants and the tremendous lack of qualified people in the field.

She had worked with several accounting applications packages and several types of hardware configurations from main frame to micro. Only recently had she given serious thought to simplifying accounting for the smaller machines.

Kimberly's idea was to simplify accounting design and still have it very flexible. The accounting data could be used by several programs, and they could be changed immediately according to the latest accepted accounting principles.

A leaf fell into the water. The patterns it created reflected the sun in a scatter of color and brightness. To keep it simple was so hard, but she had to do it.

Kimberly looked at the blank paper in front of her. How could she write an article that would explain accounting in a simple way to people whose work is so complex—to programmers. She had sat there for more than an hour, and the only thing she had written was a date in the upper right-hand corner of her yellow pad.

She wanted to write this article for the trade magazine *Online*, which had even given her an advance. Kimberly looked at her watch. She decided that she wasn't going to get inspired sitting there. So she did what she always did during a crisis . . .

She began.

The problem in computer accounting programs has always been that they lacked flexibility. The first computer accounting programs written in the fifties and sixties tended to put all instructions, data, documentation, and so forth, in line in the programming code. The modular approach was for building housing and airplanes— not for computer programs. The only "structured" part of the program was that it had a beginning and, somewhere, an end. *Systems* was defined as an approach to betting blackjack.

One problem encountered by the writers of the first accounting software still persists. Much of the software is written by computer programmers, often excellent programmers, who know very little about accounting. On the other hand, most accountants and CPAs would rather spend their time learning about taxes and auditing than learning how to program accounting software. Worse, programmers of accounting software rarely completely understand the practical problems of the bookkeeper who has to input the numbers at the terminal.

Writing good accounting software requires three things:

1. A comprehensive understanding of accounting and the accounting process.
2. A comprehensive understanding of programming languages and techniques and the computer process.
3. An understanding of the practical aspects of daily computer use.

ACCOUNTING BASICS

Accounting is the process of recording and tracking business financial transactions. All accounting transactions are *financial* in nature. When you enter the name and address of a vendor in the computer or on a record, this is not an accounting transaction. If you enter the amount of *money* that you owe or pay to a vendor, this is an accounting transaction.

All transactions possible in a business accounting system fall into six different groups of accounts. The groups of accounts are:

*   Assets
*   Liabilities
*   Equity
*   Income
*   Cost of sales
*   Expenses

THE SIX GROUPS OF ACCOUNTS

Assets

Assets are what a business owns. An asset is property that is used in your business. This property contributes toward earning the income of the business, whether directly or indirectly. Assets are productive items that contribute to income and are, generally speaking, tangible property or promises of future receipt of cash (such as Accounts receivable) Assets may be investments made in the business that are not considered an expense.

The committee on terminology of the American Institute of Certified Public Accountants (AICPA), in Accounting Terminology Bulletin No. 1, defined asset as follows: "The word *asset* is not synonymous with or limited to property but includes also that part of any cost or expense incurred which is properly carried forward upon a closing of books at a specific date. . . . [An asset] represents a property right or value acquired, or an expenditure made, which has created a property right, which is properly applicable to the future. Thus plant, accounts receivable, inventory, and a deferred charge are all assets."

"Assets include the following items (accounts):

- Cash
- Accounts receivable
- Inventory
- Investments
- Prepaid expense (such as rent or utility deposits)
- Equipment
- Motor vehicles
- Furniture and fixtures
- Land and buildings
- Building improvements (or leasehold improvements if you rent or lease)
- Other tangible property
- Goodwill
- Patents and copyrights
- Organizational expenses
- Research and development

All these items can be divided into three categories: current, fixed, and other assets.

Current assets are those items that can be readily converted into cash within a one-year period. Current assets are assets in which the flow of funds is one of continuous turnover in the short run. Current assets include cash, accounts receivable, and inventory. *Fixed assets* are items of property, plant, and equipment referred to as 'fixed' because of their permanent nature and because they are not subject to rapid turnover. Fixed assets are used in connection with producing or earning revenue and are not ordinarily for sale. *Other assets* are all the assets that are not current and cannot fit into the fixed asset category (such as research and development or goodwill).

Liabilities

Liabilities are what a business owes to others. Liabilities include debts of the company, that is, amounts of money owed but not yet paid.

Liabilities include the following items (accounts):

- Accounts payable (money owed for inventory, outside labor, etc.)
- Notes payable (the notes, usually secured by some asset or personal guarantee, that require repayment such as bank debt or mortgages)
- Accrued expenses (such as income tax payable, salaries payable, rent payable—amounts that you now owe but have not paid)

- Trade payables (generally called Accounts payable)
- Provision for pensions
- Bonds
- Debentures

Liabilities are generally considered to be either current or long-term. *Current liabilities* are those debts existing as of a certain date which are due for payment within one year or within the normal operating cycle of the business. *Long-term*, or *fixed*, *liabilities* are those debts that will be paid in a period longer than one year.

Equity

Owners' equity or capital is the owners' earnings kept in the business over the years. In a *sole proprietorship* (business owned by one person), owner's equity is shown as a single balance sheet figure covering both the capital an owner has put into the business and the net earnings left there. In a *partnership*, the owners' equity is usually shown on the balance sheet classified by individual partners. In a *corporation*, the owners' equity is shown in a balance sheet in at least two parts: (1) capital stock (or paid-in capital) and (2) retained earnings. The capital stock is shown at 'par' or 'stated value.' The difference between the par value of stock and the amount paid for the stock, less costs, is shown as 'paid-in surplus.'

Owners' equity can be shown as:

- For sole proprietorships or partnerships—as equity for each owner under their name.
- For corporations—as capital stock, paid-in surplus, and retained earnings.

Income

Income (or sales or revenue) is the amount that a business receives for its goods and services. For the majority of companies, those that sell on credit, *income* is the amount billed for goods *shipped* during a given accounting period. Income may be extended to cover "fees" for services performed as well as other items of income such as commissions, rents, and royalties.

For industries that ship goods, there is normally a passing of legal title, which is evidence that a sale has in fact taken place. In other types of business transactions revenue recognition is not dependent on the passing of title. For example, service industries do not pass legal title when they perform a service for their customers.

Income usually includes the following items (accounts):

- Merchandise sales
- Rental income
- Commissions
- Royalties
- Fees for services

Expenses

Operating expenses are the costs of operating a business that are not directly related to sales. Operating expenses include all overhead costs such as salaries and rent as well as the expenses of selling the product or service. Direct costs required to produce sales such as inventory costs or manufacturing costs are not considered to be expense but "cost of sales." Expenses are period costs and not inventory costs. Operating expenses are the costs to operate a business and are more or less independent of the sales level.

Clarence Nickerson in his *Accounting Handbook for Non-Accountants* describes *expense* as "a term for a financial transaction or event resulting in a decrease in assets (such as cash) or an increase in liabilities (such as accounts payable) with a corresponding decrease in owners equity."[*]

Expenses include the following items (accounts):

- Wages and salaries
- Rental expense (including equipment or premise leases)
- Repairs
- Replacements
- Depreciation
- Bad debt
- Travel and transportation
- Business entertainment
- Interest expense (on debt repayment)
- Insurance
- Taxes (payroll, social security, personal property, real property)
- Office supplies
- Accounting and legal expense
- Utilities (heat, gas, electric, telephone, etc.)
- Advertising
- Licenses and regulatory fees
- Charitable contributions
- Donations to business organizations and industry associations
- Management survey expenses
- Lobbying expenses
- Franchise, trademark, or trade name expenses
- Educational expenses for your employees or yourself
- Commitment fees or standby charges you incur in a mortgaging agreement
- Freight and postage

Cost of Sales

Cost of sales is the cost of the merchandise sold. It does not cover the expenses of selling or shipping this merchandise nor, ordinarily, any storing, office, or general administrative expenses involved in company operations. These items are considered "operating expense."

In professional and service businesses, there are usually *no* cost of sales because these companies receive income from fees, rents, and the like, and not from the sale of inventories.

In businesses that have inventories, such as retail, wholesale, and manufacturing businesses, there *is* a cost of sales.

[*]Clarence Nickerson, *Accounting Handbook for Non-Accountants*, 2nd ed. (Boston: 1979), CBI Publishing.

Inventories are a major part of determining cost of sales. Inventory amounts include goods held for sale in the normal course of business as well as raw materials and supplies that will physically become a part of the merchandise intended for sale. In manufacturing companies the cost of labor, supplies, raw material, and certain other "factory overhead" items such as utilities make up finished inventories. Therefore, these items can be considered a cost of sales.

Cost of sales includes the following items (accounts):

- Merchandise inventory purchased and sold during the period
- Raw material
- Direct labor
- Supplies that become part of or are used up by the inventory manufacturing process
- Factory overhead including factory utility and supervisory costs
- Packaging and containers that are part of the product manufactured
- Freight-in, express-in, and cartage-in

Merchandise inventory purchased and sold during the year is usually determined by starting with the inventory at the beginning of the year, adding the purchases during the year, and subtracting out the ending inventory at the end of the year, as follows:

	Beginning inventory
plus	Purchases during the period
minus	Ending inventory at the end of the period
equals	Merchandise inventory cost of sales

The following is a summary of the accounts, in groups and separately:

ASSETS
Cash
Accounts receivable
Inventory
Investments
Pre-paid expense and deposits
Equipment
Motor vehicles
Furniture and fixtures
Land and buildings
Building improvements
Other tangible property
Goodwill
Patents and copyrights
Organizational expense
Research and development

EXPENSES
Wage and salaries
Rental expense
Repairs
Replacements

Depreciation
Bad debt
Travel and transportation
Business entertainment
Interest expense
Insurance
Taxes
Office supplies
Accounting and legal expense
Utility expense
Advertising
Licenses and regulatory fees
Charitable contributions
Donations to business organizations
     and industry associations
Management survey expense
Lobbying expense
Franchise, trademark, or trade
     name expense
Educational expense
Commitment fees
Freight and postage

LIABILITIES

Accounts payable
Notes payable
Accrued expenses
Trade payables
Provision for pensions
Bonds
Debentures

INCOME

Merchandise sales
Rental income
Commissions
Royalties
Fees for services

COST OF SALES

Merchandise inventory
Raw material
Direct labor
Supplies
Factory overhead
Packaging and containers
Freight-in, express-in, and chartage-in

CAPITAL (EQUITY)

Owners' equity
Capital stock
Paid-in surplus
Retained earnings

CHARACTERISTICS OF THE SIX GROUPS OF ACCOUNTS

Interestingly enough, these *six* groups of accounts (assets, liabilities, income and equity, cost of sales, and expense) form only *two* groups when we consider their shared characteristics. One group (three accounts) represents the *sources* of money for a business. The other group (three accounts) represents the *uses* of money. One group represents accounts that are by themselves *nonproductive* of income. The other group is those accounts that are *productive* of income. One account group is always increased by a *debit*, and the other group shows increases by a *credit*.

Dr. Alex Dhiegh once said that when you understand the image of something, you don't need words to explain it. This is another way of saying that a picture is worth a thousand words. So I have created an illustration of the accounts of a business as a circle divided into six pieces. The circle is called the *Circle of Accounts*. It is further divided into two sides of three pieces each. The left side of the circle is shaded dark; the right side is light. See Figure 1.1.

From the illustration you can see that assets, expenses, and cost of sales are on the left (shaded) side of the Accounts Circle. These three groups of accounts share certain characteristics. Assets, expenses, and cost of sales represent money *used* by the business that is *productive* of income. Each of these accounts is *always* increased by a *debit*.

On the other side of the Accounts Circle (the unshaded side) are the liability, equity, and income accounts. They also have certain characteristics in common. Their characteristics are opposite those of assets, expenses, and cost of sales. Liability, equity, and income accounts share the following: (1) they represent *sources* of money for the business; (2) they are *nonproductive* of income; and (3) they are always increased with a *credit*. Figure 1.2 shows the Accounts Circle again, but this time it lists the characteristics of each side of the circle.

Liabilities, equity, and income represent money that comes from outside the business enterprise. *Liabilities* represent money that is borrowed or a promise to pay for some asset such as equipment or inventory. If you borrow money, obviously that liability is a source of money. When a company purchases equipment or receives inventory in return for a note or an account payable each of those liabilities serves as a source for a dollar-equivalent asset. *Equity* is the amount of money that the owners put into the business, a source of money from outside the company. *Income* is also a source of money from outside the business.

Assets, expenses, and cost of sales represent money that is used within the business. If you purchase an *asset* or if you create cash or accounts receivable (also assets), you are

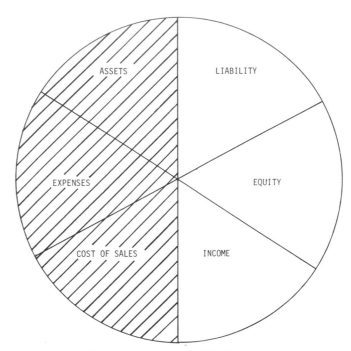

THE ACCOUNTS CIRCLE

Figure 1.1 The accounts of a business can be divided into six groups: assets, liability, equity, income, cost of sales, and expenses.

using the money inside the business. *Expenses* represent money used to pay for overhead. *Cost of sales* is money used for the purchase or production of merchandise for sale.

LEFT SIDE, RIGHT SIDE—THE DEBIT AND THE CREDIT

One of the most confusing of all accounting conventions is the use of the debit and the credit. The main reason for this confusion is that debits and credits have different meanings when applied to each side of the Accounts Circle. A debit *increases* assets, expenses, and cost of sales, but it *decreases* liabilities, equity, and income.

A debit has only *one* irrevocable characteristic—it is a written number on the *left* side of an account paper. A debit is *always* an entry on the left side of an account. No entry can be called a debit if it is on the right side of the account.

Similarly, a credit is *always* an entry on the *right* side of an account ledger. If it is a numerical entry on the right side of an account ledger, then by definition it is a credit.

Debit and credit have only one physical meaning; they are either a left entry or a right entry.

In the double-entry bookkeeping system each account has two possible entries, an entry on the left side (debit) and an entry on the right side (credit). Whether a left side (debit) entry increases the amount or decreases the amount in an account depends on each individual account. But an entry in the *left* column is always a *debit* and an entry on *right* side is always a *credit*. Some accounts receive a debit entry when they are to be increased, whereas other accounts are credited for an increase.

By now you may have guessed why assets, expenses, and cost of sales are on the *left* (debit) side and why liabilities, equity, and income are on the *right* (credit) side.

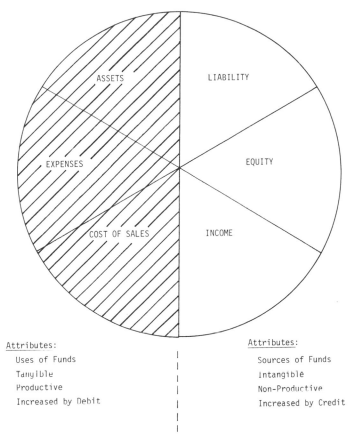

THE ACCOUNTS CIRCLE

Attributes:
Uses of Funds
Tangible
Productive
Increased by Debit

Attributes:
Sources of Funds
Intangible
Non-Productive
Increased by Credit

Figure 1.2 The six groups of accounts fall into only two larger groups based on their contrasting attributes.

All the *left* group (assets, expense, and cost of sales) are *increased* by a debit. That is to say, when you receive money for the business, this money increases (debits) the total amount you have in the asset cash. Each time you write a check for the rent, this increases (debits) the amount that you have paid for rent to date. The total in each account is cumulative—the more times you pay rent, the larger the total amount shown in that account. It is easy to see that accounts that are increased by a debit will generally have *debit balance*, that is, a debit total in that account.

Stated again: *assets*, *expenses*, and *cost of sales* generally have a *debit balance* and are *increased* by a *debit*.

The *right* group of liabilities, equity, and income, because they are opposite of the *left* group, are increased by *credit*, and they generally have a *credit balance*.

For example: Your company receives a $25,000 loan from a bank. You have increased your liabilities by $25,000. Therefore, you would *credit* liabilities (notes payable) by $25,000. You now have a *credit balance* in this loan liability account of $25,000. (This assumes that you had no other loans—the balance would be the previous loans plus $25,000 if there were other loans.)

But what happened to the $25,000 that you borrowed? That money is entered as an increase (debit) in the Cash asset account. You increase the amount of money that you now have in cash. Assuming that your cash-in-bank was not overdrawn by $25,000 or more, that cash account would now have a *debit balance*.

This example illustrates that there is no such thing as just *one* entry in accounting for each transaction (and subsequent entry in the books): there is activity in at least two accounts. Borrowing money not only increases liabilities but it also increases *cash*.

You know that:

1. The *left* group (assets, expenses, and cost of sales) is increased by a *debit* and generally has a *debit balance*.
2. The *right* group (liabilities, equity, and income) is increased by a *credit*, and the separate accounts generally have a *credit balance*.

The question then becomes: If a debit increases the left group and credit increases the right group, what decreases the amounts?

The answer is the only logical one available: If a debit increases a group, then a credit will decrease it. Conversely, if an account is increased by a credit, a decreasing entry would be a debit. From the standpoint of balance this makes sense. Opposite account groups are increased in opposite ways and are decreased in opposite ways. A *debit* increases assets, expenses, and cost of sales and decreases liabilities, equity, and income. A *credit* increases liabilities, equity, and income and decreases assets, expenses, and cost of sales. This can be summarized as shown in Figure 1.3.

Account Group	Debit	Credit
Assets	Increases	Decreases
Expense	Increases	Decreases
Cost of sales	Increases	Decreases
Liabilities	Decreases	Increases
Equity	Decreases	Increases
Income	Decreases	Increases

Figure 1.3   The interrelationships of the accounts.

In accounting if you debit one account you must credit another account. Conversely, if you credit one account you must debit another account. In this way, transactions or movements in one account effect movements in another account.

EXAMPLES OF ACCOUNT TRANSACTIONS

Let's take some examples. When an owner of a business adds to his equity, this increases (credits) his equity account and also increases (debits) the cash account. What happens is that the owner puts cash into the business. However, the accountant wants to keep track of two facts: how much the owner put in and how much is in the cash account because of this transaction. If the transaction were written in a journal, it would look like this:

Date	Explanation	Debit	Credit
1/20/80	Cash	$5,000	
	Owner's equity		$5,000
	To record the contribution of cash to the business of John Zipp.		

When a *sale* is made for *cash*, income is increased (credited) and cash is increased (debited). The journal entry would look like this:

Date	Explanation	Debit	Credit
1/21/80	Cash	$ 500	
	Income		$ 500
	To record sales for cash.		

When an expense is paid, cash is decreased (credited) because the expense has to be paid out of cash, and *expense* is increased (debited). The journal transaction would look like this:

Date	Explanation	Debit	Credit
1/22/80	Expense	$ 400	
	Cash		$ 400
	To record payment from cash of an expense.		

Assume that John Zipp, the owner of this business, is able to get inventory on credit. He pays no money for a certain period of time, but he takes possession of the inventory. This would decrease an "account payable," an account recording the money he owes. This transaction would increase (credit) *accounts payable*, a liability, and increase (debit) *inventory*, an asset. The journal entries would be:

Date	Explanation	Debit	Credit
1/23/80	Inventory	$1,000	
	Accounts payable		$1,000
	To record purchase of inventory on credit.		

GENERALIZATIONS OF ACCOUNT TRANSACTIONS

The following are some helpful generalizations:

1. Every debit requires at least one credit, and every credit at least one debit.
2. There are three types of transactions between the account groups: increase–decrease, increase–increase, and decrease–decrease. Furthermore, any transactions between any of the account groups on one side of the Accounts Circle and any of the accounts groups on the *opposite* side of the Accounts Circle will either be an increase–increase or decrease–decrease transaction. For example: debit (increase) cash and credit (increase) liability. Any transaction between groups of accounts on the *same* side of the Accounts Circle will be an increase–decrease transaction. For example: Debit (increase) expense and credit (decrease) cash.
3. Cash decreases (credit) whenever a check is written by the business.
   - Most checks are written for expense items–debit (increase) expense and credit (decrease) cash.

- The second largest number of checks are written either to purchase inventory for cash (debit merchandise inventory, credit cash) or to pay accounts payable for merchandise purchased on credit (debit accounts payable, credit cash)
- Almost every check written for debt repayment has an interest and a principal portion. The interest portion is an expense, and the principal portion is considered a reduction in debt (debit expense, debit liability, and credit cash).
- Checks are occasionally written for owners' draw or dividends [debit owners draw (or debit dividends), credit cash].

4. With the exception of a reduction in accounts receivable (asset) caused by payment on account by a customer, Cash is almost always increased (debit) by increases in the account groups on the *right* side of the Accounts Circle (liabilities, equity, income). For example: A loan calls for a debit to cash, a credit to liabilities. When sales are made for cash you debit cash and credit income. If an owner puts money into his company you debit cash and credit equity. Only very rarely is cash increased from: (1) a cash rebate on expense or cost of sales or (2) the proceeds from the sale of assets.

THE BASIC ACCOUNTING EQUATION AND PERMANENT AND TEMPORARY ACCOUNTS

Up to this point I have covered the accounting basics as you would normally learn then from any accounting book. There are other basic accounting structural ideas that are rarely discussed in detail, but which have great implications for a computerized accounting system. These ideas have to do with the basic accounting equation and the concept of permanent and temporary accounts.

The basic accounting equation, the formula from which all accounting logic proceeds, is:

$$ASSETS = LIABILITIES + EQUITY \text{ (owner's capital)}$$

Using the rules of algebra, this can also be stated as:

$$ASSETS - LIABILITIES = EQUITY$$
or
$$ASSETS - EQUITY = LIABILITIES$$
or
$$ASSETS - EQUITY - LIABILITIES = 0 \text{ (zero)}$$

In other words, the total dollar amount of assets equals the total dollar amount of equity plus liabilities. The dollar amount of assets minus the dollar amount of liabilities (or equity) equals the total dollar amount of equity (or liabilities). If you subtract the total dollar volume of liabilities and capital from assets, you get zero.

Both sides of the equation are in *balance*: The total of one side (assets) equals the total of the other side (liabilities + equity). When these three accounts are put in document form, it is called a *balance sheet*, one of the basic documents of accounting.

The equation means that the value of the properties a business owns (assets) are equal to the value of the rights in those properties (liabilities and equity). Liabilities are the creditors' (banks, trade, etc.) rights in the business. Equity is the owners' right in the business. So rights in properties equal the amount of properties.

When I say that the entire field of accounting is encompassed by this simple equation, you might be surprised. You might be surprised because I've spent almost a whole article telling how accounting has six groups of accounts—not three.

Your surprise might increase if I tell you that those other groups of accounts—that is, income, expense, and cost of sales—are actually part of the *equity* account.

The equity account reflects the owners' investment and retention of capital in the business. The equity account increases if the company makes a profit, and it decreases if the company suffers a loss. The money that is left in the business from the net profit less taxes, owners' draw, principal loan repayment, and other cash outflows are taken out, is called *retained earnings*. Retained earnings are earnings (profit) kept in the business. Retained earnings is the ever-changing component of owners' equity. *Net profit* is income less cost of sales and expenses. The equity account is actually composed of owners' equity at the beginning of the period *plus* income *minus* cost of sales minus expenses *minus* other cash costs.

Income, cost of sales, and expenses are components of the equity account. The result of taking income and subtracting cost of sales, expenses, and dividends is either an increase (caused by net profit) or a decrease (caused by net loss) in the equity account.

Income, cost of sales, and expenses fit into the basic accounting equation—Assets = Liabilities + Equity—by being part of the equity account.

Let's expand the basic accounting equation to include income, expense, and cost of sales. The equation can then be restated:

ASSETS = LIABILITIES + previous EQUITY + INCOME − COST OF SALES − COSTS°

If that last surprise is not enough, here's another one. Of all the six account groups, only three are accounts that continue from year to year. These three account groups (assets, liabilities, and equity) will begin an accounting period with some dollar value balance. When the accounting period is over, these accounts still have a dollar balance.

For example: At the beginning of the year your company has accounts receivable, you owe the banks some money, and you still have in the business the money with which you originally started. At the end of the year you will still have accounts receivable, you will still probably owe the bank money, and you still will have some of your own money in the company. Since assets, liabilities, and equity always have a balance in them, they are considered to be *permanent* accounts.

The income, expense, and cost of sales accounts are a part of the equity account, *but* only a temporary part. Income less cost of sales less expense is only posted to *equity once* per period. If the accounting period for a business is one year, the income statement accounts (income, expense, and cost of sales) only become *incorporated into equity once per year*. It would be much too troublesome to constantly incorporate these three large groups of accounts into equity. This would cause the equity account to have a larger number of entries than the Cash account. In short, it is accounting convention to incorporate income, cost of sales, and expense into equity no more than once per accounting period (month, quarter, annual).

When income, cost of sales, and expense (the income statement accounts) are "posted" or put as part of equity, the separate accounts are zeroed out. All the entries in the income statement accounts are made zero, and they start out with zero in the account to begin the next period.

°Costs are money such as taxes and dividends that are not expenses but represent real cash outflow plus expenses.

The following is an example of an end-of-the-period journal entry, closing various income and expense accounts to the income and expense summary, an equity account:

Date	Explanation	Debit	Credit
12/31/80	Income	$150,000	
	Income and expense		
	Summary	$150,000	
	Income and expense summary	142,000	
	Merchandise purchases		120,000
	Salary expense		10,000
	Rental expense		4,000
	Utilities		2,000
	Supplies		1,000
	Taxes		500
	Accounting		1,200
	Entertainment		2,300
	Transportation and travel		1,000
	To record transfer of accounts to		
	Income and expense summary.		

Income, expense, and cost of sales accounts are zeroed out and closed once per period. Therefore they are considered *temporary* accounts.

Assets, liabilities, and equity (to which the temporary accounts are closed once per period) are considered *permanent* accounts because they are never closed or zeroed out at the end of a period. These accounts are the basic accounts of the business. The only time they will be zero is if they are physically reduced by some event such as selling off an asset, spending all the cash in the bank, paying off a debt, or totaling all the money out of equity.

If all the assets are sold and all the asset accounts are reduced to zero, the business ceases to exist. If all the equity account equals zero, the business has as much debt as assets, meaning the business is in trouble. If there is zero debt (no liabilities), the company would be considered unusual, and this circumstance generally exists only when a business is just starting. In short, it is a rare instance when any of the three permanent account groups (assets, liabilities, and equity) are zero.

Now for the last surprise. The permanent accounts—assets, liabilities, and equity—happen to be the accounts that appear on the business balance sheet, and the temporary accounts—income, expense, and cost of sales—are the accounts that constitute the income statement (profit and loss statement). Figure 1.4 shows the Accounts Circle and how this all comes together.

SUMMARY

There are six groups of accounts. They are:

- Assets
- Liabilities
- Equity
- Income
- Cost of sales
- Expenses

THE ACCOUNTS CIRCLE

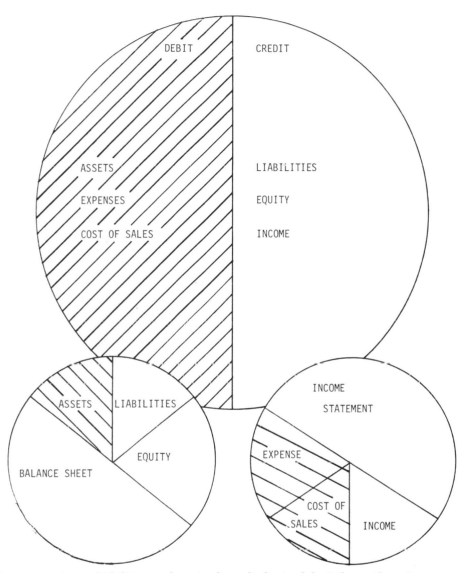

Figure 1.4   Assets, liabilities, and equity form the basis of the Balance Sheet. Income, cost of sales, and expenses are the basis of the income statement.

The groups of accounts fall into different categories. Assets, cost of sales, and expenses are money used inside the business—they are basically a USE of money. All these accounts are *increased* by a *debit* and *decreased* by a *credit*.

Liabilities, equity, and income, on the other hand, are sources of money. They are *increased* by a *credit* and *decreased* by a *debit*.

Assets, liabilities, and equity are the constituent accounts of the basic account equation:

$$\text{ASSETS} = \text{LIABILITIES} + \text{EQUITY}$$

Assets, liabilities, and equity are *permanent* accounts—they are never closed out in accounting, but continue to be open as long as the business exists. Assets, liabilities, and equity are also the groups of accounts that make up the balance sheet.

Income, cost of sales, and expenses are the group of accounts that make up the profit and loss statement (income statement). They are *temporary* accounts that are closed out at the end of each accounting period. They are all closed out to the equity account, which is a permanent account.

         o o o o

Kimberly read back through her article. It was dark now. She could barely see the words. The article was complete. But it still wasn't simple.

Chapter Two

A Computerized Accounting System for Hero Manufacturing

Kimberly Rogers was looking forward to her appointment at Hero Manufacturing. And she was in a hurry. But she couldn't help stopping near the front door and looking at her new dress in the big, heavy-framed mirror. "Girl," she said aloud to herself while turning her body from left to right, "if you don't knock them dead today, those boys just have to be blind."

She got into her sports car, tossing her briefcase into the passenger seat. She opened her briefcase and glanced at her itinerary for the day. Her first stop was Hero Manufacturing on the east side of town.

Her job was to set up a computerized accounting system for Hero and write the necessary interfaces to tie the accounting system into the company's present inventory system. Kimberly was an independent software consultant who worked for a consortium of independent consultants called Earthapple Business Systems. Earthapple would contract the job, sell the hardware, and subcontract the software to independents such as Kimberly. Kimberly had written most of her software for DEC LSI computers, but she had worked with 8080/Z-80 assembly language.

Originally Kimberly was interested primarily in accounting. When she was working on her MBA, she had received many accounting credits but she had hated computers. She couldn't stand dealing with them. She figured that as an executive she wouldn't have to bother with them. Then a funny thing happened. Fresh out of grad school she was working for a Big Eight accounting firm. One of the employees at the firm, a friend of hers, was very interested in computers and had bought and assembled one of the early Altar 8080-chip computers.

Whenever she visited her friend, he always seemed to be working on his computer. He programmed it in assembly language because at that time there was no higher-level language that would run on the Altar. Over a period of three to four months of constant exposure, Kimberly caught the fever that her friend was experiencing. She started programming computers and learning as much as she could about them. At one point she talked about computers so much that her friends didn't want to talk to her anymore. "Computers are boring," they would tell her.

Little by little she learned about computers. She even went back to school to get a M.S. degree in information systems.

Kimberly pulled into the parking lot of Hero Manufacturing. Kimberly always entered through the plant door when she went to visit a client. This let her see the production people at work and get an idea of the flow of the operation before she met the management. There were racks of steel products in every part of the facility. There were a few people working on milling machines. A truck was loading at the dock.

Kimberly walked through the offices at the front of the shop and into the lobby. She asked for John Jones, the owner, and sat down to read a trade magazine laying on the chair.

John Jones came to the front lobby, and was clearly a little surprised that his anticipated consultant was not only female, but Black. After the introductory handshake and the offer of coffee, they got down to business.

Kimberly began by explaining, "My job is to put together an accounting system for you. I will not write all the software myself. . . ." Kimberly paused and asked John Jones, "Do you understand what software is?"

"Well, I think it's what the computer is programmed with to make it run . . . er. . . . But I must admit that I really don't understand it too well."

"Well," Kimberly continued, "we'll get to that a little later. Let me continue. I won't write all of this 'software' myself. I'll use some software that is now available and modify it for your needs. Even though the available software for your machine is not perfect, it will do.

THE TROUBLE WITH COMP-AIRE

"Brad Mayer of Earthapple told me that you are using our system to replace a previous machine and software. Could you tell me about that?" Kimberly asked.

"Sure," Jones began.

"Before Earthapple put in the DEC LSI-11 computer, we had a system based on a Z-80. But it never ran right. It was an inventory system that we had. The company that put it in, Comp-aire, is now out of business. I was one of their first customers. They used to work for Quantell.

Comp-aire was recommended to me by a friend when they first started. He said that all the guys there were real computer geniuses. I don't know about that now. But when I talked to them, they really sounded sharp. They said that the computer would pretty well solve all my inventory problems.

I asked them for a system that had all the present inventory listed and would allow me to put in each new order as it was received. It was suppose to have customer records in addition to inventory records. The system was suppose to:

1. print an invoice register containing the cost and gross profit on each invoice as well as sales journal totals;
2. keep track of accounts receivable by posting to both a master file and the individual customer files;
3. post payments made to accounts receivable (master and customer);
4. update the inventory files for new inventory purchases.

In fact, by the time the machine was working, I had to settle for a lot less from Comp-aire. Now, Earthapple has designed a system for me that does all this. That's the one I'm using now. But Comp-aire—boy, what a mess they made.

The software from Comp-aire was supposed to cost $17,000. Well, they changed our ironclad contract from $17,000 to $40,000. And even at that, the damn system never produced an invoice in what Comp-aire called a "real-time mode." We had trouble changing customer files, and the inventory figures were never totally accurate or satisfactory.

It had other problems, too. Whenever more than two TV screens, those CRTs, were operating, the system almost stopped. Sometimes it would take five minutes to enter one sales order. Whenever the printer was working, that was it. It was impossible to use the TV, I mean CRT, at the same time.

The chronological order of events went something like this. In June of the year before last I signed a contract with Comp-aire. I was told that the system would be completely set up and would require me to hire more people. In January of last year we took delivery of the hardware. But the hardware was not operational because there was testing that still had to be done.

Comp-aire allowed us to postpone payment until March, because that's how long it would take, they said, to get everything running. We paid in March—except for the software costs. From March to September the programmers kept saying, "We'll be operational next month." In October of last year, I was getting pretty fed up. I told them that I wanted at least the basics to work by November. The basics were to keep track of my in-house inventory, what came in, what went out, and how much was left. I also wanted a master list of accounts receivable and accounts payable.

From October through November the people from Comp-aire went through extensive testing for the system. All the programs tested individually appeared all right. After the system was running, we had a lot of problems with the CRTs, and the system made weird errors. Comp-aire kept mentioning "read errors" every time they input information for certain inventory items. But it worked for others. In February of this year the head programmer from Comp-aire threw up his arms in frustration and quit. I hired the other assistant programmer who was working for Comp-aire. I also called in another software house, and they told me that they would have to start from scratch. Remember, I had already spent $40,000 for software. The outside software house told me that there was no system documentation, the programs were not modular, and they were falling apart. The reports didn't balance properly, and customer files were erased. Plus there were hardware problems. It was impossible to have simultaneous operation of input and report printing. The system didn't operate properly whenever more than two terminals were running.

So I called several companies. From each vendor I asked for:

1. detailed specification of all pertinent hardware and software.
2. a full-scale demonstration of the equipment on at least one of my principal applications.
3. a detailed proposal that spelled out exactly what equipment, software, and technical support would be supplied.
4. estimated processing times for each of my applications.
5. all responsibilities of the vendor.
6. the total purchase price.
7. a list of the users of your machine and system in this geographical area.

Earthapple impressed me the most, and I think you guys know what you're doing. But I've gone through the wars, and I'm not going to be fooled anymore.

TYPES OF COMPUTER SOFTWARE

Kimberly looked at Jones. "That's quite an ordeal. I hope this installation will be nowhere near that problematic. How's the DEC 11 and the software designed by Earthapple doing?"

"It runs very well," John Jones replied. "So far the people at Earthapple have done a good job. Brad Mayer did a very good job. He seems like a nice guy."

"Well, before we get into the accounting stuff, is there anything you'd like to ask me?" Kimberly questioned.

"Yes," John answered. "You said you were going to explain software to me. I've heard the term for a long time, but I don't quite understand it."

"Okay," Kimberly said, "I'll try to be brief. It's hard for me to hold back at times. Systems software is the set of programs that allows the computer to function as a coherent system. There are three types of software in your computer. These are: (1) operating system software, (2) high-level language software, and finally, (3) applications software—the kind I'll be writing."

Operating System Software

The operating system is the software heart of a computer. It coordinates all the different parts of a computer, including the central processing unit (CPU), peripherals (such as CRTS and disks), the high-level language, and the applications program. Since most small businesses have magnetic storage systems, the operating system is a *disk operating system* (DOS).

An applications programmer—that's what I am—doesn't like to bother with the DOS. But I do demand programmer-oriented documentation. This permits modifications and adaptations whenever needed. It also allows adequate error tracing when necessary. I am concerned that the DOS be compatible with the high-level language that I want to use for my applications programming. You cannot assume that there is compatibility because many high-level languages are designed to work with only one certain DOS, and no others. Much of the applications software that you buy "off the shelf" must have a certain specified operating system in order to work.

The most important function of the DOS is the storage and manipulation of programs and data. A good DOS should make efficient use of the available storage on the disk. Another function of the DOS is to transfer files to other disks or peripherals, the CRT, printer, and so on. It also can restructure files by processes such as merging, concatenating (linking together), or extracting subsets of files.

Higher-Level Languages

The only language that a computer understands is sequences of ones and zeros. This is called *machine language*. Although you could program all your business applications in this language, it would take a long, long, long time. I understand English best. It would be most efficient to program in English. But you can't program in English. So halfway languages were designed. They are somewhere between what I understand and what the machine understands. They called these programming languages FORTRAN, BASIC, COBOL, and so forth.

The most available and commonly used language for small business computers is BASIC. Nearly all the applications programs for these computers are written in BASIC. But that is not as simple as it sounds. An applications program written in one dialect of a language will not necessarily run with any other dialect of the language. Language standardization is practically nonexistent except for theoretical discussions at high levels. With BASIC, for example, there are as many versions or dialects as there are manufacturers.

An applications program which is written in one dialect may be adapted to another dialect, but only if the source code is provided with the program. Unfortunately, most applications people are afraid to provide a source code because they think someone will steal their programs.

The actual workings of the high-level language (BASIC) program must be such that errors in how the language is used (syntax) are caught before they get into the operating system. An example of a syntax error is when the operator makes a typographical error trying to input data.

For business programs, an important feature of a high-level language is that it has diversity of formats for generating invoices, purchase orders, accounting reports, checks, or whatever is routinely needed. Closely related to the print format is horizontal and vertical tabulation. This should allow any desired column of line to be selected and forms to be tabulated. Tabulation makes graphics possible. I will, as an applications programmer, do all your programming in a high-level language like BASIC.

Applications Software

Although the machine, operating system, and programming language are the foundation upon which the applications program rests, it is the program itself that does the work. That work includes accounting, text editing, inventory control, etc.

Applications programs, including the custom software that I am writing, will represent the largest computer expenditure over the long run. It will progress as the computer is used for increasing workloads. The hardware and system software, by contrast, represent one-time costs.

Applications software comes from two sources: programs "off the shelf" (packaged for retail), or custom programming. The "off the shelf" programs are the cheapest. On the other hand, the available selection is often insufficient for a particular business. This is the case with Hero.

With the modified applications programs that I will design you will receive modular software that has been adequately documented, tested, and debugged. The software will be fully compatible with the underlying hardware and software.

DOCUMENTATION

Of these requirements, as you must have guessed by now, adequate documentation is the most important. If your needs change, or if the applications program has to be modified, it is documentation that will make the task difficult or easy. There are two types of documentation: programmer documentation and end-user documentation.

Programmer Documentation

Programmer documentation, sometimes called *application technical documentation*, is required to enable future maintenance, modifications, expansion, and error correction by other programmers. Errors may appear years later, and it would be impossible to track them down without clear explanations of the program design and function. This programmer documentation should include two formats: (1) a programmer manual and (2) remarks in the code itself.

The programmer manual should include a description of overall program design complete with flowcharts and module charts. The form of the manual differs from company to company, but I use the following format (it is suggested by the American Institute of Certified Public Accountants°):

- *Application overview.* A description of the application's functions, the files it maintains, its input, and its output.

°*Guidelines for General System Specifications for a Computer System*, 1975, by the Computer Applications Subcommittee of the American Institute of Certified Public Accountants.

- *Systems flowchart.*   A graphic representation of the relationship between the files, input, programs and output.
- *System flow narrative.*   A narrative description of each process illustrated by the system flowchart. Its function is to elaborate upon the flowchart in words.
- *File description.*   A detailed description of the purpose, contents, and organization of each file used in the system.
- *Input description.*   A description of each piece of information you wish to enter into the system.
- *Output description.*   A description of each report or printout from the system.
- *Processing description.*   A description of the general operation of each program in the system.

Comments in the applications programming code itself (REMark statements in BASIC) should be generous enough to explain major program and subroutine details.

End-User Documentation

End-user documentation is designed to allow the program to be used by the business-person. The description of the program and instructions for its use must anticipate the questions of the nonprofessional. A person totally new to the program should be able to operate the program accurately without help from a professional.

End-user documentation is very important. If anything goes wrong, the first people who will try to set things right are not likely to know very much about computers. At sometime there will be mistakes made from careless operation. The programmer must allow for the inevitable. Mistakes that shift the operations from one level of software to another (i.e., from the user program to machine language) must be easily corrected by the operator. Restart procedures, reconfigurations of the system, fallback procedures, or anything that's allowed on-site have to be absolutely cookbook and foolproof.

User procedure documentation is a user's manual. The manual will include the following information (as suggested by the AICPA°):

- *Application overview.*   A nontechnical description of the application. This generally explains the functions; it identifies the files it maintains and defines the content of its input and output.
- *Input preparation procedures.*   Detailed procedure instructions for preparing input source documents and for their conversion to machine processing form.
- *Input control procedures.*   Instructions for establishing data controls before submitting input for processing.
- *Input transmittal procedures.*   Instructions for submitting the input to be processed.
- *Output document descriptions.*   Examples of all output reports and other documents. This is accompanied by (1) a general narrative description of each output, (2) an explanation of the purpose of each output, and (3) an indication of the frequency of each output.
- *Output control procedures*   Instructions for verifying the completeness and accuracy of each output.
- *Error correction procedures*   A listing of possible error conditions and procedures for correction and/or reentry.

° *Guidelines for General System Specifications for a Computer System,* 1975, by the Computer Applications Subcommittee of the American Institute of Certified Public Accountants

TESTING AND DEBUGGING

One of the most important factors influencing the reliability of the computer system you have is the applications program.

After the coding of each module (seperate, independent part of a program) is complete, the debugging and testing of the module begin. *Debugging* is the detection and subsequent correction of the more obvious errors. Testing is initiated only after each module is working without obvious errors. This testing procedure requires that each section of code in the module be exercised for all working conditions.

The total time spent debugging should occupy only a small fraction of the total time expended up to that point. Excessive debugging time indicates insufficient design integrity. In other words the program has not been designed logically and clearly. Testing occurs after debugging. A perfectly functioning program may need no debugging, but it still needs complete and thorough testing. This testing might be time consuming. There is no shortcut to ascertain that the program is running properly.

"Does that explain software well enough for you?" Kimberly asked.

"Very nice." John Jones answered. "I think I got it. There are three types of software: operating system software, language software, and applications software. The operating system software makes sure all the peripherals are working and maintains the files. Language software comes in BASIC, FORTRAN, and other flavors. It is the language that you use to program the applications such as accounting or inventory control.

The most important software from a business standpoint is the applications software. The applications software tells the computer how to do the application—it tells it how to account. The important areas of applications software are adequate documentation, good style, proper debugging and testing, and, of course, compatibility with the rest of the hardware and software."

"All right," Kimberly said, "now let's talk about how I'm going to set up an accounting system for your company. Let's start with the output . . ."

SYSTEM OUTPUT

The starting point of all computer software design is to carefully define the output required by the user. Unfortunately, in a great many cases, the user doesn't know what he wants, or what he needs for output. Then I, as the analyst, must find out. To get all this right I like to use two basic tools—logical data layouts and the Warnier-Orr data diagrams.

This illustration (Figure 2.1) shows a logical output layout for an invoice. The next illustration (Figure 2.2) shows what a CRT screen output would be for a General Journal transaction register.

What these illustrations show is not the physical columns and rows in which the data are placed, but the logical relationship of the information on the page.

The other tool we like to use is the Warnier-Orr diagrams. Figure 2.3 is an illustration of the invoice in Figure 2.1.

The Warnier–Orr diagrams are used to show the hierarchy and logical structure of the output. What makes this type of diagram particularly important is that it orders the number of logical possibilities. The diagram helps communicate the user's intent in a logical and complete way.

What we need from Hero Manufacturing are copies of all the standard formats and forms you use for accounting. I will take these forms and the type of output you are using and discuss them with you. Then we will put that data into the Warnier–Orr diagram and logical output formats.

```
          ┌─                         ─┐
             HERO MANUFACTURING
          └─                         ─┘

             ┌─             ─┐
                 INVOICE
             └─             ─┘

┌─                ─┐   ┌─               ─┐   ┌─                  ─┐
  CUSTOMER NO.         CUSTOMER NAME         CUSTOMER ADDRESS
└─                ─┘   └─               ─┘   └─                  ─┘

   ┌─          ─┐      ┌─                              ─┐
     ORDER NO.           SHIP TO:   NAME AND ADDRESS
   └─          ─┘      └─                              ─┘

     ┌─              ─┐   ┌─                      ─┐
        ORDER DATE          DELIVERY DATE
     └─              ─┘   └─                      ─┘

┌─              ─┐  ┌─             ─┐  ┌─          ─┐  ┌─           ─┐
  PRODUCT NAME       PRODUCT NO.        QUANTITY       UNIT/PRICE
└─              ─┘  └─             ─┘  └─          ─┘  └─           ─┘

                   ┌─             ─┐  ┌─          ─┐  ┌─           ─┐
                   └─             ─┘  └─          ─┘  └─           ─┘

                   ┌─             ─┐  ┌─          ─┐  ┌─           ─┐
                   └─             ─┘  └─          ─┘  └─           ─┘

                                      ┌─                          ─┐
                                          TOTAL AMOUNT
                                      └─                          ─┘
```

Figure 2.1   Average logical layout for invoice output.

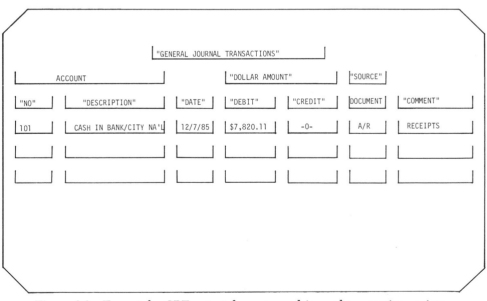

Figure 2.2   Format for CRT output for a general journal transaction register.

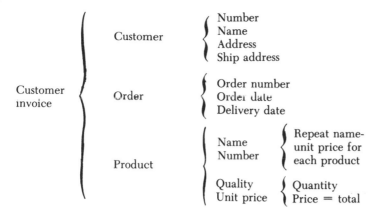

Figure 2.3   Warnier diagram of invoice in Figure 2.1.

DATA BASE

The second most important thing in designing a computer system is the data base. The *data base* is all the data you input which the computer then acts upon to perform the accounting, inventory, customer file, and other operations.

There are two ways to handle this data. You can create separate data files for each computer application such as accounting. Or you can use one data file for *all* applications. The traditional approach has been to create a new data file each time you have a new application. In the case of Hero Manufacturing that would mean that you would have one set of files for inventory and another set for accounting. A newer approach, the one we use, is to have one set of data files to which any application has access. This system is called a *Data Base Management System (DBMS)*.

A data base management system is a software package designed to interact with a collection of computer-stored files (a data base). The idea is to use the same files or data groupings for several applications. Figure 2.4 shows how several applications may share one group of data. Figure 2.5 shows how the same individual data items may be required by a number of records and documents.

A typical data base management system includes the following:

- Schema.   A high-level language such as BASIC, FORTRAN, COBOL, etc.
- Data Manipulation Subroutines.   Special miniprograms that can be 'called' by the programming language (schema). They are used to manipulate and extract data from the data base.
- Utility Programs.   Programs stored on the disks used to load the data base on the disk and to duplicate the data base as a backup.

John Jones looked like he was about to fall asleep. "I'm sorry," Kimberly apologized, "but I *do* go on when I start talking about the kind of system that I like. But I think anything beyond this point should be reserved for programmers and other computer junkies. I usually keep the greater detail for my lectures. Do you understand what I need and what I'm trying to do?" Kimberly asked Jones.

"You need some copies of the types of accounting forms we have." John answered. "You also said you were going to put all the data in one place so they would be easier to get at. That's data base management. I've heard of it."

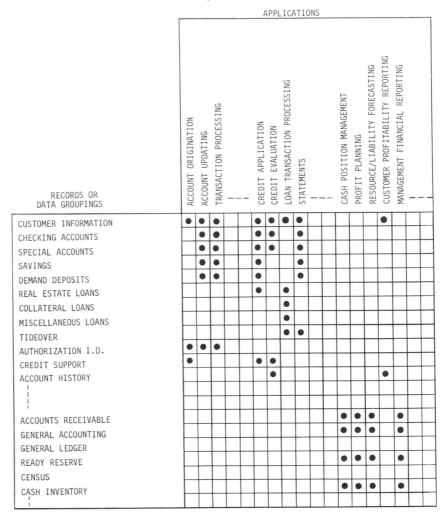

Figure 2.4 Many applications may share one piece of data. For example, customer information is shared by programs to perform account origination, account updating, transaction processing, credit application, credit evaluation, statements, and so on.

"Well, on one count you misunderstood me," Kimberly replied. "I need more than just your accounting records for output. I also need other information from you now such as this questionnaire." Kimberly held up several pieces of paper (Figure 2.6). "Also, when I get all this information I want to take it to my office and design how I intend to handle the whole works. Then, within two weeks, I will come back to see you. We'll review the design, the output formats and documents, and the information that you will input. When you understand all of this, I'll start writing the program."

"Here's the questionnaire I need filled out," Kimberly said. John Jones and Kimberly Rogers began work on the questionnaire.

SUMMARY

"Wait," Kimberly said. "Don't start yet. I want to make sure you understand what we've talked about, so I would like to summarize if I may."

"Certainly," John replied.

"You said that to find Earthapple you asked for certain information from each of the

RECORDS AND DOCUMENTS

DATA ITEMS	ORDER FROM CUSTOMER	CUSTOMER FILE	WAREHOUSE ORDER	WAREHOUSE TICKET	INVOICE	WEEKLY TOTAL SHIPMENT REPORT	WEEKLY ITEM SHIPMENT REPORT	YEAR-TO-DATE SHIPMENT REPORT	YEAR-TO-DATE ITEM REPORT	ITEM FILE	WEEKLY ITEM INVENTORY REPORT	INVENTORY FILE	BRANCH FILE	MONTHLY BRANCH SUMMARY	YEAR-TO-DATE SALES REPORT	ITEM ON ORDER REPORT	TOTAL ON-ORDER REPORT	MONTHLY CUSTOMER REPORT	CUSTOMER PAYMENT	ACCOUNTS RECEIVABLE	OVERDUE ACCOUNTS	OVERDUE NOTICES
CUSTOMER NUMBER	•	•	•		•													•	•	•	•	•
CUSTOMER ORDER NUMBER	•		•		•														•	•	•	•
ITEM NUMBER	•		•	•	•		•		•	•	•	•				•		•				•
ITEM TYPE AND SIZE	•		•	•	•		•		•	•	•	•				•		•				•
CORPORATE ORDER NUMBER			•	•	•													•		•	•	•
INVOICE NUMBER					•													•	•	•	•	•
BRANCH OFFICE NUMBER	•				•								•	•	•		•	•		•	•	•
CUSTOMER NAME	•	•			•										•			•	•	•	•	•
ITEM NAME	•		•	•	•		•		•	•	•	•				•	•	•				•
DATE OF INVOICE					•															•	•	•
QUANTITY ORDERED	•		•	•	•				•		•	•				•		•				•
QUANTITY SHIPPED			•	•	•	•	•	•										•		•	•	•
QUANTITY OUT OF STOCK			•	•	•	•	•	•	•			•						•				
SHIPPING INSTRUCTIONS			•	•	•																	
CODE FOR SHIPPING			•	•	•																	
CUSTOMER ADDRESS		•			•																	
BRANCH OFFICE NAME	•	•			•								•	•	•		•	•				•
BRANCH OFFICE ADDRESS	•				•								•									•
PRICE					•	•	•	•	•	•									•	•	•	•
INVOICE LINE VALUE					•															•	•	•
DISCOUNT RATE					•				•											•	•	•
INVOICE LINE DISCOUNT					•																	•
C.O.D. OR CREDIT CODE	•	•			•													•				•
WEEKLY TOTAL OF ITEM SHIPPED						•	•	•	•			•										
WEEKLY VALUE OF ITEM SHIPPED						•	•	•	•													

Figure 2.5 Certain data items may be used in several different documents. For example, customer number is used in order forms, customer files, warehouse orders, and so on.

vendors. This information included detailed descriptions of equipment and software, a proposal of services including allowances for the time it would take, a demonstration of the system, the price, and a list of our customer-users. This is the best procedure.

"We talked extensively about the types of software there are: (1) operating system, (2) high-level languages like BASIC, and (3) the all important applications software. Just as important as this software and the integration required is the documentation of the system. Documentation includes material for the programmer (programmer documentation) and for the user (user documentation). Program documentation should include an application overview, a system flowchart and narrative, and a description of files, inputs, output, and processing. User documentation should include applications overview; procedures for input preparation, control, and transmittal; output document descriptions and control procedures; and error correction procedures.

"The starting point of all computer software design has to be defining the output required by the user, Hero Manufacturing. That's why I need you to fill out this questionnaire (Figure 2.6). I'll find out what your output needs are, and using Warnier-

LOCATION OF PLANTS AND OFFICES

Type of Operation
No. of Employees

CORPORATE ORGANIZATION AND REPORTING STRUCTURE, COMPUTER UNIT RECORD DATA ENTRY EQUIPMENT CONFIGURATION—INCLUDING TERMINALS, LINES, AND MODEMS

Vendor
Machine/Feature
Description
Rental Amount
Maintenance Amount
OT Amount
Tax Amount
Tax Amount
Purchase
Lease

DATA PROCESSING ORGANIZATION AND REPORTING STRUCTURE (DOCUMENT FLOWS)
VOLUME STATISTICS
FILE STATISTICS
EXISTING APPLICATIONS
PRODUCTS HANDLED

COMPANY NAME: _____

SURVEY VOLUME QUESTIONNAIRE

ACCOUNTS RECEIVABLE

_____ 1. Number of customers?
_____ 2. Any open item customers?
_____ 3. Average age of A/R in days?
_____ 4. Number of invoices per month? (Maximum)
_____ 5. Number of invoices per day? (Maximum)

INVENTORY MANAGEMENT

_____ 1. Do you have more than one warehouse?
_____ 2. Do you wish order tracking management reports?
_____ 3. Will you use a
_____ 4. Number of items inventoried?
_____ 5. Number of total items for all warehouses?
_____ 6. Number of items on order (purchase and/or
_____   shop order) at any one time?
_____ 7. Number of transactions per day?

ORDER ENTRY/INVOICES

_____ 1. Installing inventory application?
_____ 2. Number of customers?
_____ 3. Number of items inventoried?
_____ 4. Number of total items for all warehouses?
_____ 5. Number of different ship-to name & addresses?
_____ 6. Number of quantity price discount items?
_____ 7. Number of fixed-price contracts by items?
_____ 8. Number of invoices per month? (Maximum)
_____ 9. Number of invoices per day? (Maximum)
_____ 10. Number of new orders per month? (Maximum)
_____ 11. Number of new orders per day? (Maximum)

_____ 12. Maximum number of open orders at any one time?
_____ 13. Average number of line items per order?

GENERAL LEDGER

_____ 1. Number of G/L accounts in chart of accounts?
_____ 2. Do you wish to retain budget amounts?

ACCOUNTS PAYABLE

_____ 1. Do you wish to reconcile checks?
_____ 2. Number of vendors active per year?
_____ 3. Number of invoices received per month?
_____ 4. Number of checks written per month?
_____ 5. Number of invoices entered at any one time?
_____ 6. Number of account numbers in your chart of accounts?

PAYROLL

_____ 1. Do you require G/L distribution?
_____ 2. Do you want to enter hours by day?
_____ 3. Maximum number or regular hours per day?
_____ 4. Do you require union reporting?
_____ 5. Do you require state distribution for tax purposes?
_____ 6. Do you require city/local distribution for tax purposes?
_____ 7. Do you wish to reconcile payroll checks on the system?
_____ 8. Number of total persons employed in a year?
_____ 9. Number of misc. deductions per employee? (Average)
_____ 10. Number of total payroll checks per mo. (hourly, salary, executive)
_____ 11. Number of payroll checks written any one time? (Maximum)
_____ 12. Number of time input transactions per day per employee? (Average)
_____ 13. Number of days per pay period an average employee works?
_____ 14. Number of accounts in chart of accounts?
_____ 15. Number of total dept./work center combinations?
_____ 16. Total number of unions?
_____ 17. Maximum no. of deduction types for any one union?

PRODUCTION STATUS AND COSTING

_____ 1. Do you wish to maintain & select basic items from job select file?
_____ 2. Edited transactions to interfere from payroll?
_____ 3. Edited transactions to interfere from payroll?
_____ 4. Edited transactions to interface from inventory?
_____ 5. Number of jobs active at any one time?
_____ 6. Average number of operations per job?
_____ 7. Average number of material and/or misc. costs per job?
_____ 8. Number of repetitive basic items?
_____ 9. Average number of material/misc. transactions per job per week?

SALES ANALYSIS

_____ 1. Installing accounts receivable application?
_____ 2. Installing order entry and invoicing application?
_____ 3. Installing inventory application?
_____ 4. Number of salespersons
_____ 5. Do you want daily salespersons recap?
_____ 6. Maximum number of invoices written in any one month?
_____ 7. Maximum number of invoices written in any one day?

PRODUCT DEFINITION/COSTING

_____ 1. Number of item numbers in product master file?
_____ 2. Number of single level assemblies?
_____ 3. Average no. of components per single level assembly?

Figure 2.6 Feasibility study facts checklist.

Orr diagrams I'll chart your needs. We at Earthapple use a data base management system to make data integration easier. Our system for data bases includes a schema (BASIC and FORTRAN), data manipulation subroutines, and utility programs.

"Any questions?" Kimberly concluded.

"Yeah. This questionnaire is a bear. Can't you fill it out for me?" John Jones asked.

Chapter Three
Assets, Cash, and Accounts Receivable

It may appear strange that accountants stick together. But it seems to be true. Whereas the average person probably has, at most, one friend who is in the accounting field, Kimberly has six. Six of her close friends—including her current boyfriend—are accountants. Five of them are CPAs.

Kimberly likes to hear the inside stories of how H. L. Hunt used all the available tax laws to pay very little taxes. Or how such-and-such company has accounting skeletons in their executive cloak closet. The most depressing of these stories is the one that Kimberly had heard many times. The small business company president, knowing nothing of accounting, hires a "recommended" bookkeeper, who then absconds with two years' profits. Usually it is the small company that doesn't take advantage of the tax laws or ends up with a charlatan "accountant" who does much more harm than good.

It was to these people, the small business people, that Kimberly's boyfriend, Udjat Her, lectured. Kimberly liked to hear his lectures. It was interesting to learn what the concerns of small businesses were. And besides, she could keep an eye on him at the same time. Udjat was from Egypt. Since the Tutankhamen tour and the Middle East peace accords, Egyptian men had become fascinating to Kimberly.

Tonight Udjat was lecturing on the subject of assets. Of all the groups of accounts, assets, without a doubt, is the most important and the most complicated. Assets include cash, inventory, and accounts receivable—all of which are very essential items for business. How a business manages these resources determines, to a large degree, the success of the business.

Then you must consider fixed assets such as equipment and the investment tax credits and the depreciation that go along with them. Obviously, depreciation and income tax credits have a strong influence on what equipment is purchased or what property improvements are made.

The lecture on assets was the first in a series on accounting that was to be given by Udjat. There was standing room only in the classroom as he began.

ASSETS

Assets are what a company owns. Assets are productive items that contribute to income. They are, generally speaking, tangible property or promises of future receipts of cash (like accounts receivable or investments).

Assets include the following items (accounts):

- Cash
- Accounts receivable
- Inventory
- Investments
- Prepaid expense (such as last month's rent or utility deposits)
- Equipment
- Motor vehicles
- Furniture and fixtures
- Land and buildings
- Building improvements (called leasehold improvements if you are a renter)
- Other tangible property
- Goodwill
- Patents and copyrights
- Organizational expense
- Research and development

All these items can be divided into three categories: (1) current, (2) fixed, and (3) other assets.

Current assets are those items that can be readily converted into cash within a one-year period. Current assets are assets in which the flow of funds is one of continuous circulation or turnover in the short run.

Fixed assets are items of property, plant, and equipment and are referred to as "fixed" because of their permanent nature and because they are not subject to rapid turnover. Fixed assets are used in connection with producing or earning revenue and are not for sale in the ordinary course of business.

Other assets are all the assets that are not current and cannot fit into the fixed asset category (such as research and development, or goodwill).

Current assets include:

- Cash
- Accounts receivable
- Inventory
- Investments or Notes receivable that can be converted to cash within one year
- Prepaid expense

Fixed assets include:

- Equipment
- Motor vehicles
- Furniture and fixtures
- Land and buildings
- Leasehold improvements (or building improvements)
- Any other property that you could consider tangible or long-lasting.

Other assets include:

- Goodwill
- Patents and copyrights

- Research and development
- Organizational expense
- *Sometimes* prototype costs

This lecture will cover the most important current assets—cash and accounts receivable.

CASH

The cash account is the most active of all business accounts. Receipts from sales (either in cash or payment of accounts receivable), receipts from the sale of assets, receipts from capital investment of the owners, and receipts of loan proceeds all go through the cash account. So will disbursement for payment of expenses, cost of goods sold, repayment of a liability, payment of dividends or owner's draw, and the purchase of assets.

The cash account is the *only* account that is used in transactions with all the other groups of accounts: assets, liabilities, capital, cost of goods sold, income, and expenses.

Cash transactions in the cash account can be roughly divided into (1) cash receipts and payments and (2) cash documentation in original vouchers, journals, and ledgers. Cash receipts come from sales of products or assets, investment in the business, or proceeds from borrowing. Cash documentation involves all bookkeeping records from the original transaction document (such as a sales receipt) to the journal to the ledgers.

Cash Receipts and Payments. The principal cash events and their related original transaction documents are shown in Figure 3.1. These original transaction documents initiate the processing of cash information. A cash receipt document indicates that the firm has received cash, and a check indicates that a payment has been made.

The concept of cash receipt, relocation, and disbursement can be illustrated in terms of how it affects journal entries, as shown in Figure 3.2.

Event	Original Transaction Document
Cash is received	1. Receipt (sales receipt, check, cash)
	2. Draft (bank deposit slip)
Cash is relocated or	3. Record of deposit (relocation of cash to a bank account)
	4. Transfer (relocation of cash from one business or division to another, or from one bank account to another)
Cash is disbursed	5. Bank adjustment (reduction from bank account for bank services, charges, and adjustments)
	6. Petty cash fund
	7. Check or money order

Figure 3.1 Cash events and original transaction documents.

Event/Voucher		Notation	Accounts	Debit	Credit
Cash is received					
1. Receipt voucher	(a)	Cash provided as equity from owners	Cash Equity	5,000	5,000
	(b)	Cash provided by long-term creditors	Cash Long-term liab.	2,500	2,500
	(c)	Customer pays cash on account	Cash Accts. rec.	150	150
	(d)	Fixed assets sold for cash	Cash Fixed asset	1,000	1,000
	(e)	A sale is made for cash	Cash Income	1,500	1,500
Cash is relocated					
3. Deposit	(f)	Cash is deposited in Bank	X Bank Cash	9,750	9,750
	(g)	Cash is transfered from X Bank to Y Bank	Y Bank X Bank	5,000	5,000
Cash is disbursed					
5. Adjustment	(h)	X Bank service charges are recorded	Bank chgs. X Bank	5	5
6. Petty cash	(i)	Postage stamps are purchased	Misc. expense Cash	50	50
7. Checks	(j)	Merchandise is purchased with a check from X Bank	Inventory X Bank	900	900
	(k)	A payment is made to long-term creditors from X Bank	Long-term liab. X Bank	500	500
	(l)	Owner takes draw from Y Bank	Owner draw (equity) Y Bank	1,000	1,000
	(m)	Payment is made to vendor from Y Bank	Accts. pay. Y Bank	250	250
	(n)	A fixed asset is purchased with a check from Y Bank	Fixed asset Y Bank	2,500	2,500
	(o)	Wages, rent, & other expense is paid	Expense Y Bank	1,000	1,000

Figure 3.2   Cash actions and journal entries.

The following is a list of typical origins of cash receipts and disbursements:

Receipts
1.   From customers, that is, collections of accounts receivable or notes payable.
2.   From cash sales.
3.   From miscellaneous repetitive sources, for example, rent income, interest income, dividends, and royalties.
4.   From miscellaneous repetitive sources, for example, sale of surplus assets or

investments and new sources of finance (bank borrowings, loans, equity investment from outside).

Payments

1. To suppliers of raw materials or other supplies, that is, reduction of accounts payable or notes payable.
2. To employees for salaries and labor-related expenses, for example, taxes, insurance, and pensions.
3. Utilities and other services where payment is made on a regular basis (telephone, accounting, maintenance, etc.).
4. Other operating expenses (supplies, small tools, fees, etc.).
5. Settlement of tax liabilities (federal, state, and local).
6. For capital expenditures, for example, the acquisition of land, buildings, plant, and equipment: representing significant but irregular payments.
7. To meet financial obligations:
    (a) Of a regular nature, for example, interest and dividend payments.
    (b) Of an irregular nature, for example, repayment of loans.
8. For any other purpose of a significant, irregular, or extraordinary nature, for example, settlement of litigation.

THE CASH TANK METHOD OF CASH MANAGEMENT

W. C. F. Hartley, in his book *Cash: Planning, Forecasting, and Control,*° describes an easy-to-visualize method of cash management called the *cash tank.* The level of liquid (cash) in the tank can only be controlled by one of two courses of action:

1. reducing or eliminating outflows by adjusting the valves on one or more of the outlet pipes;
2. increasing inflows by adjusting the valves on one or more of the inlet pipes.

A schematic diagram of such a liquid flow system appears in Figure 3.3. Shown are the main tank, feeder tanks, inlet pipes, and outlet pipes with the control valves pictured as a spoked wheel. The control valve regulates both the rate and timing of the flow.

Against the background of this physical model of liquid flow it is easy to visualize a cash flow system that adopts the same concepts. The main elements of such a system are incorporated into the second schematic diagram also shown in Figure 3.3. Only three feeder tanks have been used, representing the three major sources: income from operations, new financing (from debt or capital injection), and liquidation of assets.

Similarly, each group of inflows has its counterpart group of outflows: (1) appropriations of profit (payment of all expenses out of income, plus payment of taxes, owners' draw, dividends, etc.); (2) servicing or repayment of borrowings; and (3) acquisition of assets. If management is to control the level of cash in the tank, these are the three primary groups of inflow and outflow to be addressed.

FORECASTING CASH MOVEMENTS

Because cash flow is critical to a firm, it is essential that management attempt to forecast the likely pattern of future cash flows, if only as a precaution against business

°London: Business Books Limited, 1976.

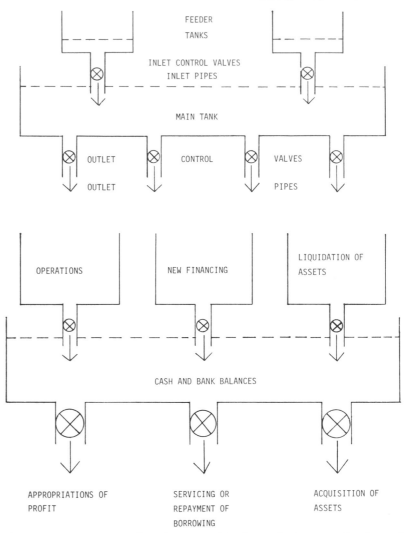

Figure 3.3 Cash is likened to a liquid system of feeder tanks (representing incoming cash), a main tank that holds the cash (representing cash now available to the company), and outlet pipes (representing, with their outlet control valves, the cash management process). The second diagram shows the sources of cash (operations, new financing, and liquidation of assets) and the uses of cash (expense and cost of sales expenditures, the appropriations of profit; repayment of borrowings, and aquisitions of assets).

failure. This forecast will not always prove to be precisely accurate, but it will still create reliable signals to indicate whether, when, and what type of action needs to be taken. A "good" forecast is not the one that turns out to be "right," but the one that provides the basis for guiding timely management action.

There are two types of forecasts:

- the short-term forecast, and
- the long-term forecast.

The Short-Term Cash Forecast

The short-term (or short-range) cash budget covers the length of a cycle from investment of cash to its recovery in such terms as inventory and receivables. The period covered is generally one year.

The prime objective of a short-term cash forecast is to ensure that a firm can pay its debts in the immediate future. It is oriented toward the guidance of appropriate management control action in the short term. For this reason, it needs to be up to date and reasonably detailed. It should be prepared at frequent intervals over the next 6 to 12 months.

The Long-Term Cash Forecast

A long-term (or long-range) cash forecast covers the length of a cycle from investment of cash to its recovery from such items as plant and equipment, market development, and research. The period most commonly used for this purpose is from three to five years, because this is viewed as being the maximum length of time in which sales trends, technology, and the products of market development and research can be projected. In cases where long-term cash flow is certain, as with ground rents, mortgage loans, or long-term leases, cash flow may be projected accurately for longer periods.

The object of preparing a cash forecast over the longer term is to indicate the future financial consequences of present courses of action. The long-term forecast is usually prepared annually. Its orientation is toward the financial consequences of and interrelationships of strategic management decisions.

MANAGEMENT CASH CONTROL

There are generally considered to be two types of control in the cash system: (1) stewardship controls and (2) management controls.

Stewardship Controls

Stewardship controls are designed to accomplish two things:

1. The proper receipt of all cash by the organization.
2. The proper disbursement of all cash by the organization.

Cash is more susceptible to theft than any other asset. Udjat repeated the phrase he had just said. Cash is more susceptible to theft than any other asset. . . . Remember this.

Strict stewardship controls are needed to prevent misappropriation of cash. Two forms of embezzlement should be noted:

- *Lapping.* The theft of cash received from one customer, but credited to that customer's account at a later date by using cash received from another customer.
- *Kiting.*
  (a)   Cashing an unrecorded check in one bank, and covering it with a check drawn on another bank.
  (b)   Opening a bank account with a fraudulent check (usually originating in a different city or state to lengthen clearing time), and then drawing most of the amount out before the bank discovers the error.

Embezzlement using the methods above, as well as other techniques, may be guarded against by maintaining a system of internal controls over the handling of cash. The following are general principles for controlling cash receipts and cash disbursements.

Some *general principles* for controlling *cash receipts* are:

1. The immediate separation of cash from its documentation. For instance, people who record cash transactions should not write checks or make deposits. Documentation is channeled to the accounting department and cash to the cashier. Their records can be compared.
2. The function of cash handling must be distinct from maintaining the accounting records. Neither party should have access to or supervise the recordkeeping of the other.
3. If possible, there should be a daily deposit of all cash receipts into the bank.
4. The person responsible for cash receipts should not be responsible for cash disbursements.

The following are *general principles* for controlling *cash disbursements*:

1. All disbursements should be made by check. Issuing a check should require approval of more than one person. A cancelled check is proof that payment was made, and payment by check provides a permanent record of disbursements.
2. Checks should be prenumbered. Spoiled checks should be marked "void."
3. If possible, checks should be signed by one person and countersigned by another.
4. Supporting invoices and other documentation should be perforated or marked "paid," in order to prevent double payment for the same item.
5. A system for approving payments should underlie the issuance of checks. The person who approved payment should not be the person who issues the check.

Note that stewardship controls place a repeated emphasis on the principle of *separation of duties*. Underlying this principle is the fact that the probability of embezzlement is decreased significantly where an act of dishonesty requires the collusion of two or more persons.

Management Controls

Management control has as its principal purpose *optimizing* the company's cash position. This is true if the company has a cash surplus or a cash deficit.

Excess cash may denote poor management because these cash resources can usually produce a higher return if they are converted to some other form of asset (such as investments). Contrary to popular thinking, a large cash balance is not a reliable indicator of an organization's good state of health; it may be just the opposite. Too little cash is also hazardous and may require unscheduled borrowing of funds or the untimely sale of the firm's assets.

Cash forecasts and budgets are the principal techniques for management control of cash. They serve as management controls for the following reasons:

1. They emphasize the timing of future cash events.
2. They indicate periods when cash surpluses or shortages are likely to occur, thus enabling management to:
    (a) convert temporary surplus cash into investments;
    (b) arrange in advance for financing for periods where shortages are indicated.
3. They facilitate the scheduling of loan repayments.

4. By distinguishing postponable from nonpostponable expenditures, they provide management with a basis for deciding priorities and for relating postponable needs to periods where better financing is available.

5. They provide guidelines for controlling disbursements, in that expenditures for a particular account cannot exceed budget without special approval.

MONEY FLOAT

Money *float* is also a very effective management cash control technique. "Float" is cash in transit. For example, the period between the time a check is written and the time it "clears" is a cash float. Many large companies pay their employees on the west coast with checks drawn on east coast banks so that the time between when the check is written, cashed at a west coast bank, shipped to an east coast bank, and subtracted from the company's account is lengthy. The company can use the cash during this time interval. Here are some more examples of float:

1. *Disneyland coupons.* Visitors to Disneyland exchange money for coupons at the gate. They may not use all of the coupons in one day, so they keep the rest for a return visit days, weeks, months (or never) in the future. Disneyland, of course, has been paid for the unused coupons so that it gets float on the money.

2. *Traveler's checks.* Bank of America, City Bank, Cooks, and American Express Company trade their traveler's checks for cash (the money you pay for the checks, if any, goes to the bank as a handling fee). The person who exchanges his or her cash for traveler's checks takes a vacation, during which he or she periodically cashes the traveler's checks. Meanwhile, the issuing company (American Express) has invested the cash it received. With a continuing stream of clients, the issuing company always has a substantial amount of 'float' invested, the earnings from which constitute the company's source of income.

3. *Trade dollars.* A group of merchants wish to encourage business among themselves as a group. The promoters issue trade association dollars in exchange for real money. For as long as the "trade dollars" remain in circulation within the group, the promoters can benefit from the investment of the "float."

4. *Gift certificates.* Rather than purchase an item from a retail store, many people buy gift certificates for relatives and friends. Until the relatives and friends spend these certificates, however, the company that issues them (the retailer) can use the money as "float."

The above are examples of how float can be created. While most businesses do not create float, they can use it. For example, analysis of check-clearing processes can permit a pairing of cash reserves.

Float works two ways in a checking account: When deposits are made, a float of from two to three days is usually required before the checks clear the payor's account. This is "negative float," for until the deposits are cleared the firm may not issue checks or make withdrawals. On the other hand, checks issued by the firm are "float" until they have cleared the firm's bank account. This is "positive float." To refine our measurement of float you can analyze checks outstanding at the end of each month and 'age' them according to the various time periods shown in Figure 3.4.

With sufficient aging data and experience, you have a basis for calculating probable float. You can calculate the percentage of total checks cashed in less than 30 days, less than 60 days, and so on. You could then figure that a certain amount of your checks are

Checks Outstanding	0–30 Days	31–60 Days	61–90 Days	Over 90 Days
No. 1012				$ 500
1015			$1,000	
1023			500	
1032		$1,500		
1035		500		
1041	$ 500			
1046	2,000			
1048	2,500			
	5,000	$2,000	$1,500	$ 500

Figure 3.4 "Aging" checks outstanding.

going to be outstanding, so that you could actually write checks for that percentage more than your cash balance in the bank. You could also get an idea of how long a certain company takes to cash checks, etc. Float analysis can in this way be a useful management cash control tool.

RECEIVABLES

The term *receivables* indicates claims for money and goods due from other businesses. There are various types or categories of receivables, including:

- Accounts receivable (due from customers)
- Notes receivable (due from those who owe money and who have signed a negotiable instrument or note)
- Deposits receivable or returnable
- Claims against various parties (governments, lawsuits)
- Advances to employees, officers, stockholders

Current Versus Noncurrent

Receivables may be listed as current assets or as long-term assets. To be classified as a current asset, a receivable should be convertible into cash within one year's time. Otherwise it should be classified as a noncurrent asset.

Receivables should be stated at their net realizable cash value. Initially, receivables may be stated at the invoice price of the sale if, for example, a credit sale for $100 is recorded. However, not all receivables are collectable; therefore, to state receivables at their net realizable cash value requires an estimate of the amounts of receivables that will not be collected. In other words, an *allowance for bad debts* or an *allowance for uncollectable accounts* should be deducted from receivables.

Discounting

It is commonly understood that a dollar today is worth more than a dollar tomorrow. This is because a dollar today can be invested or loaned, and thus interest can be earned. For example, if you have $100 and you can lend this money at 6%, at the end of a year you will have $106. On the other hand, if a customer buys some goods from you worth $100, but says that he will pay in one year's time, you don't have a $100 sale. You only sold $94.00 (100 × 0.94), assuming that you could have loaned the money at 6% interest.

A ruling issued in 1971 by the Accounting Principles Board (APB),° *APB Opinion No. 21*, requires that interest be imputed on receivables. This means that if you sell to a customer and allow liberal or lengthy terms for payment (1) without interest on the amounts owed, or (2) interest at an unrealistically low amount, then the amount of the sale and the amount of the receivable should both be reduced. They are reduced by a realistic level of interest on the amounts receivable. This interest is taken into account over the term of the receivable.

Example.   A company sells a machine to a customer for $1,000 with the following terms: $100 down, balance payable in three annual installments of $300 each, plus accrued interest. The unpaid balance will accrue at 4%. However, similar loans to another class of customers would normally require interest at 6%.

Amount of sale: $968 composed of:
                    $100 down payment
                     900 receivable
                    ___72 interest at 4%°
                  $1,072
                   _(104) less interest at 6%†
                  $ 968

Amount of receivable composed of: $868
                    Amount of sale $968
                    Less: Cash down   100
                                     _____
                                     $808

At the end of the first year you would record cash received of $336. And interest income of $52.

°Note that reducing sales and receivables for imputed interest is required for companies that issue financial statements that conform to generally accepted accounting principles. This is not a procedure that is acceptable for tax purposes, except in certain limited circumstances.

Bad Debts Expense

When you sell on credit, you must expect some customers not to pay, unless you have an extraordinarily effective collection procedure.

°The APB was the official rule-making body of the accounting between 1959 and 1973. It has been replaced by the Financial Standards Board.
†(900 × 0.04) + (600 × 0.04) + (300 × 0.04).
††(900 × 0.06) + (600 × 0.06) + (300 × 0.06).

There are four principal methods of calculating estimates of bad debt expense:

- Percentage of sales
- Percentage of credit sales
- Percentage of outstanding receivables
- Aging receivables

All of these methods are currently in use. The percentage of credit sales and percentage of outstanding receivables are most commonly used. The aging method probably gives the most accurate figure for bad debts expense, and with increased use of computers, it should become widely used.

Percentage of Credit Sales. When a percentage of sales approach is employed, a company's past experience with uncollectable accounts is analyzed. Assuming that there is a stable relationship between a previous year's charge sales and bad debts, that relationship can be turned into a percentage and used to determine the current year's bad debt expense (see Figure 3.5).

Percentage of Outstanding Receivables. Using past experience, a company can estimate the percentage of its outstanding accounts receivable that will become uncollectable. This procedure provides a reasonably accurate picture of the value of the receivables at any time, but it does not fit the concept of matching costs and revenues as well as the percentage of sales approach. This is because in the percentage of outstanding receivables method you must rely on the past to predict the future (see Figure 3.6).

Aging of Accounts Receivable

A more sophisticated approach than the percentage of outstanding receivables method is to set up an aging schedule. Such a schedule indicates which accounts require special attention by providing the age of the receivable (see Figure 3.7).

From Figure 3.7 you can see that the amount $189.00 indicates the bad debt expense to be reported for the year. But only if this is the first year the company has been in operation. In subsequent years, the allowance for doubtful accounts is adjusted to the amount determined by the aging schedule. An aging schedule is not only prepared to determine bad debts expense, but it may also serve as a control device to determine the composition of receivables and to identify delinquent accounts. The estimated loss

Year	Credit Sales	Actual Bad Debts
19x3	$1,000,000	$15,000
19x2	900,000	12,000
19x1	800,000	12,000
Total	$2,700,000	$39,000

Percentages $= \dfrac{\$39,000}{2,700,000} = 1.44\%$

19x4   Credit sales: $1,200,000
19x4   Estimated bad debt expense: 1.44% $\times$ $1,200 = $17,280

Figure 3.5   Calculation of bad debt by historical credit sales bases expected performance on past performance.

Year	Accounts Receivable (End of Year)	Accounts Receivable that Become Bad Debts
19x3	$150,000	$15,000
19x2	140,000	12,000
19x1	135,000	12,000
Total	$425,000	$39,000

Percentage: $\dfrac{\$39,000}{\$425,000} = 9.2\%$

19x4   Ending Accounts Receivable: $160,000
19x4   Estimated bad debt expense: 9.2% $\times$ $160,000 = $14,720

Figure 3.6   Calculating bad debt as a percentage of accounts receivable is another historical predictive technique.

Aging Schedule

Name of Customer	Balance 12/31	Under 60 days	61–90 Days	91–120 Days	Over 120 Days
Customer A	$1,000	$ 800	$200	$	$
Customer B	3,000	3,000			
Customer C	600				600
Customer D	750			150	
	$5,350	$4,400	$200	$150	$600

Summary

Age	Amount	Percentage	
Under 60 days	$4,400	1%	$ 44.00
61–90 days	200	5%	10.00
91–120 days	150	10%	15.00
Over 120 days	600	20%	120.00
Bad debts expense or allowance for doubtful accounts:			$189.00

Figure 3.7   To fully understand who owes you what for how long, the illustrated aging schedule is used.

percentage developed for each age category is based on previous loss experience and the advice of persons in your business who are responsible for granting credit.

The aging approach is sensitive to the actual status of receivables, but as with all estimates, it may overstate or understate the actual loss from uncollectable accounts.

DESIGNING A CREDIT POLICY

Receivables result from selling on credit, and the essence of credit sales lies in the tradeoff between increased sales and increased collection costs. Credit sales can be increased indefinitely in most businesses simply by liberalizing credit agreements. However, the increased sales become unprofitable when the costs of collection exceed the profit margin. Therefore, a balance between increased sales and collection costs must be sought.

Credit rating services, such as Dun and Bradstreet and TRW Credit Data, are helpful for making credit decisions, but rating services cannot themselves make credit granting decisions. They only provide the historical background on a prospective customer.

Receivables Information System

A credit policy should be based on the typical credit terms in your industry. You should expect to meet the terms offered by the competition in the industry. Customers that are poor credit risks require stricter terms. One way to formulate a sound credit policy is to develop a *credit information system*, sometimes called a *credit scoring system*. This is based on the five Cs of credit: character, capital, capacity, collateral, and conditions.

- *Character* Defined as the probability that a customer will try to honor his obligations, character is measured by past payment history. Interviews and references can supply relevant information.
- *Capital* Measured by the financial position of the firm as indicated by total assets, net worth, or debt to equity ratio.
- *Collateral* Represented by assets the customer may offer as security.
- *Capacity* Measured by the consistency of profitable operations.
- *Conditions* The state of the economy and the state of the industry in which the customer operates.

An illustration of a credit scoring sheet appears in Figure 3.8.

How to Develop Credit Scores

Based on data supplied in the customer's credit applications, assign points in each rating category. Then decide a cutoff point. The sum of the points in each category provides the customer's credit score. (In the example in Figure 3.8, points range from 1 to 5, but you can set your own range to suit the facts of your industry.)

As previously indicated, aging accounts is a useful technique because it directs attention to the most troublesome areas, and it may indicate necessary changes in credit granting policy. If the data are available, another useful technique would be analysis of payment history by customer class or category. Results of this technique may disclose that certain categories of customers are more trouble than they are worth and that credit should either not be granted or granted only on restricted terms.

Character					Points
Subjective measure	Excellent	Good	Fair	Marginal	
Points	5	3	1	0	☐
Capacity:	15+	10–15	5–10	2–5	
Years of profit	5	4	3	2	☐
Capital:	0–.010	0.10–0.25	0.25–0.80	0.50–1.00	
Debt/equity ratio	5	3	3	1	☐
Collateral:	Mortgage	Securities	Pledge	None	
Type	5	4	2	1	☐
Conditions:	Growth in	Growth in	Stable	Decline	
Sales growth in	past four	past two			
customer's industry	quarters	quarters			
	5	4	2	0	☐
Total score					☐

Figure 3.8   Sample credit scoring system based on common indicators of credit worthiness.

Ways to speed up the payment of receivables include:

- Discounts for early payment
- Add on interest for payment after a certain date
- Dunning letters that become increasingly threatening as time passes
- Personal telephone calls
- Outside collection services
- Legal action

You would like to stimulate payment with the method that costs least in terms of expense and customer alienation. There is a tradeoff between the severity of the stimulation technique and maintenance of customer satisfaction. You should relate the severity of the technique to the age of the receivable.

Bad Debts and the IRS. The tax law divides potential bad debts into three general categories:

1. Business bad debts.
2. Nonbusiness bad debts.
3. Personal bad debts.

Personal bad debts are generally not deductible at all unless they are fully supported by signed, legal agreements for repayment and evidence a business purpose. These agreements convert the bad debt from a personal one into a nonbusiness bad debt with an investment purpose. For example, a father makes a loan to his son so that the son can start a business. If there are no signed agreements, with specific repayment terms, the debt would not be deductible in the event the son could not repay. However, if the agreement is specific as to times and terms of repayment, if the father did expect repayment, and if the son could not repay, then the debt would be deductible as a capital loss. This capital loss from personal bad debts could offset capital gains by being subtracted in arriving at adjusted gross income (up to a limit of $1,000 per year).

Business bad debts are deductible in full against ordinary income. There are two methods used to determine the amount of the bad debt deduction. One is the *specific debt method*. Under the specific debt method the taxpayer deducts in each year the specific debts that become uncollectable in that year. This is used primarily by taxpayers who do not want to estimate a reserve for bad debts. It is not a generally accepted accounting principle for audited statements, and therefore it should be used only by businesses not issuing audited statements.

DEFERRING TAX ON INSTALLMENT SALES RECEIVABLE

Though it is not a generally accepted accounting principle to which auditors will attach a clean opinion, the *Internal Revenue Code* provides that the installment method of accounting can be used for tax purposes. This means that taxes on the uncollected portion of installment contracts receivable do not have to be paid until the cash is collected. This provision is available to all dealers in personal property who regularly sell on the installment basis, and to others who occasionally sell real property or personal property, if the amount received in the year of sale is 30% or less of the selling price.

Example. An individual sells a house for $100,000. The buyer assumes a $20,000 mortgage, makes a down payment of $30,000, and agrees to pay the balance of $50,000 over 10 years. The house cost the seller $60,000. How much profit would the individual report in the year of sale?

Answer: $15,000.

Explanation: The gross profit is $40,000 ($100,000 − $60,000). The installment method of reporting may be used because the cash received ($30,000) is not greater than 30% of the selling price ($100,000). The profit to be reported is the ratio of the gross profit ($40,000) divided by the contract price ($80,000, which is $100,000 − $20,000 mortgage assumed) times the cash received ($30,000).

ACCOUNTS RECEIVABLE FINANCING AND FACTORING

If you are in a business that is growing rapidly, you may find that there is a need for additional working capital, but that your balance sheet does not support unsecured borrowing from a bank. It is often possible, in similar circumstances, to borrow on a secured basis by pledging or assigning valid accounts receivable as collateral for the loan.

This type of loan is available from your bank or from a subsidiary of the banks that specialize in commercial financing. For businesses with higher degrees of risk, commercial finance companies or factors may be the appropriate source of funds.

The type of financing and the terms of the loan will vary by the character of the industry you are in and by the institution providing the financing. The two basic categories of receivable financing are (1) accounts receivable financing and (2) factoring.

Accounts Receivable Financing

In accounts receivable financing receivables act as collateral for a loan. The companies that apply for this type of financing are generally fast growing, highly seasonal, and in need of operating cash. Lenders will take great care to determine the value of that company's accounts receivable—the bigger and higher quality the customer is (e.g., IBM) the better. The cost of receivable financing is high compared to the cost of term loans. Term loan rates are usually the prime interest rate plus 1 or 2%. Accounts receivable loans may be prime plus 4 to 6%.

There are considerations that make receivable loans attractive. Interest is computed on an average daily balance basis (you only pay for what you use). No compensating balances (amount the company must maintain in checking at no interest) are required with receivable financing.

Factoring

Factoring is distinguished from receivables financing by the fact that in factoring the outstanding receivables are sold outright, and without recourse, to the factor. There are two types of factoring: *maturity factoring* and *discount factoring*.

In maturity factoring no funds are remitted by the factor until the receivables are collected. The factor, in essence, serves as the credit department of his customer. Typically the factor knows the customers of the client better than the client knows them and is able to determine the credit worthiness of a customer and the collectability of the receivable. The factor maintains credit files on customers in industries where factoring is common and has staffs of auditor and loan officers to assist collection procedures. In discount factoring, the factor in essence buys the receivables for cash, at a discount.

For the services the client pays approximately 1% of outstanding receivables as a factoring fee, but is relieved of collection and credit burdens. Factoring is not widespread outside of the textile and garment industries.

Improvement of Financial Ratios by Factoring.   Balance sheet financial ratios may be made to appear more favorable through factoring. Figure 3.9 presents an example of comparative balance sheets, with and without factoring. Without factoring, the company requires a $100,000 bank loan and incurs $200,000 of payables, while having $300,000 of receivables outstanding. The *current ratio* (current assets divided by current liabilities) is 1.53 : 1 without factoring. With factoring, the receivables are sold, and $200,000 is applied to reduce the accounts payable to $100,000 and pay off the note. The current ratio is increased to 2.6:1.

Questions on Cash

Udjat Her paused and then asked for questions. A gentleman in the middle of the room asked, "When you were discussing cash control, you said that the person who handles cash deposits should not handle cash receipts. I run a small company and all I have is a secretary, a bookkeeper, and a few warehouse people. What should I do?"

"The principal of managing cash receipts is not to allow the same person to write checks and make deposits. As far as personnel, instead of having your bookkeeper make the deposits, either you or your secretary can make them. When your bookkeeper makes out the checks, you should verify them before signing. Who are they made out to? Is it full payment or partial payment? Do all checks that are made out get recorded? It would be a good idea if someone other than your bookkeeper made out the checks, at least occasionally. You could have your spouse, yourself, or even your warehouse personnel make out the checks," Udjat answered.

Another person asked, "How do I find out how long on the average it takes for people to cash the checks I send them?"

Udjat Her answered, "The best way to do that is to look at your statement and original checks when you receive them from the bank. This will tell you how many checks were outstanding on the statement date (these are the checks that were not returned with the statement but were written before the statement date). You then 'age' the checks outstanding to see how long a time has lapsed between the time you wrote the check and the statement date. You will find some checks that were written as much as two weeks or more before the closing date are still outstanding. If the pattern is consistent every month, you can plan your actual cash deposits and checks accordingly."

Kimberly Rogers decided to ask a question, too. After all, when they were together they very seldom talked about accounting. "How does the new Financial Accounting

Assets		Liabilities		With Factoring			
				Assets		Liabilities	
Cash	$ 10,000	Accounts payable	$200,000	Cash	$ 10,000	Accounts payable	$100,000
Accounts receivable	300,000	Note payable	100,000	Due from factor	100,000		
Inventory	150,000	Net worth	160,000	Inventory	150,000	Net worth	160,000
Total	$460,000	Total	$460,000	Total	$260,000	Total	$260,000

Figure 3.9   A demonstration of the effect factoring has on a balance sheet. Total assets and liabilities are higher without factoring.

Standard Board's ruling on inflation accounting affect assets?" Kimberly asked with a smile.

ASSETS AND INFLATION

"The lady wants to know about inflation and assets," Udjat repeated. "Well, most of the people in this class will be happy to learn that right now this ruling only affects companies exceeding either $125 million of inventory and gross property, plant, and equipment or $1 billion in total assets. Does anyone here qualify?" Udjat paused as if he were looking for a show of hands. "But the lady is right in assuming that some time in the future this might affect a much larger segment of business.

"The reason for the ruling is that when inflation is not considered in the increase in the value of inventory and equipment and other fixed assets held over a period of time, you will overstate profits. According to the Department of Commerce data computed in 1979, corporate profits in that year could have been overstated by an astonishing $50 billion. This means that a gap of 30 to 40% existed between the amounts the companies reported and the 'real' economic earnings.

"Inflation accounting is a two-step process. Key balance sheet assets such as plant, equipment, and inventories are adjusted upward to reflect the ravages of inflation. On the income statement these upward adjustments translate into sharply higher depreciation expenses and cost of goods sold.

"The opinion requires that companies must come up with a supplemental Income Statement that contrasts three sets of numbers:

1. Historical cost figures such as those always used in accounting and still being used by companies under $125 million in current assets.
2. Constant-dollar figures, which are determined by taking the historical cost figures and adjusting them by a general price-level index such as the consumer price index.
3. Current cost figures calculated from today's replacement cost of each fixed asset and item of inventory."

SUMMARY

The students shifted from left to right, looking at their watches. Udjat looked at his watch. He was running one minute late. People were eager to leave. "Okay," he said, "I'll give you a one-minute summary, and then we can all disappear into the parking lot."

"Assets are what a company owns. Assets include cash, accounts receivable, inventory, investments, prepaid expense, equipment, motor vehicles, furniture and fixtures, land and buildings, building improvements (leasehold improvements for leasor), goodwill, patents and copyrights, organizational expense, and research and development.

"Current assets are the easily cash-convertible items such as cash, inventory, and accounts receivable. Cash is the most active of the accounts in bookkeeping. Into the cash account comes most of the money a business receives (income, debt, or equity), and from it is subtracted the costs of a business (expenses, cost of sales, asset purchases, and owners' income). It is sometimes helpful to visualize cash as a big tank holding money. The tank fills up when cash sales or collections of accounts receivable are made. The tank also fills from outside sources such as debt, equity investment, or asset conversion. The tank goes down when expenses are paid, inventory is paid for, debt is repaid, owners are rewarded, or assets are purchased.

"Cash is more susceptible to theft than any other asset. Therefore cash controls are needed by business to ensure that the cash they earn stays in the business. There are two types of cash controls. First, stewardship controls cash receipts by seperating cash from its documentation (the person who deposits the money does not keep the books for deposits) and controls cash payments by paying monies by check, marking the bill when paid, and having bills approved by a person other than the one who signs the check. Second, management controls are controls of budgeting and personnel to avoid cash loss.

"Cash 'float' is cash in transit. The time between when a check is written and when it is cashed is float. Float is also paying for something that you don't use until later. Disneyland coupons, traveler's checks, trade dollars, and gift certificates use float.

"Receivables are claims for money and goods due from customers and others. Discounting is when you sell to a customer and allow lengthy terms for repayment. If this happens, when you are paid, you have to declare the income as a smaller dollar amount than you receive, the difference being 'imputed' interest. Bad debt expense is the amount you allow for receivables that are bad, that is, not paid in full. You must declare as gross income any merchandise that is shipped, whether it is paid for in cash or you take an account receivable for it. If the account receivable is not paid, you write off the bad debt against your gross sales (which already includes that receivable as income). The three methods for determining bad debt expense are percentage of credit sales, percentage of outstanding receivables, and aging of accounts receivable.

"Since you must collect receivables to get cash, we discussed the advantages of a credit policy. You may use a numerical credit-scoring system for all new customers and make an organized effort for collections (discounts for early payment, interest for late payments, correspondence, telephoning, etc.).

"From time to time a business may need immediate cash and cannot wait for its accounts receivable to be paid. In this instance, the company might want to consider accounts receivable financing or factoring. Accounts receivable financing is an arrangement whereby a lender uses accounts receivable as collateral and loans a certain percentage of their value to the business to be paid back by endorsing the customer's payment check to the lender. Factoring is the process by which a business sells outright its accounts receivable to a factor. The factor notifies the customers that they own the accounts receivable and the customer pays them directly."

When everyone had left but Udjat and Kimberly, Udjat put his arm around her shoulder and said, "You just wait until I come to your class and put you on the line about data base management."

Chapter Four
Inventory, Fixed Assets, and Depreciation

Kimberly Rogers sat alone at an "outdoors" table of a health food restaurant in the bowels of a large 50-story downtown complex. Kimberly relaxed and watched as people rushed past. She watched their eyes. Some walked with downcast eyes, some walked with their eyes looking into the faces of others, and some people walked as though they were in a dream.

She thought about the project at Hero Manufacturing. She thought about the perfect software system. She thought about stillness. Her daily life was not without frustration. Like most people she had worries—about work, about her boyfriend, Udjat, about her car. The one thing that always helped to put things in proper perspective was a few moments of quiet reflection.

Soon Kimberly felt good. Soon she was sitting still, lost in her own thoughts. Her reverie was interrupted only when she felt a friendly hand on her shoulder. She quickly turned—it was Udjat Her. He was smiling. "I'm sorry I'm late. Ready for one of my celebrated lectures?"

Kimberly and Udjat arrived at the classroom earlier than the students. They talked for a while until most of the students arrived and one reminded Udjat that it was time to start.

Udjat began, "Last week we talked about cash and accounts receivable. In addition to cash and accounts receivable, there are other assets that are important to business.

"The other important current asset is inventory. How inventory is calculated and valued (last-in, first-out, and first-in, first-out, etc.) affects net profit directly. Unlike cash, accounts receivable, and other assets, inventories appear both on the balance sheet and on the income statement (profit and loss statement).

The most important consideration for fixed assets such as equipment, leasehold improvements, buildings, and so on, is the determination of their value and their depreciation. Depreciation is the allowance for wear-and-tear on assets determined by the tax code and accounting principles. The method of depreciation directly affects net profit. The higher the depreciation, the faster the fixed assets are depreciated, and the less profit the company will show. Also, since depreciation is the only expense that does not require a cash outlay, it figures predominantly in cash planning. Similar expenses are investment tax credit, depletion, and amortization.

I will discuss these topics in depth in this lecture.

INVENTORIES

Inventories are defined as (1) assets that are held for sale in the ordinary course of business, or (2) goods that will be used or consumed in the production of goods to be sold. Assets that are to be resold are excluded from inventory because they are not normally sold in the ordinary course of business. Assets held for resale might include building and equipment items that are being retired or stocks and bonds held for investment.

Inventories are typically considered within the setting of a trading business. A trading business purchases its merchandise in a ready-to-sell form and considers unsold units on hand at the end of the period as merchandise inventory. Usually only one inventory account appears in the financial statements of a trading business.

Most larger businesses are not merchandising operations, but rather are manufacturing concerns whose purpose is to produce goods to be sold to merchandising firms (either wholesale or retail). A manufacturing firm normally has three inventory accounts—raw accounts—raw materials, work in process, and finished goods.

The cost of goods and materials on hand, but not yet placed into production, is considered *raw materials inventory*. For example, raw materials are items such as plastic to make toys or steel to make a car. These materials can be traced directly to the end product. At any given point in time in a continuous production process, some units are not completely processed. The cost of the raw material for a partially completed product, plus the cost of labor applied specifically to the material and a share of the overhead costs, constitute the *work in process inventory*. The costs of completed but unsold units on hand at the end of the period are reported as *finished goods inventory*.

An example of categories of inventories:

Inventories

Finished goods	$200,000
Work in process	15,000
Raw materials	20,000
Other materials and supplies	30,000

The distinction between *inventories* and *supplies* lies in the fact that inventories typically become products to be sold, or at least part of a product to be sold, and supplies are consumed. Supplies would include lubrication oil for a machine, while inventory would include products manufactured by the machine.

The investment in inventories is usually the largest current asset in manufacturing and retail firms, and it may often be a significant portion of the firm's total assets. If unsalable items accumulate in inventory, a potential loss exists. If products ordered or desired by the customers are not readily available in the style, quality, and quantity required, sales and customers may be lost. Inefficient purchasing, faulty manufacturing, or inadequate sales efforts result in excessive or unsalable inventories.

Inventories are more sensitive to general business fluctuations than other assets. When sales demand is great, merchandise can be disposed of quickly, and large quantities of inventories are appropriate. However, during a downward trend in the business cycle, lines of merchandise will move slowly, stocks will pile up, and product obsolescence becomes a specter hovering over the manager's shoulder.

One essential of inventory planning and control is an accounting of information required by management to make manufacturing, merchandising, and financial decisions. Such an accounting system is often referred to as a *perpetual inventory system*.

In a perpetual inventory system, information is available at any time on the quantity of each item of material or type of merchandise on hand. There are basically two types of perpetual inventory systems: detailed inventory records that support the general ledger inventory account or detailed records that constitute an information system outside the accounting double-entry system.

In the first type of perpetual inventory system, purchases of raw materials or inventory are debited directly to an inventory account. As the inventory is sold or transferred to a work in process account, it is credited from the inventory account and debited to a work in process or cost of sales account. Thus, the balance in the inventory account at any time should equal the dollar value of inventory on hand. Figure 4.1 shows an example of this perpetual inventory system.

In the second type of perpetual inventory system, the records are similar to the first type. The basic difference is that dollar values are not maintained, and debits or credits do not enter into the accounting system.

Computers have greatly facilitated the process of inventory control and planning. Because of the data processing capability of computers, additional information can be kept and maintained in the perpetual inventory system. Some types of information that you might want to maintain are: a description of the inventory item, item number, location, minimum and maximum quantities to be maintained in inventory, vendor, amount on order, and amount and cost of items on hand.

Regardless of whether the perpetual inventory system is tied into the accounting system, or is a separate information system, it is necessary to periodically take a *physical inventory*. A physical count must be taken at least once a year for all inventories. Merchandising firms take inventories more often in order to maintain control over inventories that can be stolen easily by customers or employees.

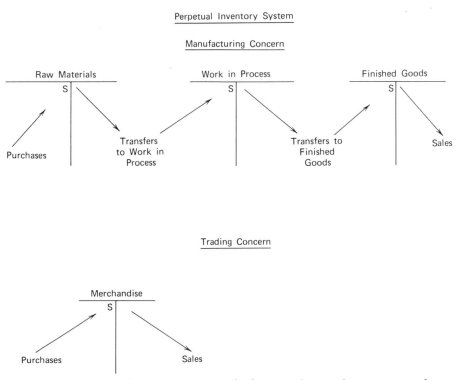

Figure 4.1   In a perpetual inventory system the business knows the quantity and type of inventory at all times. Manufacturers must keep track of three types of inventory—raw materials, work in process, and finished goods.

In recent years, some companies have developed inventory controls that are effective in determining inventory quantities. These methods are typically based on statistical sampling. The methods may be reliable enough so that an annual physical count of each inventory item is unnecessary.

Another inventory control possibility is to take the physical inventories throughout the year on a rotating basis. Thus, instead of taking one annual physical inventory, there is a continued physical inventory throughout the year so that all inventory items are counted and the detail records corrected at least once during the year.

FIFO VERSUS LIFO

There are three primary methods of valuing inventory and costs of goods sold for accounting and for tax purposes: (1) first-in, first-out (FIFO), (2) weighted average, and (3) last-in, first-out (LIFO).

Figure 4.2 presents an example of the calculation of the ending inventory values and the cost of goods sold under the three methods. As you can see, in a period of rising prices, LIFO produces a cost of goods sold dollar figure that is higher than the cost of goods sold produced by FIFO. This is the principal advantage of LIFO. In inflationary times, the effect of LIFO is to increase cost of goods sold, thereby reducing your reported net income and your tax burden.

	Units	Unit Cost	Total
Assume			
Beginning inventory	2	$10	$20
Purchases			
1	1	11	11
2	1	10	10
3	1	12	12
4	1	13	13
Cost of goods available for sale			$66
Total quantity available for sale	6		
Total sold during period	4		
Ending inventory units	2		
Weighted Average			
Cost of goods available for sale		$66	
Total units available for sale		6	
Average cost		$11	
Ending inventory value (2 × $11)		$22	
Cost of goods sold (4 × $11)		$44	
First-in, First-out (FIFO)			
Ending Inventory: 1 at $13 = $13			
1 at 12 = 12		$25	
Cost of goods sold			
Cost of goods available for sale	$66		
Less: Value of ending inventory	25	$41	
Last-in, First-out (LIFO)			
Ending inventory: 2 at $10 = $20			
Cost of goods sold			
Cost of goods available for sale	$66		
Less: Value of ending inventory	20	$46	

Figure 4.2 The three methods of inventory valuation—weighted average, FIFO, and LIFO—illustrated.

In certain situations, the LIFO cost flow will be representative of the physical flow of the goods into and out of the inventory. In most situations, however, LIFO will simply be an accounting and tax convention and will not be useful for control of inventory. An advantage of the LIFO method is that it reflects current disposable income. Essentially, though, LIFO has become popular for a practical reason: the income tax benefits.

As long as the price level of inventories increases and the inventory quantities do not decrease, an indefinite deferral of income taxes occurs with LIFO. Even if the price level later decreases, your company will have been given a temporary deferral of its income taxes.

There are some criticisms of LIFO that I must mention. *First*, the inventory valuation on the balance sheet is outdated and irrelevant because the oldest costs remain in the inventory. This causes several problems, especially regarding the measurement of working capital in the company. The difference between identical companies, one on FIFO and one on LIFO, with respect to working capital will be that in general the working capital under LIFO will be smaller.

Second, LIFO does not measure "real income" in the economic sense. In order to measure "real income" as opposed to monetary income, the cost of goods sold should consist of the costs required to replace goods that have been sold. The S.E.C., through its Accounting Series Release No. 190, requires an estimate of this "real income" number for approximately the 1,000 largest companies in the United States.

Third, with LIFO you face the involuntary liquidation problem. The involuntary liquidation problem occurs if the base layers, which have the old costs, are sold (liquidated). There can be bizarre results on income because old costs lead to an overstatement of reported income for the period and detrimental income tax consequences.

Fourth, in an attempt to avoid the negative consequences of the third criticism above, management may be led to make poor judgments with respect to inventory purchases. At year end, unnecessary purchases may be made in order to restore liquidated LIFO inventory base layers.

RETAIL INVENTORY

Retail merchants often have difficulties when it comes to financial control, decision making, and the tax consequences of inventories. A special method of inventory measurement and valuation has been developed to aid the retail merchant. This method is called the *conventional retail method*. There is also a LIFO variation on the conventional retail method.

Under the conventional retail method, goods in inventory are valued at the *retail selling price*. This inventory value is then reduced to approximate cost through multiplication by a cost-to-retail ratio! A separate ratio must be determined for each department or class of goods. Figure 4.3 presents an example of a conventional retail method calculation of ending inventory.

As you look at Figure 4.3 notice that all costs—including costs in the beginning inventory, freight-in, and purchases—are added to the cost side (or numerator) of the ratio. The retail value of the beginning inventory, the retail value of the purchases, and additional markups are added to form the retail side (denominator). The ratio is applied to the ending retail inventory to convert it to inventory at cost.

NONCURRENT ASSETS AND DEPRECIATION

The primary category of noncurrent assets for most businesses is property, plant, and equipment, which is also referred to as *fixed assets*. Fixed assets are machines, desks,

	Cost	Retail
Beginning inventory	$10,000	$ 20,000
Purchases	80,000	160,000
Freight-in	500	
Purchase returns	(2,000)	(4,000)
Markups		1,000
	$88,500	$177,000

Cost/retail ratio: $\dfrac{88,500}{177,000} = 0.50$

	Cost		Retail
Sales			(100,000)
Markdowns			(1,500)
Ending inventory	$37,750	0.50	$ 75,500

Figure 4.3   Conventional retail inventory method.

typewriters, buildings, trucks, and land. Virtually all businesses have fixed assets of some sort.

The interesting thing about fixed assets is that all of them except land are subject to depreciation. That is, the fixed assets wear out from use at some point. Even apartment or office buildings, which seem to appreciate rather than depreciate in value, wear out at some point. Therefore, the Internal Revenue Code allows a deduction on all fixed assets for depreciation.

The remainder of my lecture covers the topic of depreciation. Depreciation, and the related topics of depletion and amortization, are defined as follows:

- *Depreciation.*   In accounting terms, depreciation is defined as the process of allocating the cost expiration of tangible property against income. Depreciation also carries the connotation of decline in value due to use or wear or tear.
- *Depletion.*   Depletion is defined as the process of allocating against revenue the cost expiration of a natural resource, such as an oil well.
- *Amortization.*   Amortization is defined as the process of allocating the cost expiration of intangibles (such as patents or leaseholds) against revenue.

In order to determine the amount of depreciation, depletion, or amortization to be recorded for a period, or to be deducted for tax purposes, it is essential to know first:

1. The cost of the asset.
2. The estimated economic useful life of the asset.
3. The estimated salvage or residual value of the asset at the end of its useful life.

DETERMINING THE COST OF AN ASSET

The acquisition cost of an asset is measured by the cash outlay made to acquire the asset. If something other than cash is exchanged for the asset, the fair market value of the noncash consideration at the time of the transaction is the measure of cost. If the fair market value of the noncash consideration cannot be determined, the asset is recorded at *its* fair market value.

An asset is generally not considered to be acquired for accounting or tax purposes until it has been placed in the position where it is ready to be used. Thus, all reasonable and legitimate costs incurred in placing an asset in service are considered to be part of the cost.

Cash Purchase

If an asset is purchased for cash, any other necessary outlay, including installation costs, should be capitalized, that is, made into a depreciable asset. The costs to be capitalized (made an asset) include the invoice price plus incidental costs (such as insurance during transit, freight, duties, title search, registration fees, and installation costs).

Credit Purchases

For assets acquired on a deferred payment basis, the cash equivalent price of the asset, excluding interest, should be capitalized. Actual or imputed interest on the note payable or other liability should be charged to current expense when it is paid or accrued. Even if the purchase contract does not specify interest on the liability, imputed interest should be deducted in determining the cost of the asset.

Example.   To illustrate the purchase of an asset on credit, assume that a machine was purchased under contract that required equal payments of $3,154.70 at the end of each of four years when the prevailing interest rate was 10% per annum. To record the asset at $12,618.80 ($3,154.70 times four years) would include interest in the cost of the asset. The actual cost of the asset is the present value of the four payments discounted at 10%:

$$\text{actual cost} = \text{annual payment} \times \text{present value of the annuity}°$$
$$\$3,154.70 \times 3.1699 = \$10,000$$

Therefore, the cost of the machine would be $10,000. Likewise, the difference between the $10,000 cost and the total of the installment payments ($12,618.80) represents interest expense (of $2,618.80) that can be deducted as paid.

Assets Acquired in Exchange for Other Assets

If assets are acquired in exchange for other assets, further problems arise regarding the determination of the cost of the acquired assets. Items of property, plant, and equipment are frequently acquired by trading in an old asset in full or part payment for another asset. In some cases, an asset is acquired by exchanging another asset plus cash. Cash paid or received in an exchange transaction is often referred to as *boot*.

For tax purposes, the cost basis of an asset acquired through an exchange is equal to the cost of the asset given up, plus any cash boot given.

Example.   Your company acquired a truck three years ago for $9,000. It had an estimated life of six years, with *no* salvage value, and you used straight-line depreciation. The current *book value*, or *basis*, of the truck would be $4,500, calculated as follows:

°The present value of an annuity is found by taking the amount of the payment ($3,154.70), the term of the payments (4 years), and the prevailing interest rate (10%), then consulting an annuity table or using the proper formula to determine the value today (present value) of that income stream over that term.

1. $\dfrac{9,000}{6} = \$1,500$ depreciation per year.

2. 3 years $\times$ \$1,500 = \$4,500 depreciation for 3 years.

3. \$9,000 cost - \$4,500 depreciation = \$4,500 basis.

If a person traded in the old truck for a new truck and paid \$3,000 in cash in addition, this person would then have a new truck with a book value, or basis, of \$7,500,° despite the fact that the new truck might have a list price higher or lower than that amount.

Investment Tax Credit

It is important to determine the cost of an asset not only for depreciation purposes but also for an equally valuable tax reason, namely, the *investment tax credit*. The investment tax credit was established by Congress to stimulate the purchase of machinery and equipment throughout the economy. It was created in 1962 and has been modified subsequently several times. An investment credit is allowed against a person's tax liability when qualified business property is placed into service. The credit also may apply to progress payments made during the course of building or acquiring qualified property. The credit has no effect on regular depreciation.

Taxpayers can take a 10% credit for investments in qualified business property acquired after January 2, 1975. A corporate taxpayer may elect an 11% credit in an amount equal to 1% of the investment if it is contributed to an *Employee Stock Ownership Plan*. The maximum amount of credit that can be taken in any one taxable year is \$50,000, plus one-half of your tax liability in excess of \$50,000. The credit can be deferred up to seven years.

Example. Your company's tax liability before the investment tax credit is \$100,000. The maximum credit allowable is \$75,000 (\$50,000 + one-half of \$50,000). If you buy qualified property costing \$200,000, your credit would be \$20,000 and your tax liability would be \$80,000.

The amount of qualified investment depends on the useful life of the property to which the credit applies. Useful life is determined from the cost of the property. This is why the cost of an asset, discussed previously, is quite important.

Example. If you trade in a machine with a book value of \$4,000 and pay \$1,000, in additional cash, for a new machine, the cost of the new machine would be \$5,000, and you would be allowed an investment credit of \$500 (10% of \$5,000).

However, if the machine you acquire is used, rather than new, then only the excess cost above the book value qualifies for the investment credit. Therefore, in the example above, your investment credit would be reduced to \$100 (\$5,000 - \$4,000 times 10%).

The rule about property applies even if you sell an asset and then later reinvest the proceeds in a used asset of a similar type.

Example. If you sell a truck, which has a book value of \$3,000, and then later you buy a truck for \$5,000, the amount of cost that qualifies for the investment credit is limited to \$2,000 (\$5,000 - \$3,000).

The investment tax credit applies to *depreciable tangible personal property*. This means it applies to property used in your trade or business that has a physical existence

°\$4,500 basis (present 'book' value) of truck traded plus \$3,000 cash.

and that is not inventory, supplies, or real estate. Livestock of a farmer, except for horses, is considered to be qualified property.

Examples of qualified property include: office equipment, machinery in a factory, computers in a store, and neon signs for advertising. Even the cost of producing a motion picture or TV film has been considered to be qualified property, though it is more intangible than tangible.

The investment credit does apply to real property in certain circumstances. In order to qualify, the real property must be an integral part of either a manufacturing, production, mining, or utility operation, or constitute a research facility, or a facility for bulk storage of commodities. Examples of real property qualifying for the investment credit include: blast furnaces, oil derricks, oil and gas pipelines, broadcasting towers, and railroad tracks.

The credit is allowed for the year that the qualifying property is placed into service. This is the earlier of either (1) the first year that depreciation on the asset can be taken, or (2) the year the asset becomes ready for its intended purpose.

There is a limit on the amount of investment in used property and equipment that will qualify for the investment tax credit. The limit is $100,000 for corporations and the same for individuals. However, if you are married and file a separate tax return, the limit is $50,000. For a partnership, the limitation is $100,000 for the partnership as a whole.

No investment credit is allowed for property with a useful life of less than three years. Used property will not be qualified if, after you acquire it, it is used by the person from whom you acquired it. An example of this might be a sale and lease-back arrangement. Property which you have used before or property you have repossessed will not qualify. Property which you acquire from your subsidiary, or from your parent company if you are a more than 50%-owned subsidiary, would not qualify. If you sell or give personally owned property to a business which you control, the business cannot take a credit.

No credit is allowed for property that is used primarily for housing or to provide lodging, such as a hotel or motel. However, facilities related to housing or lodging may qualify, such as a restaurant in a hotel, or laundry machines in an apartment building.

USEFUL LIFE LIMITATIONS

In order to qualify for the full investment credit, the useful life of the asset must be at least seven years. If the useful life is five or six years, then only two-thirds of the cost of the asset qualifies for the credit. If the useful life is three or four years, then only one-third of the cost qualifies. If the useful life is less than three years, the asset does not qualify for the credit.

Example. Assume that you purchase a delivery truck, a small computer, and a lathe. The amounts qualified for investment credit are calculated as shown in the accompanying table.

Asset	Useful life	Cost	Percentage	Qualified amount
Delivery truck	3	$ 9,000	33⅓%	$ 3,000
Computer	5	12,000	66⅔%	8,000
Lathe	7	15,000	100%	15,000
				$26,000

The total investment credit is therefore $26,000 × 10% = $2600.

If the credit is not used in the period when it is earned, it may be carried back to offset taxes already paid up to three years previously, and it may be carried forward up to seven years.

The investment credit may have to be recaptured if the asset is not held at least seven years. Even if the asset is destroyed, recapture of the credit will occur.

Example. You bought a machine in 1978. It has a useful life of 10 years and cost $8,000. In 1978 you could have taken an $800 credit. However, if the machine is destroyed by fire in 1980, the $800 will be added to your tax liability for 1980.

DEPRECIATION

Once you have acquired a fixed asset and have determined its cost, then the question of depreciation arises. The Internal Revenue Code recognizes that a depreciation allowance is necessary because property gradually approaches a point when its usefulness is exhausted. Therefore, depreciation is allowed only on property that has a definitely limited useful life. Depreciation may even be allowed on fruit trees if it can be shown that the trees have a limited life.

Intangible property can be depreciated if its use in a business is of limited duration. Examples of depreciable intangibles include licenses, franchises, patents, and copyrights. Ordinarily, depreciation of intangibles is referred to as amortization.

Depreciation Methods

The Internal Revenue Code specifies three particular methods of computing depreciation. However, others may be used. The three methods are:

1. straight-line,
2. declining-balance, and
3. sum-of-the-years' digits.

You do not have to use the same method for all your depreciable property, but once you choose a method for a particular property you must continue using that method unless you obtain approval from the Internal Revenue Service to change. Obtaining approval is not a problem. You simply file Form 3115 during the first 180 days of the year of the change.

Useful Life and Salvage Value

You may enter into an agreement with the IRS as to the useful life, depreciation method, and salvage value of any property. However, there are classes of property that have been established by Internal Revenue Regulations. These classes each have asset depreciation ranges. If you choose a useful life within the limits of the asset depreciation range for a given asset, you will not be challenged by the IRS.

Salvage value, established at the point when property is acquired, is the amount that can be realized when the property is no longer useful to the taxpayer. It may be no more than junk value, or it may be a large portion of the original cost, depending on the length of time before the end of the asset's useful economic life. The length of time for useful life is determined by when the taxpayer plans to dispose of the property. An estimated salvage value of *less than 10%* of the original cost may be *disregarded* in computing depreciation. However, no asset may be depreciated below a reasonable salvage value.

Salvage value must be subtracted from original cost in computing straight-line and sum-of-the-years' digits depreciation. It is not subtracted in computing declining-balance depreciation.

Example. A machine is purchased for $10,000. It has a salvage value of $2,000 and a useful life of five years. The first year of depreciation under each of the three methods is (each term is defined in the paragraphs that follow):

- *Straight line*

$$\frac{\$10,000 - \$2,000}{5} = \$1,600$$

- *Sum-of-the-years' digits*

$$(\$10,000 - \$2,000)\frac{5}{15} = \$2,667$$

- *Double declining-balance*

$$\$10,000 \ (40\%) = \$4,000$$

Depreciation Examples

Straight-Line. The formula for straight-line depreciation is: cost minus salvage value divided by useful life equals depreciation for each year.

Sum-of-the-Years' Digits. Sum-of-the-years' digits depreciation allocates a declining portion of the total cost to depreciation expense in each year. In the example just mentioned where a machine was purchased for $10,000 and had a salvage value of $2,000 and a useful life of five years, sum-of-the-years' digits depreciation would be calculated as follows:

Year	Factor	$\times$	Cost minus salvage	$=$	Depreciation expense
1	5/15		$8,000		$2,667
2	4/15		8,000		2,133
3	3/15		8,000		1,600
4	2/15		8,000		1,067
5	1/15		8,000		533
					$8,000

The formula for calculating the denominator of the sum-of-the-years' digits fraction (which is 15 in the above example) is:

$$\frac{n \ (n + 1)}{2}$$

where n = useful life.

Example:

$$\text{useful life} = 5 \text{ years}$$
$$\text{denominator} = \frac{5 \times (5 + 1)}{2} = \frac{30}{2} = 15$$

Sum-of-the-years' digits cannot be used for real estate, except for new residential rental buildings such as apartment houses.

Declining-Balance. The declining-balance method applies a constant percentage to the declining book value of the asset.

Example. Same assumptions as above. Cost of machine = $10,000; useful life = five years.

Double Declining Balance

Year	Percentage	Book value	Depreciation
1	40%	$10,000	$4,000
2	40%	6,000	2,400
3	40%	3,600	1,440
4	40%	2,160	864
5	40%	1,296	518.40

Note that the total depreciation exceeds the original cost minus salvage value of $8,000. This would *not* be allowed for tax purposes. Therefore, in year four only $160 of depreciation could be taken (in order to bring the book value equal to the salvage value), and in year five no depreciation would be taken.

The maximum rate on declining-balance depreciation is specified by the following table. The factor is multiplied by the straight-line rate in order to find the maximum declining-balance rate.

Type of property	Factor
New equipment	2
Used equipment	1½
New real estate	1½
Used real estate	1
Used residential rental property	1¼

Example. You buy a new apartment building with a 50-year useful life. The maximum percentage you can use on declining balance depreciation is 3% (1½ times ¹⁄₅₀).

Depreciation for Periods Shorter than One Year

Usually when you acquire an asset during a year, you prorate the depreciation that you owe on the asset.

Example. On April 1, you acquire a machine for $12,000. It has a useful life of 10 years. You decide to use straight-line depreciation. The depreciation expense for the year of acquisition would be $900: ($12,000/10 $\times$ 9/12).

GAINS AND LOSSES ON SALES

The rules regarding the computation of gains and losses upon sale or retirement of depreciable assets are somewhat complicated. In general, capital gains and losses are taxed at different rates than gains and losses on the sale of other assets. Depreciable property is not a capital asset. Therefore, capital gains and losses are not allowable when depreciable property is sold. However, Congress decided in Section 1231 of the

Internal Revenue Code to extend capital gain treatment to depreciable assets while preserving the benefits of ordinary loss treatment. Later, Congress changed its mind and added Section 1245 of the Code which provides that for equipment that you sell, you have ordinary gain treatment to the extent of any depreciation taken on the equipment.

Example. You buy a machine in 1978 for $10,000 and decide to depreciate it on the straight-line method over 10 years. By the end of 1980 you have taken $2,000 in depreciation. If you then sell the machine for $11,000, you must record $2,000 of ordinary income gain and $1,000 of capital gain.

Another Example. On January 1, 1971 you bought a machine for $6,000. You claimed $600 depreciation on it for each year and sold it for $2,000 on July 1, 1980. Your adjusted basis on the date of sale was $300 [$6,000 less $5,700, which represents $600 per year depreciation between 1971 and 1980 (nine years) plus $300 for the half year in 1980]. Therefore, your gain was $1,700 on the sale. Since the gain ($1,700) was less than the total depreciation ($5,700), the entire gain must be included as ordinary income.

On *real property*, gain or loss is calculated in the same way as for personal property if the following apply:

- You compute depreciation on the property using the straight-line method (or any other method resulting in depreciation not in excess of that computed by the straight-line method), and you have held the property more than a year.
- You realize a loss on the sale of property.

Otherwise, real property disposal by sale or exchange must be calculated by a special formula to determine what portion of the gain is to be treated as ordinary income.

SUMMARY

Udjat Her stopped and looked around the room. "Let me summarize. LIFO inventory shows a lower profit in time of inflation. FIFO shows a higher profit in times of inflation. If you want to show a higher profit use FIFO; if you want to show a lower profit, use LIFO. Inventory is in three stages. First the raw material comes in the door—the people in the factory turn it into finished products and that becomes 'finished goods inventory.' When inventory is counted the goods that are only half finished are considered 'work in process inventory.' There are ways to keep track of your inventory on an ongoing basis—that's called using a 'perpetual inventory system.' This is done by an ongoing count and documentation.

"All fixed assets and some intangible assets have a value that can be depreciated for tax and accounting purposes. The cost of an asset is the amount you pay for it plus tax plus shipping plus installation. If you buy an asset for something besides cash (e.g., in exchange for inventory), the value of the asset is equal to the value of the things you exchange (the inventory).

"The cost of an asset acquired through an exchange is equal to the cost of the asset given up plus any additional cash paid, regardless of the value of the asset purchased. If I trade an old truck with a book value of $4,500 plus $3,000 in cash for a *new* truck, the new truck is worth $7,500. It doesn't matter what price the new truck lists for.

"I can take an income tax credit of 10% on all new property I buy that has a life of over at least seven years.

"Assets have different expected lives according to the length of time you expect to wait before you dispose of the property, and assuming it is not less than IRS guidelines. Whatever value that you think the assets will have at the end of their life is the salvage value. "There are three methods of depreciation that are usually used: straight-line, declining-balance, and sum-of-the-years' digits.

"The formula for straight-line depreciation, the simplest form, is: value of asset minus salvage value divided by the number of years in the asset's life. The formula for double declining-balance depreciation is: value of the asset times the number of years life times two divided by 100."

The class filed out. Udjat took Kimberly's hand as he turned out the classroom lights. "Now let's go take inventory at a little late night spot I know."

Chapter Five
The New Bookkeeper
—Computerized Accounting

Kimberly Rogers's eyes scanned the audience. There were fewer people than at her other lectures. There were four women in attendance. She checked her overhead projector for the figures and began:

Accounting systems and computers are *comparable* in many ways:

- Manipulation of numbers is their central concern.
- They are both essentially binary systems. The computer "computes" by allowing conduction of electrons from component to component, each component being in either an "on" or "off" state. All accounting activities of a business are also concerned with only two states: *assets* (one side of a balance sheet) and *equities* (liabilities and owners' equity, which are the other side of a balance sheet). See Figure 5.1.
- Accounting systems and computers are both man-made, and therefore artificial systems.
- Computers and accounting are affected by largely unpredictable outside events. Federal (SEC, IRS, etc.) and industry (AICPA, etc.) rulings both affect accounting systems. Power failures, magnets, operator mistakes, and coffee spills on circuit boards will negatively affect a computer. An accounting system that works well one year might be inadequate the next because of government or industry pronouncements. A computer that is chugging along one minute might be all garbage the next if something external happens to the system.

ASSETS = EQUITY

ASSETS = LIABILITIES +
(Owners' capital + income − cost of sales − operating expense − non operating cash payments + depreciation)

ASSETS = LIABILITIES + (Owners' capital
                                       + retained earnings

Figure 5.1 **The basic components of accounting are assets and equities (liabilities and equity of owners). Owner's capital includes the money that is retained in the company as a result of operations.**

Computers and accounting systems also *differ* in important ways:

- Computers have been in use less than 40 years whereas accounting has been developed over 5,000 years.
- Accounting is based on real-world economic events. Computers are designed around theoretical mathematical models.
- Accounting is primarily a system to *gather* data. Computers are best used to *analyze* and *manipulate* data.

The table in Figure 5.2 summarizes the similarities and differences of the two systems.

ACCOUNTING TECHNOLOGY AND ACCOUNTING SYSTEMS

Before we proceed further in our exploration of accounting and computer technology, I am going to differentiate between accounting technology and accounting systems.

The *technology* of accounting consists of the physical artifacts that are employed to process accounting data. These artifacts range all the way from quill pens to computer systems. Accounting *systems*, on the other hand, are the instructions and rules for classifying and structuring accounting data. Accounting systems are concerned with grouping accounts representing ownership, equity, cost, and income. It is possible to change the accounting technology without changing the accounting system.

I make a clear distinction between system and technology because many people think that because you have changed the accounting technology (to computers) this automatically makes dramatic changes in the accounting system. This is *not* so. Computer technology provides a dramatic improvement in the speed and control of accounting, but it does not directly affect the accounting system.

ADVANTAGES OF COMPUTER ACCOUNTING SYSTEMS OVER MANUAL SYSTEMS

The advantages of computer accounting systems over manual systems are:

1. The computer can immediately post the transaction data to the accounts. Therefore the account balances are updated automatically as soon as the journal data is entered.
2. The computer can perform calculations at speeds of millions to billions of calculations per second.

COMPUTERS AND ACCOUNTING SYSTEMS

Similarities between	Differences between
• Use numbers	• Term of historical use
• Binary systems	• Real-world versus modeled events
• Man-made systems	• Gathering versus manipulating data
• Affected by outside events	

Figure 5.2 A comparison of the similarities and dissimilarities between computer systems and accounting.

3. If the data have been entered properly, the computer rarely makes errors and can be instructed to 'trap' certain types of errors that might be present in the data if entered improperly.

4. The computer can prepare accounting statements immediately at the close of an accounting period rather than requiring several hours or days of manual work.

5. With proper programming the computer prints a flexible array of output formats.

CONSIDERATIONS IN CONVERTING FROM MANUAL TO COMPUTER SYSTEMS

It is unusual for a company to switch directly from a manual bookkeeping system to a computer system. There is usually a gradual conversion of functions from manual to computer. Moreover, it is always good practice to run a manual system parallel to the computer system until the computer system is totally "debugged."

For the purposes of this lecture, however, the significant characteristics of a computer system are best illustrated by comparing them directly with a manual system.

Designing the System

A manual bookkeeping system can be set up easily by purchasing journals and ledgers and designing a chart of accounts which lists all the accounts by number. If there are unusual accounting items, a decision on procedure may be postponed until these items start to appear. In short, little design work is required for a manual system.

Before installing a computer system, one needs to prepare a detailed preliminary analysis of the application, paying particular attention to unusual or nonroutine items. Applications must consider output, input, application statistics, details of the computer system, and layout of files. A flow diagram and documentation must be designed and kept. One must write a computer program to process all of this detail long before the first input document arrives in the installation. Consequently, it takes much longer to set up a computer system than a manual accounting system.

A less obvious, but sometimes very important, consideration is that the computer system is more likely to be designed by a computer programmer than by an accountant. A manual system is never designed by a programmer, but always by an accountant.

Entering the Data into the System

With a manual accounting system the input data are recorded directly into the books, by the individual item in the journals and by totals posted to the ledgers. These entries are not checked for errors until a trial balance is made at the end of a period. With computer systems, the entry is only made once into a "journal," and the entry is checked for error as it is being made. That is, the computer input program checks for such errors as an imbalance in debits and credits, an alphabetic character where a numeric is required, or a posting to a nonexistent account.

Costing

For management the purpose of the accounting system is to provide a detailed analysis of costs. A manual system will provide analysis on a limited basis by placing each amount into a specific ledger account. This degree of analysis might have been adequate in the past, but it is too elementary to satisfy today's information needs. In a computer system, if you have the initial data, it may be quickly manipulated in any desired way.

Sequential Processing

In a manual accounting system an original document may pass through many hands. For example, a purchase invoice would start with a salesperson, be passed to manufacturing, then shipping, and then accounts receivable clerks. This division of labor discourages the possibility of fraud but at the same time it increases the possibility of error.

A computer system works differently. Once the data have been entered, all subsequent processing such as sorting, calculating, posting, and recording is done automatically. This illustrates one of the major advantages of the computer. Each separate operation using the computer can be performed with speed and accuracy greater than humanly possible.

Centralized Files

As a consequence of installing a computer system files tend to become centralized. In a manual system, each department might have its own set of files. Since centralized data processing tends to encourage centralized accounting, separate department files disappear.

Random Inquiries and Data Analysis

A random inquiry for data from a manual system might be answered faster than a similar request from a computer. If the information required is on disks or tapes not being actively used, you must wait until the computer is available to search these old disks or tapes. In a manual system, the person making the inquiry need only go to the files and look it up. In this case speed is greater for the manual system. This, of course, assumes that the data required have been filed properly and the files are not stored in a warehouse.

If the computer has drawbacks when answering random inquiries, this is easily compensated for by its advantages in compiling statistical reports.

STRUCTURE OF A COMPUTER ACCOUNTING SYSTEM

The first programs that were developed for accounting uses were written by computer programmers—probably engineers by profession. In the earliest accounting systems everything had to be programmed in either machine language or assembly language. Therefore, the accounting almost had to be programmed by an engineer or a scientist trained in this precise language. But even though times have changed, the program accounting systems have not. Most accounting programs are still written by engineers and not by accountants.

An owner of one software company told me, "I don't know *any* really good computer people who understand accounting." When asked how his company had prepared their software when he didn't have a thorough grounding in accounting, he answered, "I can design the hell out of accounting systems because it isn't necessary to know about accounting. I just look at the flow of information. I find out what the input is and what output is needed and I design around that flow of information. I don't need to know what a Sources and Application of Funds Statement is, I just need to know what it does."

This line of thinking does not take into consideration the fact that accounting is a changing—not a static—system. Sometimes the accounting system and the records required may have to change radically. When the Financial Accounting Standards Board (FASB) of the American Institute of Certified Public Accountants (AICPA) makes an announcement, it has the sanction of all the CPAs in the United States. FASB pronouncements may require that companies keep inflation-adjusted records of their assets, or require that previous lease expenses now be considered assets, and so on. Changes in accounting require changes in accounting systems. Most accounting systems are not written to accommodate these special controls.

One important aspect of accounting is the maintenance of controls. Controls should keep track of all entries so that they can be recalled when needed. This is an audit trail. Controls could be something as basic as verifying that the figures entered for a series of transactions all balance before they are posted.

The model of a computer accounting system shown in Figure 5.3 takes controls into account.

Accounting System Model

Figure 5.3 shows a model of what a computer accounting system might look like. For simplicity, I will break it into three components for explanation: input, processing and files, and output.

Inputs in the accounting system are of two types: accounting and business data (such as customer or personnel information) and control information (accounting controls, output form controls, creation of chart of accounts, etc.). Accounting and business data would include: monetary data (sales, expenses); nonmonetary data (names, addresses, and identifiers of customers, suppliers, and personnel); future plans (budget data); and "what if" simulations (what if sales were . . . what would costs be?). Control infor-

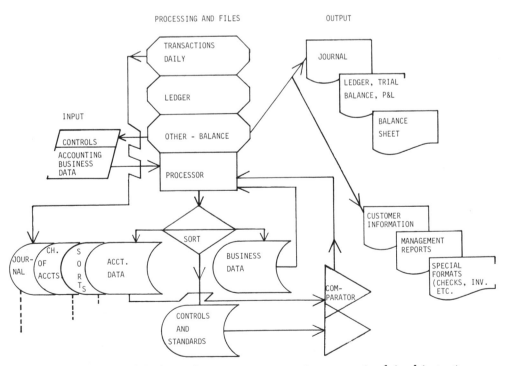

Figure 5.3   Model of sample computer accounting system (explained in text).

mation could include: accounting postulates, principles, and procedures (e.g., calculation of depreciation); selected output formats; and chart of account creation and modification (e.g., Cash is assigned the chart of account number 10000). Control input will be subject to more frequent modifications than accounting and business data.

Outputs are the financial statements; management reports; information about customers, suppliers, personnel, and budgets; and special formats such as checks, invoices, and so on. Outputs are influenced not only by the accounting and business data inputs, but also by the controls. Before output is produced, the raw data are compared with the controls and standards and processed.

The *processor* transforms input into output. The processor is instructed by the *comparator* which compares accounting data, business data, and controls for the proper response. In the illustration (Figure 5.3) the processor has attached to it three programs. These programs illustrate the minimum needed for a General Ledger accounting system: (1) daily transactions program which allows journal (daily) entries to be made of each transaction; (2) a ledger program which posts the accounts entered serially in program (1) above into individual account headings (such as rent); and (3) the balance and other programs which close out the ledgers and identify and carry forward the accounts that have to be preserved for the next accounting cycle (the Balance Sheet accounts). In other words, the job of the programs is to allow original entries (1), then separate them by specific account type (2), and then manipulate the result into some meaningful form (3). The posting program which takes the journal entries and puts them into ledger accounts involves several processes. The program reads the file journal, sorts or groups the records according to their account number, writes these totals to each ledger account into a sorted file, and prepares a trial balance. Figure 5.4 shows the flow of documents in a manual accounting system for comparison.

In summary, there are a minimum of three programs and four files. The operator manually enters raw data in the first file. With little human intervention, the program then derives from this information all the remaining files and reports. The more sophisticated systems will allow many operator options such as input controls, selection of formats, selection of "what if" criteria, and so forth. The sophisticated system will also have files for inventory and other direct-access recording functions.

Sorts

It is estimated that 25% of business computer time is devoted to sorting. Items are usually sorted according to some common characteristic, such as an account number. It is a business convention to use a chart of accounts, which in a simple example might group all cash transactions, all charges, all inventory, etc.

To the accountant, each transaction is a journal entry. To the programmer, each entry is a *record*. A collection of records may be called a journal or a *transaction file*. Each record contains several pieces of information, called *fields*. Several similar records make up a file. Figure 5.5 outlines a general ledger/journal record as it would appear in the transaction file.

Note that the accounting record is not a single record, but a dual record. Every accounting transaction requires at least two entries—a debit and a credit. If the transaction is to pay $1,500 for rent, the entry has to be a debit to rent expense of $1,500 and a credit to cash of $1,500.

The record structure in Figure 5.5 also has several *fields*. These fields include one each for the account number, the date, the dollar amount, the description, and one for other descriptors. The accounting programs are going to be reading this file—many times—as a series of alpha-numeric variables. The fields are read in sequential order— the account number, date, dollar amount, etc. The fields are kept separate so that data

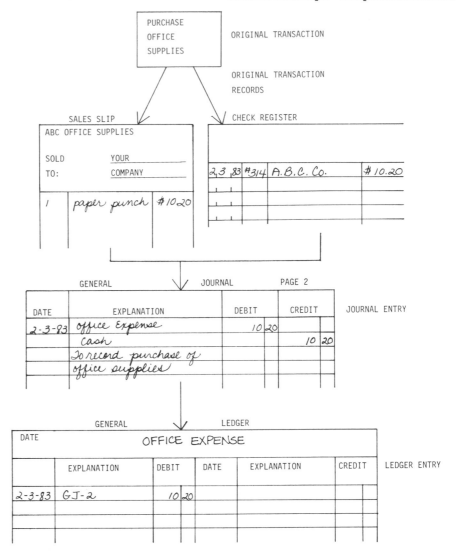

Figure 5.4   Documents in the manual accounting process.

contained in a particular field can be extracted and sorted with data in the same field of other records.

Accounting System Data Flow

The data flow of a simple accounting system is illustrated in Figure 5.6. After the beginning of the program, the *program menu* (listing of application programs) and command interpreter come into computer memory. The *command interpreter* allows the operator to edit text and files by using a simplified command language. The operator tells the computer that the operator wants to make journal entries. After the entries are made, the operator has a chance to modify them through the use of the command interpreter if entries are wrong. The program may be one that checks for proper debit and credit balances, or accepts only numeric or alphabetic characters into particular fields, or checks to see if that particular account combination is possible— automatically. If errors are found the program might prompt the operator to change the input.

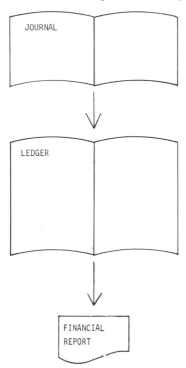

Fig 5.4   Continued

If all the entries are correct the journal records are sorted into account groups and numbers and put into the general ledger. The new balances in the general ledger are then printed and the operator, either manually or through computer prompt, may again change the material. If the material is correct, all the accounting statements (income, balance sheet, general ledger, etc.) are printed. If no corrections are neces-

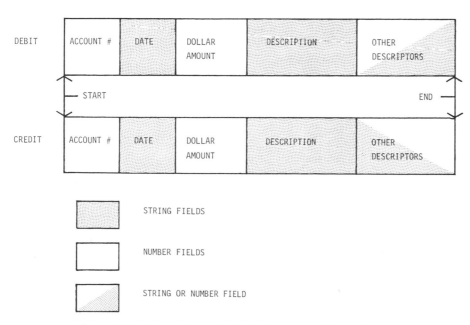

Figure 5.5   Computer equivalent of a manual journal entry.

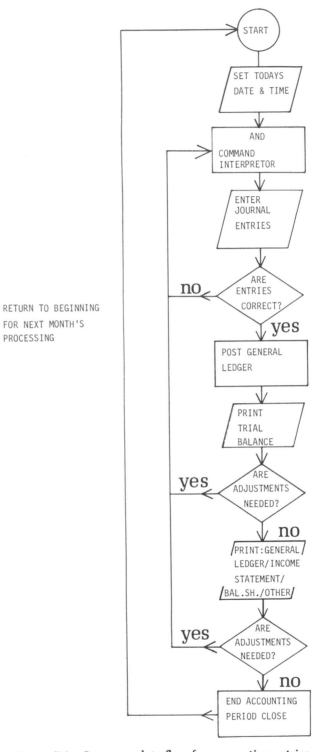

RETURN TO BEGINNING
FOR NEXT MONTH'S
PROCESSING

Figure 5.6   Computer data flow for accounting entries.

sary, the operator may signal to close the books for that accounting period and summarize or close the ledger accounts.

The menu used in a simple system should do the following:

1. Set dates.
2. Enter journal transactions.
3. Correct journal, ledger, or other material.
4. Print journal transactions.
5. Post journal transactions to ledgers.
6. Print financial reports.
7. Close accounting period.
8. Create new files, add to chart of accounts, etc.
9. Exit accounting system.

Possible Account Combinations—Input Controls

When I talked about the accounting data flow model, I mentioned that the computer applications program might be able to automatically prompt the operator if a mistake is made. Sometimes an operator enters a letter "o" instead of the number zero "0". This problem is eliminated by allowing only numeric information in *number* fields and only alphabetic information in *letter* (alphabetic or *string*) fields. To make sure that all the debits and credits balance, the program could search the dollar amount fields and compare the total debits with the total credits to see if the entries balance.

Another automatic checking technique is to check if the *account combination* is possible. For example, if we examine the account groups, we know that there can never be any transaction that will involve a debit or credit to an Income account and a corresponding credit or debit to an expense account. As a matter of fact, the Income accounts will never have a transaction of any sort with any expense account. If the operator entered a transaction as:

Income account 4001	$18,136.00	
Expense account 6045		$18,136.00

the applications program would declare this an impossible combination and require that the operator reenter the account numbers and description.

The table presented as Figure 5.7 was developed by Hayes and Baker. It shows all the possible combinations of accounts on a debit and credit basis. The table shows that there can be only 26 possible combinations of accounts. The table lists the transactions by account group. The first action (debit or credit) has a corresponding reaction (credit or debit). Both the first action and the reaction are considered. The table also lists the individual accounts (cash, inventory, notes payable) that are most often involved in the action–reaction.

For example, the only transactions that occur with an asset group account are:

1. Debit asset (particularly cash or inventory), credit liability (particularly accounts payable and notes payable).
2. Debit assets (cash and fixed assets usually), credit equity.
3. Debit assets (cash and accounts receivable), credit income.
4. Credit asset (cash), debit liability (accounts payable and notes payable).
5. Credit assets (cash), debit asset (accounts receivable and fixed assets most common).

Action Account Group	Dr./Cr.	Indiv. Acct.	Reaction Account Group	Dr./Cr.	Indiv. Acct.
Asset	DR	C-Inv.	Liability	CR	Debt, A.P.
	DR	C-FA	Equity	CR	Equ.
	DR	C-A.R	Income	CR	Income
	CR	Cash	Liability	DR	Debt, A.P.
	CR	Cash	Asset	DR	A.R., F.A.
	CR	Cash	Expense	DR	All
	CR	Cash	Cost of sales	DR	All
	CR	All	Equity	DR	Equity°
Liability	DR	A.P./Debt	Assets	CR	Cash
	DR	A.P.	Cost of sales	CR	All
	CR	Debt, A.P.	Assets	DR	C-Inv.
	CR	A.P.	Cost of sales	DR	All
	CR	Misc. Pay.	Expense	DR	All
Equity	DR	Equity	Asset	CR	All°
	DR	Equity	Expense	CR	All°
	DR	Equity	Cost of sales	CR	All°
	CR	Equity	Assets	DR	C-F.A.
Income	CR	Income	Equity	CR	Equity°
	CR	Income	Asset	CR	C-A.R.
	CR	Income	Asset	DR	C-A.R.
Expense	DR	All	Assets	CR	C
	DR	All	Liabilities	CR	Misc. Pay.
	CR	All	Equity	DR	Equity
Cost of sales	DR	All	Assets	CR	C
	DR	All	Liabilities	CR	A.P.
	CR	All	Equity	DR	Equity°

°Decreases in any asset = decrease in equity but only posted at period end and then to the I and Ex summary.

Key to Individual Accounts

C	= Cash	F.A.	= Fixed asset
Inv.	= Inventory	Equi.	= Owner's equity
Debt	= Note payable	Inc.	= Income
A.P.	= Account payable	All	= All accounts in groups
Misc. Pay.	= Miscellaneous payables—Salary payable, Taxes payable, etc.		

Figure 5.7 All possible debit-credit accounting transactions are illustrated in this Hayes-Baker table.

6. Credit assets (cash) and debit expense (all.).
7. Credit assets (cash) and debit cost of sales (all).
8. Credit assets (all), debit to equity.

And so on. The proof is in this hand out.°

Further input checking features might be built around the fact that the majority of the transactions involve a particular account. The programmer can determine by testing or by historical data what percentage of total transactions involve an individual account (like cash). You may then design a statistical test that prompts the operator when the entry is a possible one, but not one that is statistically likely. For example,

°Authors' note: The hand out material appears in the appendix of this book.

almost all debits to an expense account involve a credit to cash. If the operator inputs a debit to expense and a credit to liabilities, the program may ask that the operator reconsider before the information is posted. When the operator inputs the debit to expense and credit to liabilities, the program might ask the operator, "Do you wish to credit to an account other than cash?"

AUDITING

An increasingly important role for an accountant is as an auditor. Auditing of computer systems has become more and more important in recent years. If you review the published literature about computers for accountants, you find that most of it concerns auditing computers.

The primary role of the computer auditor is to evaluate controls both in computerized systems and in the entire data processing environment. Although different in approach, the objectives of computer system auditing are the same as those of the traditional auditing of manual systems. The same elements of control are necessary in both computerized and manual systems.

The computer itself is one of the primary tools for auditing through the use of special auditing software packages. Skills in system design and analysis are important for the auditor who must also possess a knowledge of computer hardware and operations.

The minimum requirements of the general staff auditor should include:*

1. A basic understanding of computer systems including equipment components and their general capabilities.
2. A basic understanding of widely installed computer operating systems and software.
3. A general familiarity with file processing techniques and data structures.
4. Sufficient working knowledge of computer audit software to use existing, standardized audit packages.
5. Ability to review and interpret systems documentation including flowcharts and record definitions.
6. Sufficient working knowledge of basic EDP controls to identify and evaluate the controls in effect in a client's installation.
7. Sufficient knowledge of EDP systems to develop the audit plan and supervise its execution.
8. A general familiarity with the dynamics involved in developing and modifying programs and processing systems.

Steps in an Audit Plan

The major steps in an audit are the following:

1. *Initial planning.* The auditor must gather sufficient knowledge about the client company to plan an overall audit.
2. *Systems description.* The auditor must obtain sufficient information about the company's accounting systems to be able to document the flow of transactions, identify key reports, identify key auditing controls, and determine the primary

*Elise G. Jancura, "Technical Proficiency for Auditing Computer Processed Accounting Records," *Journal of Accountancy*, Oct. 1975, pp. 46–59.

accounting practices followed. The auditor then "walks through" the system by selecting a few transactions at their source and tracing them through the system to an entry in the general ledger and vice versa.

3. *Overall evaluation of internal control.* The accountant must obtain assurance that transactions are properly authorized, executed, and recorded. The accountant must see that assets are safeguarded.

4. *Compliance tests.* The accountant must design and perform tests to determine whether the system and controls are operating as expected.

5. *Substantive tests.* The auditor completes the design and performs substantive procedures considering the effect of each test.

6. Review and evaluate financial statements considering audit evidence gathered.

7. Issue an accountant's report.

Systems description is an important step. Documentation should be adequate to reconstruct programs or systems in the event of an emergency. The auditor should place considerable importance on procedures for security and backup data, master files, programs, and recovery equipment.

Since the primary function of the audit is to test and prove controls, obviously controls evaluation is important to the entire audit.

Processing controls, sometimes called *programmed checks*, are features incorporated into the computer programs to ensure the reliability of input and output data. Some of these controls are quantitative in nature, such as record counts and control totals. Other controls are qualitative. One qualitative control is the *composition check*, which tests the completeness of data in a record to assure that none of the data fields has been inadvertently omitted. Another is the *limit check*, which tests the reasonableness of data to assure that gross errors have not been committed. Others are the *coding check*, which tests the validity of transaction codes or employee numbers; the *combination check*, which tests the independence of data; and the *sequence check*, which tests the logical sequence of data.

Fraud Prevention Through Internal Controls

Computer fraud can be a serious problem, so one of the important considerations for the auditor is ensuring that a business has sufficient internal controls to prevent fraud. Fraud can often be prevented by a tight system of internal control. As a result, the auditor usually gives special attention to the following areas:

1. *Transaction controls.* These are controls over the generation and flow of input transactions. Computer users need to perfect means to ensure that all transactions are subject to controls and that the controls are suitable. Obvious problem areas, such as adjusting entries and error corrections, should be controlled by persons other than those responsible for the entries.

2. *Inventory controls* help spot the cause of inventory shrinkage. Many inventory frauds are conducted in an environment of large, continuing inventory losses.

3. Improved *responsibility reporting* such as management systems to alert others to possible fraudulent transactions. Buyers should receive recapitulations of orders placed, both received and paid, by time period and by vendor and type of item. All expense entries should be reported to management in sufficient detail and clarity to enable executives to spot unauthorized charges.

4. *Program controls* can be maintained by having programs that access critical programs or data subject to independent verification before the company starts using them. All program changes should go through the same sequence.
5. *File control* means having a file librarian responsible for the security of all critical program and data files.

Many of the computer frauds of the past could have been prevented by a revision of the company's organizational structure. Employees should be given positions that do not conflict or overlap with the responsibilities of others in the organization. Perhaps some of the historical fraud cases would have been impossible had separation of responsibility in data processing been practiced and enforced. Separation of responsibility means separation of the following functions:

- Input data generation
- Input control
- Computer operation
- Programming and maintenance
- Output control
- Data, program file control (librarian)

It is essential that programmers not have access to input transactions, real data, or program files and that they not operate the computer. Computer operators must not be able to change programs or gain access to data files except according to job scheduling

Auditing Direct Access (On-Line) Systems

It is realistic to believe that batch processing for accounting applications is becoming a thing of the past. All new accounting systems are designed for direct (on-line) systems. Now the operator inputs material directly into the system. Most of the batch processing accounting systems now being used are for special applications (usually in large businesses). Businesses that have come into computer accounting within the last five years do not even know what batch processing it.

From an auditing standpoint, on-line systems differ from batch processing systems in three areas: lack of audit trails, the diversity of input media, and the complexity of the operating environment. All of these factors make auditing on-line systems even more difficult than auditing batch processing systems.

The lack of audit trails in on-line systems is evidenced by the fact that many input data are introduced via telecommunication devices (modems) in machine-readable form. The data base is continually being updated, and many transactions are machine initiated (such as preparation of purchase orders) on the basis of conditions that exist in the system.

The lack of traditional audit trails (records of batch processing inputs) at first created a problem for accountants and CPAs. The CPAs, however, soon came to realize that they could not expect computerized systems to be modified to provide output that only they needed. The CPAs started the technique of auditing through the computer with the use of accounting software packages and computing experience. They modified their emphasis so that they analyzed not only the output and input, but the system that produces the input and output.

Auditing Around the Computer Program

Under this approach the accountant produces a model computer program, processes the client's data, compares his results with the client's results, and thereby evaluates the effectiveness of the client's internal control.

SUMMARY

In summary, computers and accounting are alike in that they are both man-made binary systems that are affected by unpredictable outside events. Computers and accounting are different in that accounting is based on real-world economics developed over the last 5,000 years, and computers are based on theoretical models created in the past 40 years. Accounting is primarily for gathering data, computers are primarily for number manipulation. Change in the technology of accounting from pencils and paper to computers has not changed the accounting system's set of rules for classifying and structuring accounting data.

When converting from manual to computer accounting technology, one must understand the differences between computer and manual techniques in designing the system, entering the data, costing, sequential processing, centralized files, and random inquiries and data analysis.

A model of the accounting system has three components: input, processing, and output. Inputs include control information and accounting data. The processor compares accounting input to controls, prompts for correct data, and puts data into the proper accounts. Outputs are the business and financial forms that the company uses. We discussed several ideas for input controls, from having the processor differentiate between numerical and alphabetic characters so one is not wrongly substituted for the other to the Hayes-Baker debit-credit check table.

Auditing a computer accounting system is done through software tests and comparisons. Auditors also look for system documentation and security controls. We discussed their procedures for doing that.

A loud sound, the crack of lightning and the bass of thunder, came from outside the auditorium in which Kimberly Rogers was speaking. Kimberly looked at her watch. She smiled. "Well, it took thunder and lightning to make me stop. I see that the lecture has run 10 minutes over. I'd like to thank those of you who stayed. Thank you."

Chapter Six
Hero Manufacturing's Computer Accounting System and Tax Implications

Kimberly Rogers woke up with a headache—the kind you get when you've had too much of too many things. It wasn't a terrible headache—the kind that makes toast popping up sound like a diesel truck being driven through your wall. She'd had headaches like that. Never again. But this headache was bad enough.

She had to get up early. Someone said that Einstein only slept four hours every night. But she wasn't Einstein. The smell of her first cup of coffee fully opened her eyelids. When she thought of fighting an hour of traffic to get to Hero Manufacturing she was not too happy. But her strong sense of professionalism and the thought of the money that she would earn gave her that extra lift it takes to get out the front door at 7:30 in the morning.

Kimberly shifted her sportscar into first gear, and slipped a tape of the Brandenberg Concertos into the car stereo, and headed for the expressway. She was off.

When she pulled into the Hero Manufacturing parking lot Kimberly thought she saw John Jones standing at a window holding the drapes to one side. "Oh-oh," Kimberly thought, "Am I late?" She looked at her watch. She had five minutes to spare.

Kimberly brushed her hair in the rear-view mirror and grabbed her briefcase which was about twice as heavy as usual. Her headache was still with her as she walked briskly through the lobby. Kimberly thought it best to launch right into a discussion of the business at hand. After John Jones greeted her with a brief "Hello," Kimberly said, "Let's start by reviewing the present computer situation."

"Looking at your questionnaire,° I see that you do not want a payroll system. Correct?"

"Yes, I was told that it's a pain-in-the-you-know-what. I let my bank take care of that," John commented as he took a sip of coffee.

"Personally, I agree. There are some good payroll systems, of course. The bank has these. And there are some problematic payroll software systems. This is usually the stuff that the small businessperson gets. Let's talk about the other statistics: You generally have 10 jobs active at any one time, with an average of 35 operations per job which includes 14 costs. Is this correct?"

"Let me see that questionnaire" [Figure 6.1], John asked as he took a look at it. "Yes,

°See Chapter 2.

GENERAL LEDGER

_____   1.   Number of G/L accounts in chart of accounts?
_____   2.   Do you wish to retain budget amounts?

ACCOUNTS PAYABLE

_____   1.   Do you wish to reconcile checks?
_____   2.   Number of vendors active per year?
_____   3.   Number of invoices received per month?
_____   4.   Number of checks written per month?
_____   5.   Number of invoices entered at any one time?
_____   6.   Number of account numbers in your chart of accounts?

PRODUCTION STATUS AND COSTING

_____   1.   Do you wish to maintain and select basic items from job select file?
_____   2.   Edited transactions to interface from payroll?
_____   3.   Edited transactions to interface from payroll?
_____   4.   Edited transactions to interface from inventory?
_____   5.   Number of jobs active at any one time?
_____   6.   Average number of operations per job?
_____   7.   Average number of material and/or miscellaneous costs per job?
_____   8.   Number of repetitive basic items?
_____   9.   Average number of material/miscellaneous transactions per job per week?

SALES ANALYSIS

_____   1.   Installing accounts receivable application?
_____   2.   Installing order entry and invoicing application?
_____   3.   Installing inventory application?
_____   4.   Number of salesmen?
_____   5.   Do you want daily salesman recap?
_____   6.   Maximum number of invoices written in any one month?
_____   7.   Maximum number of invoices written in any one day?

PRODUCT DEFINITION/COSTING

_____   1.   Number of item numbers in product master file?
_____   2.   Number of single level assemblies?
_____   3.   Average number of components per single level assembly?

Figure 6.1   Software client questionaire.

I remember. It's been some time since we did this. You know, these figures are approximate. It varies."

"That's okay." Kimberly continued. "In the general ledger you presently have 56 accounts plus 42 accounts for receivable customers and 25 accounts for accounts payable. You write up to 40 checks per month for accounts payable. You want to be able to select basic production items from the files, and you want this accounting system to interface with the inventory system that Earthapple has already installed. Further, for sales analysis you want accounts receivable, order entry, inventory, and salesman reports. You now have three salespeople. Is this all correct?"

"Yes," John answered. "But what does all this mean?"

"Well, computers are real specific machines. These items are the raw data that I need to write a system so that it will give you what you want. If, for instance, you want a salesman report and you have three salesmen and I allow for only one, then to correct the situation might take considerable time and money. As a matter of fact, I will allow for up to 10 salesmen for possible growth."

John asked, "Well, why don't you just allow for 100 salesmen, or some infinite number. Why do you need to be so specific?"

"In a word," Kimberly answered, "space. A given computer system has only so much storage space (on the disk drive) and only so much internal memory (in the central processing unit or CPU). It is finite. You want to use this space in the best way that you reasonably can because it is limited. Even if there is a lot of room on a disk, the CPU may not have enough memory to accommodate a long program from the disk. The disk can hold much more than the CPU memory. If you fill up one disk, you can put on another to add more information, but this involves the process of an operator taking off one disk and adding another, maybe several times per day."

"Let me discuss the accounting system that I intend to install," said Kimberly. She began with an overview of its features.

ACCOUNTING PACKAGE FEATURES

The accounting software package that we are going to use for Hero Manufacturing performs not only general ledger accounting, but also acts as a product, budget, and cost reporting system. These are its features:

- *Complete financial data base.* One accessible location for all financial information allows rapid and precise data retrieval. Financial information is constantly available for updating and reporting. Amounts are kept current; closings are automatic. Period-end reporting immediately follows the final posting run with no need for intervening system procedures.
- *User-controlled report writer.* You, as a user, can get customized reports. The report writer supplies a complete subsystem that delivers total control to the user for all reporting needs such as: (1) balance sheets, (2) income statements, (3) cost control, and (4) budgeting.
- *Budgeting.* Budget amounts can be allocated to particular accounting periods based on user-established guidelines. Figures can be revised.
- *Financial statements.* Income statements and balance sheets are produced according to your own format.
- *Auditability.* Auditor approved account and transaction validation, verification, and control are used in the system.
- *Journal entry control.* The system provides editing of every journal entry, balancing of debits and credits, and automatic reversal of accruals.
- *Recurring journal entries.* The recurring entries (such as debits or credits to cash) are produced both on demand and automatically.
- *Cost accounting.* You can control an unlimited number of cost and profit center activities to help in cost accounting and job costing.
- *Statistical accounting.* Nonmonetary data (square feet, machine hours, etc.) can be used and retained by the system for use in special reports.

These features all come from the prepackaged accounting software that we will use. I will also add programming such as inventory interface, sales reports, and invoice interfacing for accounts receivable and accounts payable.

GENERAL ACCOUNTING SOFTWARE

"That sounds okay," John Jones told Kimberly, "but can you give me a little more information on these prepackaged software programs? And why do you use them?"

Kimberly answered, "We use them primarily to save time and money. If I had to write these programs from scratch, not only would it take me a lot of time, but it would cost you a lot of money. Low-cost prepackaged software programs that perform basic business tasks are the key to using computers economically.

"Let's discuss the typical features of packaged programs. They are designed to perform five standard business paperwork functions."

1. *General ledger (GL)* programs maintain the company's chart of accounts, post journal entries to update balances, accumulate a history of recent account balances, and print various financial reports. This is the program that I am instituting for Hero Manufacturing. These programs include provisions to edit, balance, and correct transactions entered into the computer, as well as to update and maintain the computer files. The programs offer reports such as: trial balance, balance sheets, income statements, and detailed posting registers for maintaining controls.

2. *Accounts payable (A/P)* programs maintain vendor files and a file of unpaid invoices or vouchers. Transactions are processed against these files, and information is retained for distributing purchases to the proper accounts and preparing the necessary checks. Reports produced by A/P programs usually include: aged accounts payable with trial balance, check register for historical information, and open invoices list. You already have this system set up.

3. *Accounts receivable (A/R)* programs maintain customer files, post various transaction amounts to these files, generate up-to-date balances, and print invoices and statements. Reports produced by A/R programs include: aged accounts receivable with trial balance and periodic activity reports for control information. Hero Manufacturing also has an accounts receivable program.

4. *Payroll* programs calculate employee pay and employee master records, maintain and check payroll files, produce paychecks and government report forms, and other reports. Reports include end-of-month listings showing deductions and tax totals. Hero pays the bank to prepare this information.

5. *Inventory* programs maintain an inventory master file, post inventory transactions to this file, and update these balances. Reports include: inventory status, exception reports, analysis by cost, and order status. Hero Manufacturing is already using this program.

PROGRAM PREPARATION AND TESTING

"Computer software is not like making toast. You don't just put bread in a toaster and it comes out nice and done. First, software that is purchased, and that has already been tested, may not work on your computer system—no matter what they tell you. It has to be installed and tested again. Integrating the custom software with the 'off-the-shelf' software is another problem.

"This illustration [Figure 6.2] shows how we at Earthapple go about setting up your system.

"We start by studying flowcharts of the present system. We then look at the input and output that your company requires, paying special attention to controls. We then prepare a flowchart of the entire system as it will be when we finish. Only then do we start writing programs. Programs are written in this order: first the utility subroutines and then the main program. Once these programs are written, debugging begins. Debugging is the process of running the programs under all circumstances and assuring the connections between several program parts (such as inventory and general ledger,

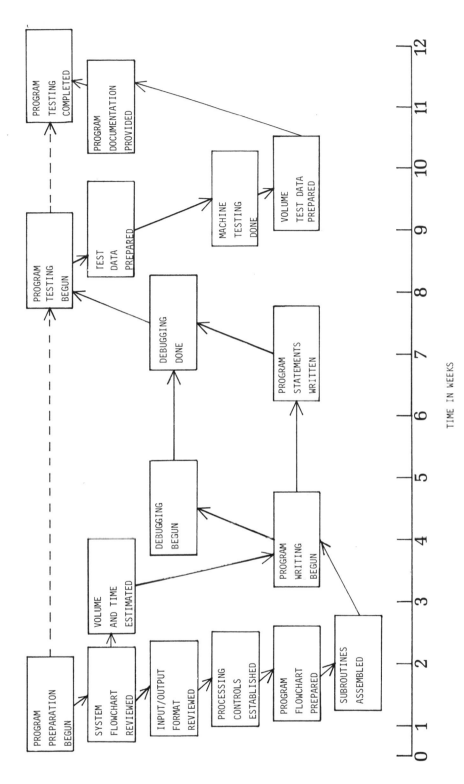

Figure 6.2   Sample program software preparation and testing procedure over time.

accounts receivable and general ledger, etc.). 'Debug' is not an insect. Debugging is the most lengthy of the steps in setting up your computer system.

"Once the debugging is done, the fun part begins. This is the part that tests the data. We first design the test, and then we test all the equipment—the hardware and the interface boards. The biggest test, which lasts for a whole day, is when we put all the data we can—in volume—through the system. You then get the documentation, operating manuals, etc., and we train the people that you want to run your system.

"As you can see from this chart [Figure 6.2], the complete process can take up to 12 weeks."

"Wait a minute!" John Jones exclaimed. "I've heard that before. It's like a self-fulfilling prophecy. If you say it *can* take 12 weeks, it *will* be 12 weeks. Let me tell you a story.

"A man believed that the last day for humanity would fall on a certain date. He believed that he should prepare himself, and all who would listen, for such an eventuality.

"When the day came, he led the others who believed as he did to the top of a mountain. As soon as they had all assembled on the summit, their combined weight caused a collapse of the mountain's fragile crust, and they were all hurled into the depths of a volcano. It was indeed their last day."

"Okay," Kimberly answered. "I get the idea. Well, sometimes it takes longer, sometimes less. This is just an average."

John Jones smiled. "Okay, continue."

Kimberly began again: "Okay, as you probably know from your experience with the present equipment, an important consideration is how easily the system can be understood and used by your employees. In other words, is the system bulletproof? Is the system designed to assume that there may be idiots on the other end, but, at the same time, does it treat them as if they were intelligent?"

IS THE SYSTEM DESIGNED FOR HUMANS?

"To make the system less fallible and more human-oriented, four types of controls are required: input controls, process controls, output controls, and system integrity controls. *Input controls* are crucial to any accounting system. Something is designed incorrectly if it is easy to make mistakes, if the operator cannot easily understand how to input information, or if the wrong people can get their hands on the wrong data.

"Our system validates all input whenever and wherever possible. It checks that numerics are used when they are required. It will check the length of entry to see if the response is too long or too short for the appropriate answer. The operator cannot type in "California" when a two-letter code "Ca." is required. Entries are checked against the files and/or control module for validity. Our software also features a bell and a blinking field when errors are indicated.

"*Processing controls* are used by our system. Programs open files for inquiry or update. Records are locked at time of update to prevent simultaneous update. Error handling programs are used in the event of abnormal program termination. Controls also allow abnormal exit routines and have the ability to cancel direct entry at any point. Control reports from the system permit balancing of summary totals in master files.

"*Output* can be regulated to offer a practical system. Report pages are numbered and dated. Registers provide audit trails. Reports are printed from *on-line* master files.

"*System integrity* is the way that the system generally hangs together. In our system all normal maintenance functions are performed under program control, with appropriate checks on file usage and dating. The system also has month, quarter, and year-end and update programs; reorganization and reindexing features; and record purging. The system gives you the ability to reprocess a day's transactions and copy the data entirely each day. There are file integrity check programs provided to verify the integrity of files following an abnormal termination of the system. A checklist is provided to ensure restart and recovery are complete. The system restarts at the last message."

"Do you have any questions before I get to work?" Kimberly Rogers asked.

"Well," John answered, "I think all my computer and systems questions are answered, at least for now. But I would like to know something that has to do with accounting more than computers."

"What's that?"

"I want to know what are the tax implications of my purchasing this computer. Can I charge off these costs? Is it better for me to lease this machine, or buy it?"

"I'm not a CPA, but I'll try to give you an idea of what the tax process is," Kimberly said. She then continued.

COMPUTERS, TAXES, AND ACCOUNTING

"From a tax standpoint, three major areas of concern should shape your decision regarding computers and systems:

- Should the computer be leased or purchased?
- Is the investment tax credit an important consideration?
- What are the tax ramifications of software packages?

"The income tax considerations involved in leasing or buying equipment are essentially the same as those that pertain to the acquisition of any other business asset. Several studies have concluded that over a five-year period the cash outflow is the same whether you buy or lease. However, the tax implications of various financing methods may differ.

Leasing

"Assuming that you've decided to lease a computer, you must make sure that the agreement you sign is a 'true lease' rather than some form of conditional sales contract. What happens at the end of the lease determines if the lease is a 'true lease' or a conditional sales contract. A problem can arise if there is an option to purchase the property once the lease expires. If the option price determined at the beginning of the lease is less than the estimated fair market value of the property at the end of the lease, the IRS could claim that the two parties intended a sale, not a lease. This is called a 'bargain option.'

"When part of the lease payments are applied to the option price, the situation is essentially the same as the 'bargain option' agreement I just mentioned.

"The American Institute of Certified Public Accountants (AICPA) is guided by an independent Financial Accounting Standards Board (FASB) that considers accounting problems and makes suggestions about how the problems are to be solved. The FASB has issued Statement No. 13 (1976) which deals exclusively and extensively with leases. Statement No. 13 is the authority on lease transactions. Generally speaking, before you sign a lease, it is a good idea to have a Certified Public Accountant and an attorney review it. Statement No. 13 is complex enough that the average business-person will have difficulty understanding all of its implications.

Investment Tax Credit

"If, instead of leasing, you decide to purchase the equipment, your company is entitled to a federal investment tax credit. Sometimes the investment tax credit can be passed through a lease, but this gets into a very tricky area that requires professional advice.

"Currently the investment tax credit is a 10% maximum. The amount of the credit is a function of the useful life and cost of the equipment. One-third of the cost is eligible if the useful life is at least five years, but less than seven. The entire cost qualifies if the useful life is seven years or more.*

Software Costs

"One of the areas of controversy in computer tax law is the treatment of software costs. The term *software* is defined to include all programs or routines that cause a computer to perform a task, as well as the documentation required to describe and maintain these programs.

"Software can be analyzed in two distinct categories:

• Deductibility
• Costs available for investment tax credit

"For income tax purposes, software costs fall into one of three categories: (1) developed software, (2) purchased software, and (3) leased software.

"*Developed software* is the cost of computer programs written by either you or your staff or an independent consultant retained by your company. In the case of developed software, you have two options. Costs may be considered as (1) expenses that are therefore deductible in the year they are incurred, or as (2) intangible assets that are capitalized and depreciated over a period of time (usually five years).

"*Purchased software* rules are more restrictive. Purchased software costs must be classified as either (1) costs included in the purchase of a computer or (2) costs stated separately and not included in the general cost of the computer. Software costs that are not stated separately are considered to be part of the computer's costs and are depreciated over the useful life of the computer. Where the software costs are stated separately, they may be treated as an intangible asset separate from the computer cost. They may be then be depreciated as a separate asset.

"If the cost of software is not separately stated, it qualifies for an investment tax credit. When software costs are stated separately, the IRS claims that these costs are not tangible personal property for investment tax purposes.

"Some state and local governments levy an *ad valorem* ('in proportion to the value') tax on tangible personal property, but not on intangible property. This may cause a conflict. For the state, you would want to characterize software costs as intangibles to avoid property tax. But classifying software as tangible property is more beneficial to you in regards to its treatment under federal tax law.

"*Leased software* payments made for the use of software are treated as a current rental expense, deductible in the year it is paid."

Kimberly paused and looked at John Jones. "Do you follow me so far?" she asked.

"Well, I'm purchasing this system and the software, as you know. I am not leasing it.

*Investment tax credits are also discussed in Chapter 4.

But I'm a little confused about this asset or expense thing you're talking about. The hardware cost is straightforward. I capitalize that as an asset and depreciate it. But what about this software stuff? I'm hiring you to develop some software for me. Therefore the costs could be considered 'developed software,' right?" John asked.

"Well, that determination generally refers to software that is developed as part of a company's research and development, but in some instances it could apply," Kimberly answered.

John continued, "On the other hand, I'm paying Earthapple for the whole show—computer, software, etc.—and they are paying you. Therefore, it could be considered 'purchased software,' right?"

"Right."

"Well, which is it? Is it purchased or developed? It can't be both can it?" John asked.

"Well," Kimberly began, "this might sound like an evasion, but this is a complex question that might affect the net profit, taxes, and equity of your company. If you need tax deductions and it can be proven that this is developed software, you might want to go that route. If, on the other hand, you want to make this cost an asset, it might be considered purchased software. At any rate, it is a smart idea to talk to a CPA."

"Well, okay," John continued, "what is the safest way to go?"

"Since you are allowed to capitalize the costs for both developed and purchased software, the most conservative route is to make assets out of software costs and depreciate them. But you should still talk to a CPA before you make that kind of a decision.

"All of the things I have just discussed are covered in FASB Statement No. 2 dealing with the treatment of research and development expenses and in Interpretation No. 6 which relates computer software to Statement No. 2 with the Statement, the Standards Board ruled that outlaws on research and development should be expensed as incurred, rather than be deferred and expensed only as income materialized from selling the resulting products. Interpretation No. 6 details when software costs are considered part of research and development," Kimberly concluded.

"If that's all the questions you have, I'll get to work," Kimberly added.

"Just one more thing. You said that you try to design the accounting software so it can be used by idiots who are treated as intelligent. Can you explain that?" John Jones was smiling. He thought this was a question that would be difficult to answer.

"Okay," Kimberly answered, "now it's my turn to tell a story. Sometimes you can give people just what they need but what they need is not necessarily what they want. I try to keep this story in mind whenever I design software for humans.

"Once there was a King who was thirsty. He did not quite know what the difficulty was, but he said: 'My throat is dry.'

"Lackeys at once ran swiftly off to find something to relieve his condition. They came back with lubricating oil. When the King drank it, his throat did not feel dry any more, but he knew that something was not right.

"The oil produced a curious sensation in his mouth. He croaked: 'My tongue feels awful—there is a curious taste—it is slippery. . . .'"

"His doctor immediately prescribed pickles and vinegar—which the King ate. Soon he had a stomachache and watering eyes to add to his sorrows.

" 'I think I must be thirsty.' he mumbled, for his sufferings had made him do some thinking.

" 'Thirst never made the eyes water,' said the courtiers to one another. But Kings are often capricious, and they ran to fetch rosewater, and scented, syrupy wines fit for a King. The King drank it all, but still he felt no better—and his digestion was ruined.

"A wise man who happened along in the middle of this crisis said: 'His Majesty needs ordinary water.'

" 'A King could never drink common water,' shouted the court in unison.

" 'Of course not,' said the King, 'and, in fact, I feel quite insulted—both as a King being offered plain water and also as a patient. After all, it must be impossible that such a dreadful and daily more complicated ailment as mine could have a simple remedy. Such a concept is contrary to logic, a disgrace to its originator, and an affront to the sick.'

"That is how the wise man came to be renamed 'The Idiot.' "°

SUMMARY

John looked at the wall for a few seconds. "You mean that even though the solution is simple, people may not like solution unless you are very careful when you give it to them."

"I couldn't say it any better." Kimberly replied. "Any other questions?"

"No. Just summarize what we talked about, if you don't mind." John took out a pencil to take it down.

"Okay. The features of our software package for accounting are a complete financial data base; user-controlled report writer; auditability; journal entry control; demand and automatic production of recurring journal entries; and software for budgeting, financial statements, cost accounting, and statistical accounting. We also include the five standard business paperwork programs: general ledger, accounts payable, accounts receivable, payroll, and inventory.

"Our program preparation and testing goes like this: (1) your present system is flowcharted, (2) we flowchart the entire system when finished, (3) write the programs, (4) debug the system, (5) give the system extensive tests, and (6) we train you and your employees to run the system. Overall, we make sure the system and the documentation are human oriented.

"Last, we discussed the various tax and accounting implications when you take possession of the computer as far as the advantage of leased versus purchased equipment, investment tax credits, and the tax implications of the money that you pay for computer software."

°Idries Shah, The Magic Monastery, (New York: E. P. Dutton & Co., 1972), pp. 43 and 44.

Chapter Seven
Liabilities

It was rainy, dreary, and cold. Kimberly Roger's toes felt like they were frozen strawberries. Kimberly moved closer to the crackling fire in the modern fireplace in her living room.

Her mind again was busy reviewing her current life. She had been thinking about the Hero Manufacturing project. But she stopped. It was a weekend and not time to think of work. She thought of Udjat Her, her boyfriend. But she would see him tonight. She reminded herself that she had an appointment with Hero's CPA next week.

The windows were rattling with the wind. Kimberly heard the windows, turned toward them, and felt even colder.

She turned back to the fire and leafed through several books. This was reading weather. But before she could even start something enjoyable, her attention was captured by a pamphlet called "Liabilities and Debt."

Kimberly sighed. "Well," she thought, "I guess it's good reading for a day like today." She glanced once more at the rain falling outside the window before she began reading. . . .

LIABILITIES

Liabilities are the amount your company owes. They are obligations that result from past transactions that require payment in the future. The amounts are either stated or implied in oral or written contracts.

Liabilities can be classified as current and noncurrent.

Current liabilities are those that are due and payable within one year. They include such things as: salaries and wages payable; other accrued expenses (utilities, taxes, supplies, etc.); accounts payable for inventories; and short-term notes payable to banks and others. Salaries and wages payable and other accrued expenses are another side of expenses and cash disbursements.

The other current liabilities usually represent debts due to banks and others. These debts are documented by a note. A note is a form of I.O.U., and it is usually a legal document. This means that the holder of the note can take you to court in order to have its provisions enforced.

Noncurrent liabilities are those that are due and payable in more than one year's time. Noncurrent liabilities are also referred to as *long-term debt*. Nearly all long-term debt is documented by a note.

°Authors' note: Cash disbursements arising from operating expenses were discussed in Chapter 3.

DEBT

Every business in the United States, regardless of size, must from time to time borrow money. Usually a business will borrow from a bank, but it may also borrow from commercial finance companies; state, local and federal governments; and the public bond market. The larger the business, the more likely it is that it can use all of these debt sources. The smaller the business, the more likely it is that it will only be able to borrow from banks and government and commercial loan sources.

Because this pamphlet is limited in scope, we shall not discuss publicly issued bonds. This is a speciality operation that requires accountants, lawyers, and underwriters. We shall limit our discussion to the traditional sources of debt capital: banks, commercial financial lenders, and government (such as Small Business Administration loans).

This pamphlet discusses financial leverage, the types of loans that are available from the different sources, the physical requirements of loan applications, and the accounting implications of debt financing.

FINANCIAL LEVERAGE

Financial leverage is the ratio of total debt to total assets. For example, a firm having assets of $1 million and total debt of $500,000 has a leverage factor of 50% ($500,000/ $1,000,000).

To understand the proper use of financial leverage you must analyze its impact on profitability under varying conditions. Let's take an example of three firms in the electronic supply industry that are identical except for their debts percentage (see Figure 7.1). Its company has used no debt and consequently has a leverage factor of zero. Hiscompany has financed their company half by debt and half by equity so they have a leverage factor of 50%. Theircompany has a leverage factor of 75%. The companies' balance sheets are shown in Figure 7.1.

How a company's capitalization affects the owners' return depends on the state of the economy. Let us assume that when the economy is depressed the firms can only earn 4% on assets because sales and profit margins are low. When the economy is brighter, the firms can earn 8%. Under normal conditions they will earn 11%, under good conditions 15% and if the economy is very good the rate of return on assets will be 20%. The table in Figure 7.2 illustrates how the use of financial leverage magnifies the impact on the firm owners' return.

As shown in Figure 7.2, when economic conditions go from normal to good, the

Itscompany			
		Total debt	$-0-
		Net worth	$100
Total assets	$100	Total liability and worth	$100
Hiscompany			
		Total debt	$ 50
		Net worth	$ 50
Total assets	$100	Total liability and worth	$100
Theircompany			
		Total debt at 8%	$ 75
		Net worth	$ 25
Total assets	$100	Total liability and worth	$100

Figure 7.1 How leverage is translated from a balance sheet.

	Very Poor	Poor	Normal	Good	Very Good
Rate of return on total assets before interest	4%	8%	11%	15%	20%
Dollar return on total assets before interest	$4	$8	$11	$15	$20
Itscompany: Leverage 0					
Earnings in dollars	$4	8	11	15	20
Less: Interest expense	$0	0	0	0	0
Gross income	$4	8	11	15	20
Taxes (50%)	$2	4	5.5	7.5	10
Available to owners	$2	4	5.5	7.5	10
Percent return on equity	2%	4%	5.5%	7.5%	10%
Hiscompany: Leverage 50%					
Earnings in dollars	$4	8	11	15	20
Less: Interest expense	$4	4	4	4	4
Gross income	$0	4	7	11	16
Taxes (50%)	$0	2	3.5	5.5	8
Available to owners	$0	2	3.5	5.5	8
Percent return on equity	0%	4%	7%	11%	16%
Theircompany: Leverage 75%					
Earnings in dollars	$4	8	11	15	20
Less: Interest expense	$6	6	6	6	6
Gross income	$(2)	2	5	9	14
Taxes (50%)	$(1)	1	2.5	4.5	7
Available to owners	$(1)	1	2.5	4.5	7
Percent return on equity	-4%	4%	10%	18%	28%

Figure 7.2   The impact of economic conditions on various leverage positions. High leverage gets the best return during very good conditions. Low leverage does best in very poor economic conditions. The tax calculation assumes tax credits for losses.

return on assets for Itscompany (no leverage) goes up 36.4%, the return for Hiscompany (50% leverage) increases 57.1%, and the return on equity for Theircompany (75% leverage) goes up a full 80%. Just the reverse happens when the economy is depressed. When the economy drops from normal to poor, Itscompany's return on equity declines only 27%. When the economy drops to poor, Hiscompany—with a higher leverage— has return on equity drop 42.9%. Theircompany, with the highest leverage, has a return on equity decline of a full 60%. In other words, the companies with the highest leverage receive the best return for owners' capital in normal or goods times, but the worst return on equity in depressed economic times. The companies with the least leverage (least debt as a percentage of total assets) reap the highest relative return in times of a depressed economy.

Wide variations in the use of financial leverage may be observed among industries and among the individual firms in each industry. Financial institutions use the most leverage because they typically have high liabilities. Public utilities have high liabilities because of large investments in fixed assets coupled with extremely stable sales. Mining and manufacturing firms use less debt because of their exposure to fluctuating sales. Small firms as a group are heavy users of debt.

In manufacturing, wide variations in leverage can be observed in the individual industries. The lowest debt compared to equity is found in textile manufacturing firms because their competitive pressures tend to be great. Low debt ratios are also found in the durable goods industries. The highest reliance on debt is found in consumer nondurable goods industries where demand is relatively insensitive to fluctuations in general business activity.

SOURCES OF DEBT CAPITAL

Not counting public debt offerings, there are basically three sources for debt capital: banks, commercial finance companies, and government agencies.

Banks

The advantages of securing a bank loan are:

1. Generally, with the exception of a few government and private programs, borrowing from a bank is the least expensive way to borrow.
2. Borrowing from a bank, as opposed to a government or commercial source, is usually better for your credit rating.
3. Banks have the widest loan breadth, that is, more types of loans and more sources.
4. Banks offer many business services including: credit references on customers or potential customers of your business; financial, investment, and estate advisory services; discount services for customers' accounts and notes payable; safe deposit boxes; night depositories.

The disadvantages of dealing with banks include:

1. The financially conservative nature of banks makes their loans the most difficult to obtain.
2. With banks that have a large number of branches, there is a tendency to have numerous replacements of the branch manager. It can be difficult to set up a long-term relationship with the branch manager.
3. The technical requirements (projected budgets, corporate and ownership information, etc.) for presenting a loan request are greater with a bank than with other sources.
4. Because banks are regulated by the federal government, and are simultaneously profit-making organizations, they have to be careful their loans do not fail. For most long-term loans, banks demand annual, semiannual, quarterly, or even monthly income statements and balance sheets so that they can carefully observe your business. Remember, they may have the records of every check that you have ever written.

What are the best and worst times to approach a bank for money? Depending on your personal or company situation, any time might be a good or bad time, irrespective of external influences and bank policies. That is, you might fall under what is called the unwritten golden rule of borrowing, which says, "If you don't need money, that's the best time to get a loan."

On an external basis (i.e., having to do with the bank and the economy only), the following are the best and worst times in which to borrow money.

The *best* environment for borrowing is:

1. When interest rates are generally low. This means (1) that the bank has more money to loan than it usually does and (2) that the borrower will get a better deal.
2. When a bank has just opened. New banks, especially independent banks, are looking for business. They love deposit business. Newly opened banks will take more chances with a marginal business because they want to build up their loan

portfolio. Sometimes you will find that new banks are conservative; but if you start building a relationship immediately, and you don't ask for money at the start, the bank will loan when they get to know you. If you have a sizable business, banking with a small independent will be advantageous because you might be their biggest depositor and they will bend over backwards to give you service.

3. When the economy is in an upturn. That is, sales all over the economy are increasing, the stock market is up, and disposable consumer income is up. This might be reflected in lower interest rates, but not necessarily.

4. When banks in a particular area are in heavy competition. This may mean that there are too many banks in a new, developing area. A sure sign of intense competition is if more than one bank visits your business with hopes of starting a financial relationship (the more, the better for you). Another sign is if there are incentives for deposits. That is, the banks are trying to outdo themselves with the premiums (toasters, calculators, etc.) they offer for deposits.

5. When banks are in a generally expansionary process. During the sixties, banks departed from their traditional conservatism and started expanding their branch systems, including international branches. Since there was more competition and a downgrading of traditional restraints, money was easier to obtain. There is a new facet of banking that might spark expansion: electronic banking devices called *automated teller machines*, or ATM's. ATMs are the electronic devices that banks put outside their branch, or in supermarkets, shopping centers, and so on. These electronic devices provide money or allow you to deposit without ever going to the bank. If the use of these devices becomes widespread, then the banks that get the most deposits will have more money to loan.

6. When there is a special program within the bank, usually a large bank, to take high-risk loans as "the bank's moral obligation." Examples are loans to minorities and special groups such as veterans, the handicapped, and, in some cases, displaced businesses or disaster victims. The large banks sometimes set aside sums for these "special high-risk" loans. But beware: Regardless of a bank's good intentions, if the economy is bad or if there is a high demand on loan funds, these special loans will be ended.

The *worst* environment for borrowing is:

1. When interest rates are high. Rates are high when there is a large demand on bank funds, and in many cases, from large, secure "Fortune 500" type firms. At this time a bank might be up to its loan limit as set by its preferred loan-to-deposit ratio (discussed shortly). High interest rates mean not only that money is more expensive, but also that there is less of it to borrow.

2. When the economy is in a recession. In recessionary times, regardless of other influences, banks tend to be more conservative in their lending. There are more chances for a business to fail in a recession. Furthermore, there is usually a high demand for money to see established businesses through the tough times.

3. When a bank is up to its lending limit, or when a bank has made a decision to decrease its dollars outstanding. When there is an extremely high demand for funds, a bank is tempted to loan at high rates and therefore make a better profit. There is a limit to how much money a bank can loan and that limit is its maximum loan-to-deposit ratio. The *loan-to-deposit ratio* is simply the total loans a bank has outstanding divided by the total number of deposits it has. During 1974, some banks had up to 75% of their deposits on loan. If only 26% of

their depositors withdrew their money, these banks would have been in serious trouble, perhaps bankruptcy. Even this 75% loan-to-deposit ratio might be misleading. Banks have to report their loan-to-deposit ratio to the federal government once a week. They can borrow money from other banks for 24 hours to raise their deposits to help the ratio. In the early part of the twentieth century, banks would very seldom go above a 33% loan-to-deposit ratio. Thus, 75% is a thin edge to walk on.

In 1975, when money supplies increased, loans did not. Although more money was available for loans, the banks wanted to keep the money to build up their loan-to-deposit ratios.

4. When there is very little bank competition for loans and deposits. A one-bank town is a perfect example. When you need money, there is only one place to go, and the competition is nil. Go to another town for financing.

5. When the parent bank is in trouble or suffers severe losses. In 1973, when United California Bank had trouble with its Swiss subsidiary, it was very difficult to get financing from the branches. If you read the business section of your newspaper, the *Wall Street Journal, Business Week*, or other business publications, you may learn about your bank's various troubles.

Of course, it is not always possible to wait for the perfect time to get a loan, and chances are good that you will need money when everyone else needs it.

Commercial Lenders

Commercial lenders, including commercial finance companies (factors, industrial time sales, leases), life insurance companies, foundations, and other private financial companies, are usually more expensive to borrow from than banks. However, they make more loans to a broader class of customers than do banks.

Commercial lenders, in general, are willing to loan to businesses that are not as strong financially as those that banks would consider. Furthermore, commercial lenders are less selective than banks in regard to collateral items, such as inventories and receivables. In short, the major advantage of commercial lenders is their flexibility.

The major disadvantage of commercial lenders is that their interest rates are generally higher, sometimes much higher, than banks.

Life insurance companies, pension funds, and foundations offer money to business for real estate, equipment, and sometimes working capital, in amounts that are usually greater than the typical bank loans. Their interest rates are usually only slightly higher than banks. The disadvantage with these companies is that they usually only make large loans (in excess of $1 million) that require that the applicant companies are financially strong. This generally eliminates most small business from consideration.

Government Loans

The largest single lender to business is the federal government, followed by state and local governments. The federal government lending program is larger than the loan programs of Bank of America, Chase Manhattan, City Bank, J. P. Morgan, and the rest of the 10 largest banks in America. The U.S. government loans over $1.852 trillion per year to business.

Without question, the cheapest loans available in this country are those made by the government. Unfortunately, only a few special businesses, under very special circumstances, qualify for these loans. Most businesses do qualify for other government loans that have interest rates at a few points over prime. The government will make loans to higher risk businesses. For instance, a start-up business that requires $100,000 in capital and has only $35,000 would not qualify for a loan at a bank at *any* interest rate. The same business, however, would qualify for a Small Business Administration (SBA) loan at rates near bank interest rates.

The equity requirements for most government loans are less than those of a bank. For a start-up business, banks usually require 50% equity, whereas government loans require from 10 to 45%. Take the example of a person who wants to start a business and has $15,000 in cash. At the bank he is eligible for a maximum loan of another $15,000, for a total of $30,000. If the same person applies for a government loan, he can receive $45,000 to $150,000, depending on the loan program. Starting a business with $45,000 instead of $30,000 can make a significant difference in its long-range success.

Government loans usually have longer repayment periods than bank loans. For this reason, your monthly payment is usually lower with a government loan than with a bank loan. If a business borrows $10,000 for three years (bank average) at 10.25%, the monthly payments are $323.85. If the same firm borrows the same amount ($10,000) at the same interest rate (10.25%) for *seven* years (government) instead of three years, the monthly payments are $67.31, or $165.54 less than the three-year loan.

There are some significant disadvantages with government loans. They may take from three months to three years to receive approval. The effort required in paperwork and research is four times as great as that with a bank loan and twice as great as that with a commercial loan. In short, the greatest disadvantages of government loans are the paperwork involved and the time required for approval.

TYPES OF LOANS AVAILABLE FROM BANKS, COMMERCIALS, AND GOVERNMENT LENDERS

The following is a review of the types of loans available and a brief discussion of the type of financing where each is used.

Bank Loans

Loans that are made for 30 to 90 days are called *short-term loans*. Short-term loans are usually employed to finance inventory on which there will be a cash return in a short period of time. New businesses very seldom receive short-term loans because they cannot turn their money around during the first few months of operations. However, short-term loans are used extensively for existing businesses.

Intermediate-term loans are for more than one year, but less than five. Equipment loans fall into this category. Most businesses will receive this type of loan unless they are financing property or getting a government-guaranteed loan. To buy an existing business or start a new one, the loan will usually be from three to five years in length.

Long-term loans are for five or more years. Government-guaranteed loans are usually for more than five years. Banks will also make long-term loans on improvements and property.

Loans are further classified into secured and unsecured loans. *Secured loans* are loans that require security. This means that you have to pledge some physical thing of value as security or collateral for the money the bank loans. A loan for buying equipment is a secured loan, because the equipment is pledged as security: The bank can repossess the equipment in the event that the borrower is unable to make the payments. Unsecured loans are made on "your good name," which means your credit in general is strong, especially with that particular bank.

Only the rare businessperson getting started or expanding will obtain an unsecured loan. Even government-guaranteed loans are "partially secured" (not totally supported by collateral, but supported with collateral to a large extent).

Secured loans in turn fall into four categories: (1) loans secured by liquid assets (stocks, bonds, or cash); (2) loans secured by accounts receivable; (3) loans secured by inventory; and (4) loans secured by fixed assets (equipment, improvements, and property).

Liquid asset loans use savings accounts, stocks, or bonds for collateral. The business leaves its stock, bonds, or savings with the bank, and the bank loans an amount equal to (for savings) or less than (with stocks and bonds whose market value fluctuates) the amount of the security. The advantage of this loan is that the interest rate is inexpensive (1 to 2% over what you are earning on savings, or near prime in the case of stocks or bonds).

Accounts receivable secured loans include both factoring and accounts receivable financing. They are not available to a business just getting started. Accounts receivable financing, and more especially factoring, tend to be expensive ways to finance a business. This financing is best used in a situation where sales are growing faster than cash flow. In accounts receivable financing (which has cheaper interest than factoring), the lender loans up to 80% of the value of your receivables (assuming all the accounts are reasonably good). The customer pays the firm, and the firm brings the endorsed check to the lender. In factoring, the lender buys the firm's accounts. When a factor buys a firm's receivables, the firm's customer receives a statement saying that the account is owned by that factor, and the customer pays the factor directly.

Inventory loans are made to businesses where there is an amount of inventory that will be tied up for a long period of time. One type of business that would use inventory loans is a car dealership. It is necessary for the dealership to retain expensive inventory (cars) in the showroom for long periods of time before it is sold. In the case of a car dealership, the company has physical possession of the inventory, but the bank owns the title. The type of inventory financing used for a new car dealership is called *flooring* (the borrower keeps the merchandise on the floor). Inventory loans are not made for inventory which comprises: (1) numerous items of different prices (grocery, hardware, and most retail businesses); (2) fast-selling items; or (3) work in process (the uncompleted goods in manufacturing).

Fixed asset secured loans are for large "capital" items like equipment, land and buildings, improvements, and fixtures. Fixed asset loans usually have the longest terms of all the secured loans previously discussed. Real estate loans are an example of secured fixed asset loans. Fixed asset loans usually exceed five years in length.

Government-guaranteed loans should interest most businesspeople. For the vast majority of small businesses, the best government-guaranteed loan is the Small Business Administration (SBA) guaranteed loan. For a bank the SBA loan guarantees 90% of the loan amount against loss. When you borrow $100,000 from a bank with an SBA guarantee, if you lose all the money in the first week, the bank will be paid 90% of the loss ($90,000) by the SBA. The SBA guaranteed loan is for high-risk types of business, that is, small, and especially new, businesses. The borrower has to meet other requirements. Information is available from your local SBA office.

Loans from Commercial Finance Companies

The types of loans available from commercial finance companies include: inventory loans; equipment and fixture loans (including industrial time financing); accounts receivable loans (including accounts receivable financing); and equipment leasing (leasing companies).

Inventory loans are available to accounts receivable and factoring clients. Such loans are frequently used to assist the customer during periods of slow product shipments and inventory buildup, or to facilitate bulk raw material purchases at advantageous prices.

Equipment loans include basically two types: money loaned against presently owned equipment, and money loaned to finance new equipment and financed on a time sales basis.

Commercial finance companies will sometimes make loans on presently owned equipment. These advances are normally amortized monthly over a period of one to five years, or even more. The proceeds from this loan may be required by the borrower to increase working capital, discount accounts payable, or simply to purchase new equipment. Very often an equipment loan is accepted in conjunction with accounts receivable or factoring arrangements.

Industrial time sales financing is the process whereby a company buys equipment from an equipment supplier and the equipment supplier sells the purchase contract to a financier.

The price you pay for buying equipment on installment is usually high—higher, in fact, than the highest interest allowable in your state. How can the additional cost of financing be higher than the maximum allowable interest rate? Because you don't pay "interest" on industrial installment loans—you pay a "time price differential."

The cost of buying on installment, called the *time price differential*, has the following rationale: A seller is presumed to have two prices. One is the cash price; the other price is the *time price*, which assumes that the purchaser, who wants credit over a period of time, must pay an added charge to compensate the seller for his additional burden. The difference between the cash price and the time price is the *time price differential*. This reasoning assumes that the seller is not a money lender. The price doctrine provides the legal mechanism to remove the time sale from the application of usury laws (the state laws that restrict the maximum interest that can be charged on secured loans). It holds that the transaction is a credit sale and is neither a loan nor a forcbearance for money.

Accounts receivable loans are the "bread and butter" of commercial finance companies, and they are originally why the commercial finance companies were founded. Accounts receivable loans fall into two categories: accounts receivable financing and factoring. See above under "Bank Loans" for details.

Leasing.   Leasing is also a type of financing. It is a way of financing the full amount of the equipment you need. Leasing is the newest addition to traditional popular funding methods, and there is still a lot of debate as to whether it is a good method for businesspeople. To add to the controversy, there is no standard way things can be leased. You can rent a piece of equipment with or without maintenance, or with partial maintenance, and you can lease by the month, year, or several years. You can also obtain leases with an option to purchase. Here are some of the advantages and disadvantages of leasing.

Advantages are:

1. Leasing offers a tax advantage. When you own something, you have to depreciate it for tax purposes over a lengthy period. Thus the cost is recovered slowly. A lot of bookkeeping has to be done to obtain a tax saving. If inflation proceeds at the same pace as in recent years, the tax saving accrues in dollars of decreasing value as the depreciation table stretches into the future. There is little reason to expect that inflation can be kept under control. Leasing expenses are operating expenses and do not have to be depreciated, stretched out, held to future years, or back-charged to years gone by.

2. If you choose to have a maintenance contract with the lease (a good example is

maintenance-included leases on copy machines), your company is freed from maintenance problems.

3. You can "walk away" from the lease—return the equipment to the lessor when the equipment becomes outmoded, without having to finish the payments. In short, leasing is more flexible than ownership.

4. You need not worry about the equipment becoming obsolete. If your lease can be cancelled you can just stop the lease.

5. The cost of the equipment is fixed by the lease agreement, and this makes the cost predictable for projections.

6. Money that might be tied up in expensive fixed assets can be used for other purposes.

The *disadvantages* of leasing include:

1. Down payments on leases were at one time cheaper than purchase down payments. Now, however, the prepayment on leases is only 2 to 5% less than the down payment required for a purchase contract.

2. The costs for purchasing or buying are about the same, and when the equipment is purchased from the leasing company at the end of the period, the costs of leasing are higher.

3. If your company loses control over maintenance, you are at the mercy of the leasing company as to when the equipment will be fixed and how the service is interpreted.

In short, leasing requires somewhat less down payment at the start, but is generally more expensive than a standard equipment purchase. Leasing is best if you need temporary use of the equipment.

Other Sources of Loans

Besides the sources mentioned above, there are other sources of capital. These include life insurance companies, credit unions, and pension funds and foundations.

Life insurance companies. Because of the striking growth of the industry, the accumulation of assets in life insurance companies has been rapid and substantial. It has been estimated that these companies are accumulating assets at the rate of $6 billion per year. The outflow of their funds can be statistically predicted. Hence, a part of their portfolio is available for long-term financing in the form of mortgages on industrial, commercial, and housing real estate. Insurance companies also make loans to businesses, but these businesses are usually substantial enterprises with long earnings records dealing in markets not subject to rapid change. The average small or medium-sized business would not qualify because life insurance companies must follow certain loan policies: (1) the borrower has to be a corporation; (2) there is a minimum time for the borrower to be in business; (3) the borrower should have sufficient historical and current earnings to meet obligations, including debt repayments. A life insurance company grants two types of loans: commercial and industrial mortgage loans and unsecured loans. Mortgages by insurance companies cost the same as more orthodox bank loans.

A prevalent type of life insurance company loan is on an unsecured basis to a business in very good financial condition. Life insurance lenders are most interested in long-range financial data demonstrated by projected sales, cash flows, and so on.

Credit unions.   If you are a member of a credit union, you can receive loans for small amounts at reasonable interest. Credit union services are offered only to members of credit unions; the credit union law restricts membership in a single credit union to a more or less homogeneous group of members having a common interest. Credit union laws restrict the rate of interest charged and the loan amount that may be made to a single borrower.

Pension funds and foundations.   Because of the money they receive, pension funds have experienced a rapid and large accumulation of assets and have a predictable outflow. Their standards of investment are similar to those of the life insurance companies, and they charge about the same interest rates. A good percentage of pension fund money is used for sale-leasehold arrangements.

Large foundations make loans in excess of $1 million for periods averaging 10 years. When they evaluate applicants, special emphasis is placed on company management, business background, and realistic projections.

ACCOUNTING IMPLICATIONS OF DEBT

When a lender loans money to a business, the immediate entry is a credit to a Notes payable account, with an explanation of the terms and length of the loan, as follows:

General Journal

Date	Comment	Debit	Credit
4/7/81	Cash	$17,000	
	Long-term notes payable		$17,000
	To record 15%, 120-month note from Bank of Amerigold; payments are $263.95 per month.		

Entries are then made in the general ledger as follows:

Bank of Amerigold Long-term Note Payable

Date	Comment	Debit	Date	Comment	Credit
			4/7/79	General journal	$17,000

Cash

Date	Comment	Debit			
4/7/81	General journal	$17,000			

Whenever a payment is made to the bank, a portion of that payment will be interest and a portion will be principal. *Interest* is the amount of money that the lender charges you for using the loan. *Principal* is the amount of the loan repayment that reduces the balance owed the bank. Interest is an expense and should be posted in an expense account. Principal is a reduction of the debt and is posted directly as a debit (a reduction in the amount owed) to the Notes payable account. Again, interest is an expense, and principal is a reduction of a liability.

Each month the lender notifies the borrower how much of the monthly payment ($263.95 in the example) is interest and how much is principal.

With a monthly payment of $263.95, the interest amount of the loan as 14%, and the amount of the loan as $17,000 (as in the example above), we get the following transactions:

General Journal

Date	Comment	Debit	Credit
5/20/81	Interest expense	$198.33	
	Long-term notes payable	65.62	
	Cash		$263.95
	To record monthly payment of note to		
	Bank of Amerigold (#12-34789-6).		

Ledgers

Date	Comment	Debit	Date	Comment	Credit
5/20/81					

Interest Expense

Date	Comment	Debit			
5/20/81	General journal	$198.33			

The interest expense can be charged against income tax in the year of entry (1981 in the examples). Principal payments are not an expense but a reduction in the balance owed on the loan. After a specified number of payments (120 in this example), the note is paid and the liability is reduced to zero.

When the firm designs a profit and loss statement and/or a balance sheet for banks, stockholders, government agencies, or other interested parties, a footnote should be included with these financial statements indicating the term and interest amount of the loan and the name of the asset secured by the note, if any.

The pamphlet on liabilities and debt stopped. It didn't end. It just stopped. Kimberly thought about the book.

Kimberly was unhappy to learn that right now appeared to be a bad time to borrow. Interest rates were high. Banks were not expanding. There was a lot of demand for money in general.

There are three basic sources of money for loans: banks, commercial financing, and the government. Kimberly knew that if she got a loan to help her consulting business she would probably get a secured loan. Her credit wasn't good enough for an unsecured loan.

SUMMARY

Kimberly tried to remember what she had read. Liabilities are the sums of money that you owe, that is, debt. Current liabilities are those that are due and payable within one year. Noncurrent liabilities are liabilities that are due after one year (like mortgages).

Financial leverage is the ratio of total debt to total assets. Under poor economic conditions, the companies with the least leverage have the best returns. In good economic conditions, the company with the highest leverage gets the best return.

Banks loan money for different terms (30 days to 30 years). A loan for less than one year is considered a short-term loan. If the loan is for more than one year it is considered an intermediate term (up to five years) or long term loan. Secured loans are loans that have collateral; unsecured loans have no collateral pledged. Secured loans fall into four categories: (1) loans secured by liquid assets (cash equivalents), (2) loans secured by accounts receivable, (3) loans secured by inventory, and (4) loans secured by fixed assets.

Leasing is a type of financing. It requires a smaller down payment but is more expensive in the long run than fixed asset purchase. Leasing is best when you have a temporary use for the equipment to be leased.

The important thing in accounting for loans is that the monthly loan repayment is both interest and principal. Interest is an expense, but principal reduction of a debt is not. Therefore, the two items must be separated.

Kimberly felt chilled and looked down at the fire. It was almost out of wood. She put some more wood into the fireplace.

Then she tossed the liability pamphlet into the fire and picked up a mystery novel.

Chapter Eight
Forms of Business Organization

"In tonight's lecture," Udjat Her began, "I will discuss the standard forms of business organization prevalent in the United States: sole proprietorships, partnerships, and corporations. I will also consider the hybrid forms of business such as trusts, joint ventures, Subchapter S corporations, and limited partnerships.

SOLE PROPRIETORSHIP

A *sole proprietorship* is the form of business organization with only one owner. In a sole proprietorship, owner and business are identical for legal, accounting, and tax purposes. Your personal assets and your business assets are in effect united, and your business income and nonbusiness income are reported to the Internal Revenue Service on the same tax form, Form 1040. Business income is simply segregated on Schedule C of Form 1040 (see Figure 8.1). About the only thing you need as a sole proprietorship is a license to do business in the place where you choose to operate.

If your business is conducted out of your home, the portion of your home that is devoted to business will be considered property used in the business. Furthermore, legitimate pension, profit sharing, and hospital and accident insurance deductions may be available.

When you own your own business there are miscellaneous taxes such as the self-employment social security tax and the quarterly tax payment that you must make to the Federal Government. These are made on Schedule SE of Form 1040 and Form 1040-ES, respectively.

PROPRIETORSHIP ACCOUNTING

There are two owner's equity accounts that you need to establish in a sole proprietorship:

1. Proprietor's capital account.
2. Proprietor's drawings account. Proprietor's drawings account is like salary, but it is considered an equity account rather than an expense account.

Profit or (Loss) From Business or Profession

(Sole Proprietorship)

Partnerships, Joint Ventures, etc., Must File Form 1065.

▶ Attach to Form 1040.   ▶ See Instructions for Schedule C (Form 1040).

1978

Name of proprietor

Social security number of proprietor

A Main business activity (see Instructions) ▶ ....; product ▶ ....

B Business name ▶ ....

C Employer identification number ▶ ....

D Business address (number and street) ▶ ....

City, State and ZIP code ▶ ....

C

E Accounting method: **(1)** ☐ Cash   **(2)** ☐ Accrual   **(3)** ☐ Other (specify) ▶ ....

F Method(s) used to value closing inventory:

(1) ☐ Cost   **(2)** ☐ Lower of cost or market   **(3)** ☐ Other (if other, attach explanation)

	Yes	No

G Was there any major change in determining quantities, costs, or valuations between opening and closing inventory? . .

If "Yes," attach explanation.

H Does this business activity involve oil or gas, movies or video tapes, or leasing personal (section 1245) property to others? (See page 25 of the Instructions.) . . . .

I Did you deduct expenses for an office in your home? . . . .

Part I   Income

1 a Gross receipts or sales	1a		
b Returns and allowances	1b		
c Balance (subtract line 1b from line 1a)	1c		
2 Cost of goods sold and/or operations (Schedule C–1, line 8)	2		
3 Gross profit (subtract line 2 from line 1c)	3		
4 Other income (attach schedule)	4		
5 Total income (add lines 3 and 4) . . . . ▶	5		

Part II   Deductions

		28 Telephone	
6 Advertising		28 Telephone	
7 Amortization		29 Travel and entertainment . . .	
8 Bad debts from sales or services .		30 Utilities	
9 Bank charges		31 a Wages	
10 Car and truck expenses		b New Jobs Credit .	
11 Commissions		c Subtract line 31b from 31a .	
12 Depletion		32 Other expenses (specify):	
13 Depreciation (explain in Schedule C–2)		a	
14 Dues and publications		b	
15 Employee benefit programs . . .		c	
16 Freight (not included on Schedule C–1)		d	
		e	
17 Insurance		f	
18 Interest on business indebtedness		g	
19 Laundry and cleaning		h	
20 Legal and professional services .		i	
21 Office supplies		j	
22 Pension and profit-sharing plans .		k	
23 Postage		l	
24 Rent on business property . . .		m	
25 Repairs		n	
26 Supplies (not included on Schedule C–1)		o	
		p	
27 Taxes		q	
		r	

33 Total deductions (add amounts in columns for lines 6 through 32r) . . . . ▶ | 33 |

34 Net profit or (loss) (subtract line 33 from line 5). Enter here and on Form 1040, line 13. **ALSO** enter on Schedule SE (Form 1040), line 5a. (For "at risk" provisions, see page 25 of Instructions.) . . . . ▶ | 34 |

Figure 8.1   IRS 1040 (Schedule C) income tax return form for proprietorships.

PARTNERSHIP

A partnership may be nothing more than two or more sole proprietors who have agreed to combine their assets and operate a business jointly. There does not have to be a formal agreement between or among the partners in order for a partnership to exist legally, or for tax purposes. However, most states have partnership laws, and written partnership agreements should be drawn up by a lawyer in conformity with the laws of your particular state. For federal income tax purposes, the term *partnership* includes: a partnership; a syndicate; a group; a pool; a joint venture; or any other unincorporated organization which carries on any business that is not a trust, an estate, or a corporation.

A partnership is not taxable as such. Only the members of the partnership are taxed in their individual capacities on their share of the partnership taxable income, whether it is distributed to them or not.

Example.   A partnership is composed of two partners sharing profits equally. In the current year, the taxable income of the business is $30,000, none of which is distributed to the partners. The partnership tax return will report the $30,000 and show shares of $15,000 for each of the partners. Each partner will report his share of the partnership taxable income on his own tax return, even though the income has not been distributed to him.

The character of the income earned by a partnership is not altered when the income passes to the partners. For example, if a partnership sells a building and realizes a long-term capital gain on the transaction, the long-term capital gain is passed through to the partners rather than being reflected as part of the partnership income. The types of income, losses, and expenses which are passed to partners include: ordinary income and loss, additional first-year depreciation, dividends, interest, short-term capital gains, long-term capital gains, and contributions.

PARTNERSHIP ACCOUNTING

If your company is a partnership, separate Capital and Drawing accounts must be kept for each partner. If no other agreement has been made, the law provides that all partnership earnings are to be shared equally. However, the partners may agree in advance to any method of sharing earnings. If they do this, but claim no losses, losses are shared in the same way as earnings.

At the end of every year, your company's profits (or losses) must be distributed to each partner's Capital account. Partners, like sole proprietors, cannot actually receive a "salary" from their company. A partner works for partnership profits. You may, however, wish to allocate "salaries" or "interest" payments, or both, to partners as a way of compensating each one fairly for time and capital invested in the business. Two methods of distributing profits are discussed below, but the same principles can be applied to any method you choose.

The easiest way to divide partnership earnings is to assign each partner a fraction, equal or otherwise. For example, two partners could take one-half each, one-quarter and three-quarters, or two-thirds and one-third.

Example.   Let's assume that Al and Sue have a partnership in which Al contributed $40,000 and Sue $20,000 in starting capital. Al is managing the business full time, and Sue works for it three-quarters of the time. They decide to divide earnings two-thirds to Al and one-third to Sue.

When $60,000 is invested, the owner's capital accounts will show the following:

Al's capital		Sue's capital	
Debit (−)	Credit (+)	Debit (−)	Credit (+)
	40,000		20,000

(Note: Cash will have been debited with the $60,000).

At the end of the year, the Al and Sue Company has earned $18,000 profit. It will be distributed as follows:

$$2/3 \times \$18,000 = \$12,000 \text{ to Al}$$
$$1/3 \times \$18,000 = \$ 6,000 \text{ to Sue}$$

If no withdrawls were made during the year, the total $18,000 would be credited to Al and Sue capital accounts as follows:

Al's capital		Sue's capital	
Debit (−)	Credit (+)	Debit (−)	Credit (+)
	40,000°		20,000°
	12,000		6,000

°Prior entry.

If withdrawls had been made by the partners during the year, they would be debited to owner's draw accounts and subtracted from net profits at the end of the year:

Net Profit: $18,000
Al's share	$12,000
Less owner's withdrawal	8,000
	$ 4,000 Al's share
Sue's share	$ 6,000
Less owner's withdrawal	5,000
	$1,000 Sue's share

LIMITED PARTNERSHIP

A *limited partnership* is a special type of partnership authorized under many state laws. A limited partnership must have at least one *general partner*, who has unlimited liability for the debts of the partnership, and who is responsible for managing the business. The *limited partners* are only liable to the extent of their partnership interests, and they must not participate in any way in the management of the business. The advantage of a limited partnership is that it may employ leverage to earn a high rate of return of the limited partners' invested capital without increasing the risk of the limited partners.

Example.   A contractor becomes the general partner in a limited partnership. He agrees to acquire land, construct a building, and sell the building when it is completed. He arranges for five investors to contribute $20,000 each to the project in exchange for limited partnership interests. On the basis of the construction plans, and the $100,000 equity, the contractor–general partner is able to arrange a bank loan for $200,000. The loan will be secured by a purchase money mortgage° and a performance bond.† Considerable leverage would be used, and most of the money contributed by the limited partners, and even the money borrowed, would be treated as a tax deductible expense in the year of the formation of the partnership.

The leverage aspect of limited partnerships is the reason why many tax shelters are constructed as limited partnerships.

Congress felt that the proliferation of tax shelters was not appropriate, and in the Tax Reform Act of 1976, tax shelters were curtailed. Basically, the Act stated that the amount of losses that could be claimed from certain investment activities could not exceed the total amount that the taxpayer had at risk in the partnership. Under the 'at risk' rule, loss deductions are limited to the amount of cash contributed to the partnership by the partner.

There is no liability for the limited partners beyond their initial investment. In the example above, when the building is sold the limited partners will share the profits.

The "at risk" rules apply to: (1) farming, other than timber, (2) oil and gas operations, (3) equipment leasing, and (4) holding, producing, or distributing motion picture films and video tapes. It is anticipated that Congress will extend the "at risk" rules to all activities other than real estate.

Real estate is still a potential type of investment for a tax shelter limited partnership, even though the rules have been changed. One method of increasing the tax deductible expenses in a real estate limited partnership was to write off interest "points," interest, and taxes during the construction period of a real estate project. The new rules state that points, interest, and taxes during construction must be capitalized and amortized over a 10-year period. This rule applies to all individuals and partnerships as well as to Subchapter S corporations.

SUBCHAPTER S CORPORATIONS

In the eyes of the law, a corporation is a person, and it can sue, be sued, and also pay taxes. Since the individuals who own the corporation also pay taxes on any dividends they receive from the corporation, there is in effect double taxation.

Many people argue that this double taxation should be eliminated. To a certain extent this has been done by the creation of Small Business Corporations, also referred to as tax option corporations, or Subchapter S corporations.

A Subchapter S corporation is a corporation that has elected, by unanimous consent of its shareholders, not to pay any corporate tax on its income, and, instead, to have the shareholders pay taxes on it, even though it is not distributed. Shareholders of a Subchapter S corporation are entitled to deduct, on their individual returns, their share of any net operating loss sustained by the corporation.

Taxable income is computed for Subchapter S companies in much the same way as it is computed for any other corporation. The shareholders are then taxed directly on this taxable income, whether or not the corporation makes any distributions to them. There is one exception to this 'no conduit' rule. The Subchapter S corporation's net capital gains or losses are passed to shareholders and are treated by them as long-term capital gains or losses on their individual returns.

Only a domestic corporation that is not a member of an affiliated group can elect

---

° A purchase money mortgage is a mortgage securing payment of all or a portion of the purchase price of real estate. A mortgage to buy a home is a purchase money mortgage.

† A performance bond is a written agreement to ensure that if the performing party does not complete his or her work, the bond beneficiary will receive reimbursement.

Subchapter S status. A qualifying Subchapter S corporation may not have more than one class of stock and more than 10 stockholders. The shareholders must all be individuals, or estates of deceased individuals who once were shareholders. As of 1977, if a Subchapter S corporation has qualified fo five consecutive years, the number of shareholders may be increased to 15.

The tax aspects of a Subchapter S corporation are somewhat complex. A Certified Public Accountant, or an attorney, should be consulted if you decide that Subchapter S status is an appropriate form of business organization for your particular business.

CORPORATIONS

Many businesses that are not designed strictly for investment purposes eventually decide to incorporate. The reasons for this include: limits on personal liability of owner-managers, financing and growth flexibility, and transferability of interest.

The first decision is where to incorporate. A corporation depends on the legal statutes of a particular state not only for its permission to exist but also for the procedure by which it will come into existence. Some state corporation laws are more attractive then others. States such as Delaware have attracted incorporations out of proportion to the actual number of corporations doing business there. This is because Delaware has had, for many years, a corporation law that offers certain privileges, advantages, and facilities for incorporation that could not be obtained elsewhere.

Recently, however, differences in corporation laws among the major commercial states have been reduced. Incorporation is often preferred in the state where the major share of the business will be done, unless business will be done throughout the country and internationally.

Although the procedure of incorporation varies in detail from state to state, the pattern is much the same everywhere. Certain steps should be taken before the incorporations draw up a charter. Included among these are: the discovery of a business opportunity, solicitation of preincorporation stock subscriptions, and reservation of a corporate name.

CORPORATE CHARTERS

Corporate charters are required to have certain clauses and are permitted to have others. Usually the first clause of a corporate charter is the *corporate name*. The name cannot conflict with any other name used in that state. If there is a conflict you may lose the right to use your own name for business purposes.

A second clause will contain the *business purpose*. This sets forth the purposes, objects, or general nature of the business. Many states permit a purpose clause to state that the corporation is formed for any lawful purpose.

A third clause of the corporate charter will outline the *capital structure*. Most corporation laws require a statement of the proposed corporation's capital structure, including: the authorized number of shares; the rights, preferences, privileges, and restrictions on the various classes and series of shares; whether the shares have a par value (I will explain this later); and the voting rights of the shares.

Other provisions appearing in the charter pertain to the location of the principal office, the number of directors, the names and addresses of the original directors, duration of the corporation, existence of preemptive rights,° powers of directors, a

---

°A preemptive right is the preferential right to purchase on the same terms as those offered by a third party.

statement that the corporation may enter into a partnership, and other provisions.

The *bylaws* of a corporation deal with the internal management rules of the corporation. They must be consistent with the charter of the corporation. Bylaws usually deal with matters such as: the duties and compensation of corporation officers; the qualifications for membership on the board of directors; executive and other director committees; the date and place of annual shareholders meetings; provisions for audits; and other matters.

COMMON STOCKHOLDER RIGHTS

The rights of the holders of common stock in a business corporation are established by the laws of the state in which the corporation is chartered and by the terms of the business's charters.

Also, collective and specific rights are usually addressed in corporate charters with respect to the rights of common stockholders:

Collective rights.   Certain *collective rights* are usually given to the hoolders of common stock. Some of the more important rights allow stockholders to amend the charter, to adopt bylaws, to elect directors, to authorize sale of major assets, to enter into mergers, to change the amount of authorized common stock, and to issue preferred stock, debentures, bonds, and other securities.

Specific rights.   Holders of common stock also have *specific rights*, as do individual owners. They have the right to vote. They may sell their ownership shares. They have the right to inspect the corporate books.

From a legal perspective, the management of a corporation derives its authority from the ownership interests of the corporation. In order to maintain and exercise this authority, a device known as the *proxy* has developed over time.

For each share of common stock owned, a stockholder has the right to cast one vote at the annual meeting of stockholders. Provision is usually made for a temporary transfer of this right to vote by the proxy. A *proxy* is defined as a transfer of the right to vote. The transfer is limited in its duration and is typically for a specific occasion such as the annual stockholder's meeting.

The Securities and Exchange Commission (SEC) supervises the use of proxies and issues frequent rules concerning them. If the proxy rules were left solely in the hands of management, there is the possibility that the incumbent management would be self-perpetuated. On the other hand, if it were easy for minority groups of stockholders and opposition stockholder factions to remove incumbent management, then it would be possible for small groups of stockholders to gain control of the corporation for their own personal ends. In order to balance these diverse interests stockholder voting for directors is regulated by law in many states.

ADVANTAGES AND DISADVANTAGES OF COMMON STOCK FINANCING

There are four principal *advantages* of using common stock as a source of financing for a corporation:

1.   Common stockholders do not receive fixed payments. As the company generates earnings, it may pay common stock dividends. In contrast to bond interest, there is no legal obligation to pay dividends.
2.   Common stock carries no fixed maturity date.

3. Since common stock provides a cushion against losses for creditors, the sale of common stock increases the credit worthiness of the firm.

4. Common stock may at times be more easily sold than debt. Common stock may have a higher expected return in periods of inflation because the return may increase, whereas the return on debt remains constant.

There are several *disadvantages* of using common stock as a source of financing for a corporation.

1. The sale of common stock extends voting rights or control to the additional stockholders. For this reason, additional equity financing is often avoided by small and new firms. The owner-managers may be unwilling to share control of their companies with outsiders.

2. Common stock gives more owners the right to share in profits.

3. The costs of underwriting and distributing common stock are usually higher than for underwriting and distributing preferred stock or debt. Underwriting costs for selling common stock are higher because the costs of investigating and equity security investment are greater than for a comparable debt security.

4. Common stock dividends are not deductible for tax purposes, but bond interest is.

PAR AND NO PAR STOCK

Common stock either has a par value or it is no par stock. *Par value* is an arbitrary amount assigned to a share of stock. Par value has no necessary relationship to the share's market value then or any other time. *No par* stock, however, is assigned a stated value per share for accounting purposes, and this is the basis on which the stock is presented in the balance sheet.

The excess price above either the par or stated value received at the time stock is sold initially is entered in an account entitled paid-in surplus, capital surplus, or capital in excess of par or stated value. This paid-in surplus appears as a separate item in the capital section of the balance sheet (see Figure 8.2).

Theoretically, and in the eyes of the law, creditors rely on a company's stated capital (at par or stated value) when granting credit to it. Actually, to the extent that creditors pay attention to financial statements at all, they rely on their appraisal of a company's working capital condition as shown by its balance sheet and on how well the company is doing judged by their analysis of its income statement.

However, the par or stated value of common stock outstanding may have never been

---

Assume 9,500 shares sold at $5 per share
Your Company Stockholder's Equity:
Common stock, $1 par value
  (Authorized: 10,000 shares;
  issued and outstanding: 9,500) $ 9,500

Capital in excess of par value   38,000

    Total stockholder's equity $47,500

Figure 8.2 Illustration of a typical paid-in surplus section of a balance sheet.

paid for in full. In this case, creditors can require that the stockholders make good the deficiency if the company fails and is unable to pay off its debts.

By selling common stock at a premium above its par or stated value, the danger to a stockholder of a possible later assessment has been avoided. To effect this, stock may be assigned a low par value, or low stated value, if the stock is no par. The low par, or low stated, values may be adopted in order to minimize the fees or taxes involved in the sale of the stock.

Corporations are created, carry on their activities, are taxed, and are dissolved under state laws. Thus, state statutes have a bearing on how a company reports ownership, as well as on how it treats other matters in its balance sheet.

PREFERRED STOCK

Preferred stock has claims or rights ahead of common stock, but behind those of debt securities. The preference may be a prior claim on earnings, or it may take the form of a prior claim on assets in the event of liquidation. It may also be a preferential position with regard to both earnings and assets. The hybrid nature of preferred stock becomes apparent when you try to classify it in relation to debt securities and common stocks. The priority feature, and the fixed dividend, indicate that preferred stock is similar to debt. Payments to preferred stockholders are limited in amount, so that common stockholders receive the advantages or disadvantages of leverage. However, if the preferred dividends are not earned, the company can forego paying them without damage of bankruptcy. In this way, preferred stock is similar to common stock.

The possible characteristics, rights, and obligations of preferred stock are similar to those of common stock. They also vary widely. As economic conditions change, new types of securities are invented. The possibilities are many, limited only by the imagination and ingenuity of the managers formulating the terms of the security issues. It is not surprising, then, that preferred stock can be found in a variety of forms. These are some of the more common features of preferred stock:

- Preference in assets and earnings
- Par or liquidation value (dividends as a percentage of par)
- Cumulative dividends (i.e., all dividends in arrears must be paid)
- Convertibility into common stock
- Participation in earnings
- Call provision

Advantages. An important advantage of preferred stock from the viewpoint of the issuer is that, in contrast to bonds, the obligation to make fixed payments is avoided. If a firm's earning power is high, higher earnings for the original owners may be obtained by selling preferred stock with a limited return rather than by selling common stock. By selling preferred stock, a company avoids the equal participation in earnings that the sale of additional common stock would require. Preferred stock also permits a company to avoid sharing control through participation in voting. In contrast to bonds, preferred stock issuance enables the company to leave mortgageable assets unencumbered. The lack of maturity date or sinking fund provision° typically makes preferred stock a more flexible financing source than bonds.

Disadvantages. The disadvantages of preferred stock include the fact that typically it must be sold at a higher yield than bonds. Furthermore, preferred stock dividends

---

°A sinking fund is a provision that facilitates the ordinary retirement of a bond issue. Typically, the sinking fund provision requires the firm to buy and retire a portion of the bond issue each year.

are not deductible for tax purposes, which increases their cost relative to bonds even more. Utility companies, such as telephone, gas, and electric providers, issue the majority of all preferred stocks. For utilities, taxes are an allowable cost for rate-making purposes; that is, higher taxes may be passed on to customers in the form of higher prices. Tax deductibility of preferred dividends is therefore not an issue.

TRANSFORMING THE STRUCTURE OF A BUSINESS

One of the few remaining ways to become a well-to-do person in the United States is to start a business enterprise, which then becomes successful. Next you take the company public in a stock offering, retaining a healthy share of the stock yourself. Then you see the stock rise significantly in price in the public market. This is, of course, a long shot; but if you win. . . .

Some lawyers, accountants, and investment bankers make a specialty out of taking new companies into the public markets. Their goal is to be part of the long shot when it comes through. The tax implications of moving away from proprietorship and partnership toward a corporation are such that generally accepted accounting principles (such as concepts of accrual, depreciation, inventory, etc.) are more frequently brought into play in corporations. The business manager in a corporate setting has to be more aware of his accounting options, and the business's accountant has to be more aware of generally accepted standards of accounting and auditing, not just taxes.

When a corporation decides to go into a public issue of stock, it may want to do many things from an accounting standpoint. For example, in a private company saving taxes may be of paramount importance. In a public company, in contrast, reported earnings may be equally important. Therefore, a company moving from private to public status may want to reassess its depreciation and amortization policy along with other accounting treatments, such as bad debt allowances, warranty reserves, inventory valuation, and so on.

Going public may mean that your company will be audited for the first time by a Certified Public Accountant. Many local CPAs are highly competent at tax returns and tax planning and preparing financial reports from client records, yet they may be only rarely engaged to perform certified audits. It is generally not possible for a CPA who is closely alllied to you, as an advisor to your business and as a preparer of your financial statements, to perform a certified audit. Going public often means you have to find a new CPA firm. This can be costly and somewhat traumatic. The benefit is obtaining a thorough review of your business, from an objective standpoint, and a general assurance that your financial statments are prepared in conformity. In addition, an unqualified opinion from a respected CPA form will enhance the marketability of the stock of your company. This can mean more money for your company if your stock is sold successfully.

A public issue of stock requires several outside consultants: an accountant and a lawyer with prior experience in public securities offerings, and a securities underwriter or investment banker. Each of these persons will have a role to play in the issuing of public securities. The accountant must prepare a certified audit opinion upon completion of his audit of your business. The lawyer will typically prepare the written parts of any forms and documents that must be filed with the Securities of Franchise Board of the state of incorporation or with the Securities and Exchange Commission (SEC).

Typically, no documents will be required if the total funds to be raised by the corporation are less than $100,000. If the total funds to be raised are between $100,000 and $500,000, then you may be able to avoid filing many of these documents by complying with Regulation A of the Securities Act of 1933, which specifies an exemption for small offerings. If the total funds to be raised are over $500,000, it will probably be necessary to undergo a complete registration statement procedure. The registration statement will be filed with and reviewed by the SEC in Washington, D.C., or by a regional field office.

Upon completion of the review, the registration is said to "go effective." Your stock then may be legally sold in the public markets. This is where the underwriter plays a role in the issuance and sale. The underwriter's job is to judge the movement of the market and to estimate the best time to begin selling the stock in the public market. As a fee, the underwriter typically receives a certain percentage of the total amount raised. Or alternatively, the underwriter will purchase the new stock at a price that is estimated to be below the market price when the stock is sold publicly. In the latter case, the risk of stock price decline is often on the underwriter, which is the reason for the name "underwriter."

Most companies which are initially required to file registration statements in conjunction with sales of stock must file additional annual, quarterly, and other update reports and must revise their registration statements, prospectuses, and proxy materials from time to time. This is an added cost in terms of the time involved for management, the accountant's and lawyer's fees, and the probable printing costs. Such costs should be considered when initially planning a public issue of stock of other securities.

SUMMARY

In summary, there are three basic forms of business organization: sole proprietorships, partnerships, and corporations.

In a sole proprietorship owner and business are identical for accounting, legal, and tax purposes. Business and nonbusiness income is reported to the IRS on the same form, form 1040.

A partnership is a business of two or more individuals. There does not have to be a formal agreement among the partners in order for a partnership to exist legally. A partnership is not taxable as such. The individual members of the partnership are taxed on their share of partnership earnings. A limited partnership is a special type of partnership that has at least one general partner, who has unlimited liability for the management and debts of the partnership, and several limited partners liable only to the extent of their share and with no management participation.

In the eyes of the law, a corporation is a person, and it can sue, be sued, and also pay taxes. A Subcharter S corporation is a corporation that has elected to have the stockholders pay taxes on corporate income instead of the corporation doing so. This makes the earnings mechanism act like a partnership. A corporation (including a Subchapter S) limits personal liability of the owners, allows financing and growth flexibility, and makes transfer of ownership interest easier. Corporate charters are required to have certain clauses, including corporate name, business purpose, capital structure, and perhaps location, number of directors, and their names and addresses. The ownership document of a corporation is stock that may be either common (voting rights but no guaranteed payments) or preferred (no voting rights but payment guaranteed).

Udjat Her finished his lecture, and his class slowly filtered out into the hall and then into the street. Udjat gathered up his notes and his books, all the time staring at Kimberly.

"You were late," he said.

"Oh, I had a little trouble getting lose from the program I was working on. I'm sorry." She smiled. "But I'm sure you can fill me in on sole proprietorships over coffee. How about it? I'll even buy."

Chapter Nine
Revenue and Expense

Kimberly couldn't make it to Udjat's class tonight because she had some midnight oil-burning to do. She didn't have the time to do her work and sit in on his class too. There was nothing wrong with that. He understood. But this was the first night that he had to face the class alone.

The school building was an old converted four-story brownstone. The only true word to describe it was "drab." Udjat found his way through the poorly lit corridor to the right door and reached inside to flip the switch. Most light switches are on the inside wall away from where the door swings open. In his classroom the light switch was *behind* the door.

He put his briefcase down near the podium, shuffled through the papers until he found the ones that he was to use that night, and he carefully laid them out. He then went down to the basement bookshop and snackbar to get a cup of coffee and a Twinkie (the only pastry available). The snackbar attendant always made the wrong change. Sometimes he would give you too much change, sometimes too little. A black-and-white television was blaring out loud from its position on top of the refrigerated case.

Udjat saw a few of the other instructors sitting on the yellow formica tables. But the basement always depressed Udjat, so he headed back to his classroom, coffee and Twinkie in hand. The room filled up slowly, and then it was starting time. He began.

REVENUE (SALES OR INCOME)

To a salesperson, a sale takes place when the salesperson receives an order from a customer. But to the accountant it is not a sale until the goods are shipped. A record or order may be kept for management purposes, but a sale is not a sale until the goods are out the door. When goods have been *shipped*, the accountant will accept the fact that delivery has been made and, accordingly, will record the event as a sale.

Thus, for the majority of companies, the word 'sales' in an income statement means goods shipped during a given accounting period.

The term *sales* may be extended to cover "fees" for services performed as well as other items of income such as commissions, rents, and royalties.

For sales involving the shipment of goods, there is normally a passing of *legal title*, which is evidence that a sale has in fact taken place. In other types of business transactions, however, revenue recognition is not dependent on the passing of title. For example, service industries such medicine or beauty care do not pass a legal title when doctors or hairdressers perform a service for their customers.

Other examples of revenue without passing legal title are situations involving long-term contracts. Legal title does not pass until the contract is completed. In the construction of a house, for example, revenue will be recognized each accounting period in accordance with the work performed during that period as measured by either: (1) percentage of completion or (2) completion of identifiable portions of work. At such times, something less than the full proportion of revenue will be recognized.

Companies selling on an installment payment basis commonly record their sales at the time goods are delivered to the customers. However, these sales are not reported for tax purposes until after their cost of merchandise has been recovered.

Where options are available that permit one type of report to the government and another to the stockholder, the natural tendency is for a company to be most conservative in computing net income for tax purposes.

Sales Discounts and Returns

In many businesses the real price charged any given buyer is determined by the application of a discount to the list or catalog price. No buyer is foolish enough to pay full price when he may be able to get a discount. Under these conditions, sales reported for accounting purposes represent revenue net of trade discounts.

The question of whether cash discounts are a financial expense, a selling expense, or a reduction in sales revenue has been debated for many years. Treating the discount as a *financial expense* assumes that it is granted in order to receive payment and to either match or better the offers of competitors. Treating the discount as a *reduction in sales revenue* may also be justified by competition. In any case, these costs are subtracted from gross sales to give a net sales figure.

The value of goods returned is another item subtracted from sales to arrive at net sales. The accounting problem caused by returns is that goods returned in the current accounting period may have been sold in the previous period. Treating them as a reduction from current sales is an incorrect matching of revenues and costs.

Unless the returns are unusually large, however, there is no serious distortion of results. The distortion of returns in one period is similar to distortions in the next period or in the previous period. In other words, these distortions will balance out over time.

An allowance for sales returns and adjustments is set as a percentage of sales. This allowance is created to allow for adjustments such as billing errors or other selling price adjustments that occur after the fact. Some companies use an allowance for trade discounts as well.

The sales journal and the accounts receivable ledger are the primary accounting systems for recording sales and revenue transactions.

Revenues and sales *cannot* be generated without incurring expenses. In order to measure the success of your business, you need to match expenses against revenue.

EXPENSES

Cost of Goods Sold

Cost of goods sold, sometimes referred to as *cost of sales*, is the cost of goods that are shipped or sold. It *does not* cover the expenses of: (1) selling or shipping these goods and (2) any storing, office, or general administrative expenses involved in company operations.

In professional and service businesses there are usually *no* costs of sales. Companies that receive income from fees, rents, commissions, and royalties do not have inventories of goods. In other businesses that have inventories, such as retail, wholesale, and manufacturing businesses, there is a cost of sales.

Inventories are a major part of determining cost of sales. Physical inventories are factors in determining the cost of goods sold. The IRS *requires* that physical inventories be taken at the beginning and end of each tax year. Inventory amounts include merchandise to be sold in the normal course of business plus raw materials and supplies that will physically become a part of that merchandise. Companies *with inventories* are *required* by the IRS to use the *accrual°* method of accounting.

Cost of goods sold is established in one of several ways: (1) *directly*, (2) by using a *gross margin* approach, or (3) by a process of *deduction*.

If detailed inventory records are maintained, the cost of goods sold can be established directly as sales take place. A good example of this is the computer cash register system used by large retailers such as Sears. The sales clerk enters the inventory number into the cash register as sales are totaled. The computer then keeps track of all the inventory as it is sold. For large manufactured goods, the cost records maintained during production are used as a substitute for cost at the time of shipment. This example illustrates the *direct* method of determining cost of sales.

A shortcut in establishing the cost of goods sold is to (1) classify sales by product groups which have the same percentage markup (gross margin) and (2) multiply the sales in each group by the appropriate percentage. This is called the *gross margin* method of determining cost of sales. For example, if the sales of a product group having a known gross margin of 30% are $100,000 for the period, the cost of goods sold would be established at 70% of this, or $70,000.

Where it is not possible or practical to establish the cost of goods directly or by the gross margin method, as above, it is necessary to determine the cost by *deduction*. An inventory record has four elements:

- What was on hand at the beginning of the period.
- What came in during the period.
- What went out during the period.
- What was left at the end of the period.

If any three of these elements are known, it is possible to find the fourth element by deduction. When using the method to determine cost of goods sold, we want to find *what went out during the period*. All companies are required to take inventory at the end of each year, so they should know what their ending inventory is and, also, what their beginning inventory (taken at the end of the last year) was. What came in represents the purchases of the company.

Figures 9.1 and 9.2 illustrate the deductive method of determining cost of goods sold. Here is a point by point explanation of Figure 9.2.

1. *Inventory at the beginning of the year* (opening inventory) for a manufacturer includes the total value of the raw material, work in process (goods not finished), finished goods, and materials and supplies used in manufacturing the goods. For retailers and wholesalers, inventory is merchandise held for sale. *Ending* inventory for *one year* is the *beginning* inventory for the *next* tax *year*.

2. *Merchandise purchased during the year* includes the cost of all raw materials or parts purchased for manufacturing into a finished product. For merchants

°In the accrual method of accounting sales are determined when goods are *shipped*, not when they are paid for. Accrual accounting determines assets, liabilities, and expense when they are incurred.

INVENTORY

ACCOUNTING TERMS

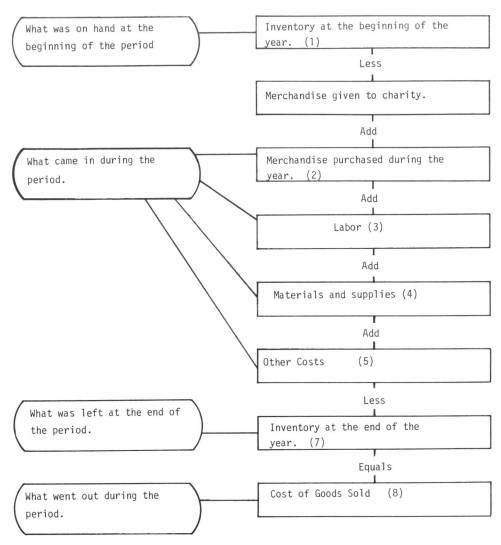

Figure 9.1 *If a business knows*: (1) inventory amount at the start of the period, (2) purchases (what came in) during the period, and (3) inventory as counted at the end of the period, then *they can deduce*: (4) inventory sold during the period or cost of sales.

purchases are all the merchandise bought for resale. Merchandise must be reported net of (1) trade discounts, (2) purchase returns and allowances, (3) merchandise withdrawn for stockholder or owner use, and sometimes (4) cash discounts.

Cash discounts can be accounted for in two ways. You can either credit them to a separate discount account, or you can deduct them from total purchases for the year. If you credit cash discounts to a separate account, the credit balance in this account at the end of the tax year must be included in your business income. Whatever method you use you must be consistent.

3. *Labor costs* are an element of cost of goods sold *only* in a manufacturing business. Labor includes both direct and indirect labor used in fabricating the raw material into a finished product. *Direct labor costs* are the wages paid to employees who spend all their time working directly on the product being

1. Inventory at the beginning of the year	$61,400	
Less: Merchandise contributed to charitable organizations	400	$ 61,000
ADD:		
2. Merchandise (or raw materials) purchased during the year	80,000	
3. Labor	20,000	
4. Materials and supplies	4,000	
5. Other costs	6,000	110,000
6. Cost of goods available for sale		171,00
SUBSTRACT:		
7. Inventory at the end of the year		35,000
RESULTS:		
8. Cost of goods sold		$136,000

Figure 9.2 A deductive calculation of cost of sales.

manufactured. *Indirect labor costs* are the wages paid to employees who perform a general factory function that does not have any immediate or direct connection with the fabrication of the product, but is a necessary part of the manufacturing process. For example, in an electronic parts factory the indirect laborer would be a janitor in the factory or people in the boxing and shipping department.

Generally, the only kinds of labor costs properly chargeable to cost of goods sold are direct or indirect labor costs, and certain other labor treated as overhead expenses to the manufacturing process.

4. *Materials and supplies*, such as hardware and chemicals, used in manufacturing goods are charged to cost of goods sold. Supplies that are *not* consumed in the manufacturing process are *not* deductible as cost of sales.

5. *Other costs* are costs incurred in connection with a manufacturing or mining process such as the cost of containers and packages; freight-in, express-in, and cartage-in; and certain overhead expenses.

If containers and packages are an *integral part* of the product manufactured, they are part of cost of goods sold. If they are *not* an integral part of the manufactured product, their costs are charged to shipping or selling expenses. *Overhead expenses* include such expenses as rent, heat, light, power, insurance, depreciation, taxes, maintenance labor, and supervision. The overhead expenses incurred as direct and necessary expenses of the manufacturing operation are included in cost of goods sold.

6. *Cost of goods available for sale* is the total of items 1 through 5. It represents the cost of goods available for sale during the year.

7. The *inventory at the end of the year* (closing inventory) should be subtracted from cost of goods available for sale (item 6).

8. *Cost of goods sold* is reached when the closing inventory is subtracted from the cost of goods available for sale. When you subtract your cost of goods sold from your adjusted total receipts or net sales for the tax year you will have determined your gross profit.

Inventory Identification

For the most part inventories determine cost of goods sold. Inventories include all finished or partly finished goods and raw materials and supplies that will physically become part of the business's merchandise intended for sale.

If you have legal title to merchandise you have purchased, you must include it in your inventory, regardless of whether or not the merchandise is physically in your possession. Inventory should also include goods under contract for sale to others or goods out on consignment.

If you sell merchandise by mail and intend that payment and delivery be C.O.D., the title passes when payment is made. Merchandise shipped C.O.D. is excluded from sales and included in your closing inventory until paid for by the buyer.

Assets such as land, buildings, and equipment used in the business, notes and accounts receivable, and similar assets are *not* to be included in inventory. Real estate dealers are allowed to inventory real estate held for sale (typically real estate is inventory in the hands of dealers in real estate). Freight-out, express-out, and cartage-out are shipping or selling expenses and are not part of the cost of goods sold.

Inventory Valuation

If the prices of the merchandise used in inventory fluctuate, a business faces the problem of deciding how to value the dollar amount of its ending inventory. For example, Z-100 digits, an important element in manufacturing your solid-state components, cost 10 cents at the beginning of the year and 12 cents at the end of the year. The question arises: Should your ending inventory of Z-100 digits be valued at 12 or 10 cents? The answer depends on the type of inventory accounting you are employing: first-in, first-out (FIFO); last-in, first-out (LIFO); or standard costing.

Standard costs are costs expected under given conditions. In a manufacturing plant, standard costing can provide the *expected* cost of material, labor, and factory overhead on each type of product. One of the uses of such standard costs is to establish the cost of goods sold for a period. Cost of sales may be determined by multiplying the quantity of each type of product sold by its standard costs. Variances between the *actual* and *standard* material, labor, and factory overhead expenses are computed each period. These variances are treated as losses or gains for the period.

When standard costing is used to determine cost of goods sold, the variance (gain or loss) in usually shown as a separate item on the income statement.

Gross Profit (Gross Margin)

Once the cost of goods sold has been established, it is subtracted from net sales to arrive at a figure for the *gross margin* (*gross profit*). This figure is the amount of revenue left after paying for the purchase or manufacturing cost of goods sold. It represents the revenue available to cover selling and administrative expenses and to provide an operating profit for the period.

For any business that has no inventory, gross sales (less returns and allowances) *is equivalent to* gross profit. Most professions and businesses that provide personal services determine gross profit as gross sales.

Since gross profit is the money available to pay for all the selling and general and administrative expenses of a corporation or business, it becomes a very important item in finance. The *gross profit percentage* (gross profit divided by net sales) is also important in determining how a particular company is doing in relation to the industry or historical averages.

Operating and Selling Expense

Operating expenses and selling expenses are listed in an income statement after the figure for gross margin. They are not included in inventory valuations. Both selling and operating expenses are sometimes listed simply under Operating expenses, General and administrative expense, or just Expenses.

Selling Expenses. Practice varies among companies with respect to the specific types of costs that are included under the title of "selling expenses." But in general, selling expenses consist of two major types: order getting (sales) and order handling (shipping). *Order-getting expenses* are those such as advertising, salesperson's salaries and commissions, and sales office costs. *Order-handling costs* are those such as order taking and filling expense, warehousing, and shipping.

The majority of costs included under the title of selling expenses do not necessarily bear any direct relationship to the sales figure. The shorter the period covered by the statement, the less likely that there is any relationship between these figures.

Operating Expense (General and Administrative Expense). General and administrative expenses (operating expenses) are costs to be deducted from the gross margin (gross profit) to arrive at net profit. From a budgeting and control standpoint, operating expenses are managed costs and, in the short run, they will be fixed costs. They are regulated over time by management decisions and do not necessarily bear any direct relationship to production or sales volume.

Items Included in Operating and Selling Expense

There are certain expenses that are tax deductible and others that are not. So for the purposes of this lecture, I will group these items into: wages and salaries; rental expense; repairs; replacements, and improvements; travel and transportation; business entertainment; interest; insurance; taxes; and other business expense. I will discuss each of these groups in turn.

Wages and Salaries

Salaries, wages, and other forms of compensation paid to employees are deductible business expenses for tax purposes if they meet the following four tests (see Figure 9.3):

Test 1. You must be able to show that salaries, wages, and other compensation are, in the words of IRS publications, ordinary and necessary expenditures directly connected with carrying on [your] business or trade. The fact that you pay your employees reasonable compensation for legitimate business purposes is not enough, by itself, to qualify the expense as a deductible expense. Remunerations of services can be deducted only if the payment is an ordinary and necessary expense of carrying on your trade or business.

Test 2. The IRS says reasonable compensation is determined by the amount that ordinarily would be paid for like services, by like enterprises, under like circumstances. The following factors are considered in determining reasonableness of compensation:

- Duties performed by the employee.
- Volume of business handled.
- Character and amount of responsibility.
- Complexities of the business.
- Amount of time required.
- General cost of living in the locality.
- Ability and achievements of the individual performing the service.
- Comparison of the compensation with the amount of gross and net income of the business.

WHAT IS A TAX DEDUCTIBLE SALARY COST?

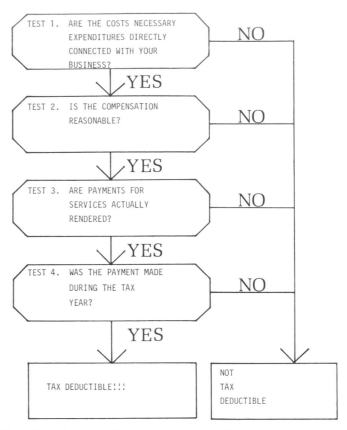

Figure 9.3 Flowchart showing the accounting tests for determining if salaries are tax deductible.

Test 3. You must be able to prove that the payments were made for services actually rendered. You must also reasonably expect your business to benefit from the service performed.

Test 4. You must have paid the compensation or incurred the expense during the tax year. If you use the cash accounting method, only the salaries actually paid during the year are deductible. If you use the accrual method of accounting, the deduction for salaries and wages is allowable in the year when the obligation to pay the compensation is established.

Bonuses you pay to employees are allowable deductions if they are intended as additional compensation, not gifts, and are paid for services actually rendered.

If, to promote employee goodwill, you distribute turkeys, hams, or other merchandise of nominal value at Christmas time and on other special occasions, the value of these gifts is not considered salary or wages paid to your employees. You can deduct the cost of these gifts as a business expense, however, under the gift category. These gifts are limited to a $25 value per person. However, if you distribute cash, gift certificates, or similar items of readily convertible cash value, the value of such gifts is considered additional wages or salary, regardless of amount.

Compensation need not be paid in cash. It may be in the form of meals, lodging, capital assets, or shares of stock in the business.

If you give stock in your company to your employees as compensation, you are entitled to deduct the fair market value of that stock as of the date given. If you transfer a capital asset or an asset used in your business to one of your employees in payment for services, its fair market value on the date of the transfer is deductible. Both of these forms of compensation are taxable income for the employee.

The cost of meals and lodging furnished to employees as part of their compensation is deductible by the employer. In some cases meals and lodging are not taxable to the employee as income. To enable the employees to exclude from their gross income the value of meals and lodging furnished them without charge by the employer, the following tests must be met:

1. The meals or lodging must be furnished on the employer's business premises.
2. The meals or lodging must be furnished for the employer's convenience.
3. In the case of lodging (but not meals), the employees must be required to accept it as a condition of their employment. This means that acceptance of the lodging is required to enable them to properly perform the duties of their employment, as when they must be available for duty at all times.

Fringe benefits such as premiums on insurance, hospitalization, and medical care for employees are deductible by the employer. This does not include life insurance premiums except under special circumstances (there is a $25,000 term insurance limit).

Contributions made for deferred compensation such as supplemental unemployment benefits, pension plans, annuity plans, profit sharing plans, bond purchase plans, and stock bonus plans are deductible if made by the employer, up to certain limits.

Rental Expenses

You may ordinarily deduct, as current expenses, rent paid or accrued for property used in your trade or business. If you allocate rental expenses to the cost of goods sold, however, you cannot include such expenses again as an operating expense.

Rent paid in property is deductible as rent to the extent of the fair market value of that property or service.

Rent paid in advance, sums paid to acquire a lease, and commissions, bonuses, fees, or other expenses you pay to obtain possession of property under a lease must be deducted over the term of the lease, or over the period covered by the advance.

Repairs, Replacements, and Improvements

Any expenditure for property or equipment may be deductible as an expense, or not, depending on whether it just maintains the property or actually adds to the value and life of the property.

Repairs, including labor, supplies, and certain other items, are deductible expenses. This is because repairs generally just maintain property. The value of your own labor expended in this repair, however, is not deductible as an expense. Examples of repairs include: patching and repairing roofs and gutters and mending leaks.

Replacements that arrest deterioration and appreciably prolong the life of the property are *not* deductible as an expense. They should be capitalized and depreciated. Major overhauls of machinery also require capitalization and depreciation.

Travel and Transportation Expenses

Travel expenses are the expenses incurred when you travel away from home overnight in pursuit of your trade or business. *Transportation expenses*, on the other hand, include only the costs of travel (not meals and lodging) directly attributable to the actual conduct of your business while you are *not* away from home overnight.

Travel expenses include:

- Meals and lodging (both en route and at your destination)
- Air, rail, and bus fares
- Baggage charges
- The cost of transporting sample cases or display materials
- The cost of maintaining and operating your automobile
- The cost of operating and maintaining your house trailer
- Reasonable cleaning and laundry expenses
- Telephone and telegraph expenses
- The cost of a public stenographer
- The cost of transportation from the airport or station to your hotel, from your hotel to the airport or station, from one customer or place of work to another
- Reasonable transportation costs from where you obtain meals and lodging to where you are working while away from home overnight
- Other similar expenses incidental to qualifying travel
- Reasonable tips incidental to any of the expenses

You can deduct travel expenses you incur for yourself, but not your family, in attending a convention. Incidental personal expenses incurred for your sightseeing, social visiting, and other entertainment are not deductible.

Transportation expenses (sometimes referred to as *local travel expenses*) include such items as train, bus, and cab fares and the expenses of operating and maintaining your business vehicle. Commuting expenses between your residence and usual place of business are not deductible regardless of the distance involved.

If you use your automobile entirely for business purposes, you can deduct all of your actual expenses for its operation, including depreciation. However, if your automobile is used only partly for business, you must apportion its expense and depreciation between business and personal usage.

If you lease a car that you use in your business, you can deduct your lease payments to the extent that they are directly attributable to your business. You cannot deduct any portion of the lease payments attributable to commuting or other personal use of the car.

Instead of using actual expenses and depreciation to determine the deductible costs of operating an automobile (including a pick-up or panel truck) for business purposes, you can use a standard mileage rate for 1980 of 20 cents a mile for the first 15,000 miles of business usage per year, and 11 cents a mile for each additional business mile in that year. To use the standard mileage rate, you must:

- Own your car
- Not use more than one car simultaneously in your business or profession
- Not use the car for hire, like as a taxi
- Not operate a fleet of cars of which two or more are used simultaneously
- Not have claimed depreciation using any method other than the straight-line method
- Not have claimed additional first-year depreciation on the car

If the car is fully depreciated you can only deduct 10 cents a mile for all miles of business usage.

Parking fees and tolls incurred during business use are deductible in addition to the standard mileage rate.

Business Entertainment Expenses

Entertainment includes any activity generally considered entertainment, amusement, or recreation. Usually, this covers entertaining guests at restaurants, theaters, sporting events, and on yachts, or on hunting or fishing vacations or similar trips. It may also include satisfying the personal or family needs of any individuals, the cost of which would otherwise be a business expense to you, such as furnishing food and beverages, or providing a hotel suite or automobile to business customers or their families.

Costs are considered business deductible entertainment expenses only if they are ordinary and necessary expenses "directly related to or associated with the active conduct of your trade or business."

Interest Expense

Interest is defined by the IRS as "the compensation allowed by law or fixed by the parties for the use (or forbearance) of money." A business can deduct all interest paid or accrued in the tax year on a business debt. This debt is generally referred to as a *liability*.

The liability must be your liability or you cannot deduct the interest paid. An individual, for instance, cannot deduct interest paid on the debt of a corporation. In the special case when you purchase property and pay interest owed by the seller, you *cannot* deduct the interest but must capitalize it (make it part of the cost of the property).

Insurance Expense

If you carry business insurance to protect your company against losses by fire or other hazards, the premiums paid are deductible as business expenses. The following are sample deductible expenses:

- Premiums on fire, theft, flood, or other casualty insurance
- Merchandise and inventory insurance
- Credit insurance
- Employee's group hospitalization and medical insurance
- Premiums on employer's liability insurance
- Malpractice insurance
- Public liability insurance
- Workman's compensation insurance
- Overhead insurance
- Use and occupancy insurance and business interruption insurance
- Employee performance bonds
- Expenses for bonds the business is required to furnish either by law or by contract
- Automobile and other vehicle insurance (unless you use the standard mileage rate to compute auto expense)

Tax Expense

Various taxes imposed by federal, state, local, and foreign governments and incurred in the ordinary course of business or trade are deductible.

Taxes that are deductible as business expenses are broken down into broad categories:

- Real property taxes
- Income tax
- Other taxes
- Employment taxes (payroll, social security, etc.)

Next to income tax, the greatest tax paid by businesspeople is *real property tax*. Ordinarily, a business can deduct all taxes imposed on real property that the business owns. Sometimes the business can elect to capitalize expenditures for taxes as a cost of the property. Those taxes that are *not* deductible include: federal income, estate, and gift taxes; state inheritance, legacy, and succession taxes; and assessments for local benefits.

"To summarize," said Udjat as he ended the lecture, "sales, or revenue, is not sales until the goods are shipped. In other words, if someone orders a computer system, that's not sales. When they pay us cash, that's not sales. It is considered a sale when the system is shipped.

"The cost of goods sold is what the cost of manufacturing is. It includes the cost of the components, the assembly labor (both assemblers and janitors), the incoming freight costs, and some overhead costs. The formula for determining the amount of inventory that went out during the year is what you have at the beginning of the year plus what you purchased and what your labor and other costs were minus what you shipped during the year: beginning inventory plus purchases and direct costs minus the goods that were sold.

"The gross profit, which is also called the gross margin, is sales minus the cost of goods.

"Operating expenses include salaries, selling expenses, shipping expenses, rents, repairs, travel, entertainment, depreciation, taxes, insurance, and interest."

The lecture was over. The students slowly moved out into the hall. Udjat Her noticed that three of the students were people he had never seen before. But this wasn't unusual. Many times people simply wandered in off the streets. But these people never caused any trouble. Most of them were foreign-born people who came to the university extension to learn. They couldn't afford to pay for the class—or even buy the books—but they came to listen. They always sat quietly at the back of the room and just listened.

As Udjat was getting his briefcase packed, a fellow teacher from down the hall walked into the classroom. "Hi, Udjat. Goin' all right?" he asked.

"Yeah. And you?" Udjat answered.

"Not too good, really. I'm gettin' tired of this place. Why should I teach here? I know that you're suppose to teach one class per quarter here and one class per quarter in the west end of town, but I can't stand this place anymore."

"Why not?" Udjat asked.

"It's stupid. First off you have to pay for parking here and not at the other facility."

"That's true," Udjat replied.

"The building is dingy and drab."

"That's also true."

"When I have the class here rather than at the Westside facility, I always have less attendance."

"My attendance is lower here, too." Udjat agreed.

"I've never made any good business contacts here."

"Me either." Udjat agreed again.

"And downtown is further away from my home than the Westside facility," the instructor concluded.

"This place is a long way from my home too." Udjat agreed with everything the instructor alleged.

"Then why are *you* here?" the instructor said in exasperation.

"The experience!" Udjat said. He couldn't think of another reason.

Chapter Ten
Accounting Records

It was very warm for December—82° outside and only one week before Christmas. Instead of going off to see Hero's CPA, Pete Popstein, Kimberly would much rather have stayed in her own air-conditioned office, out of the record-breaking heat.

But before you could write the correct accounting system for someone you need to know what system they had previously, what records were necessary, and what those records were. Popstein's accounting firm had all of Hero's records.

Popstein had his offices in a new multistory building in a prestigious part of town. That meant parking was either expensive or nearly nonexistent—probably both. Kimberly always wondered how a new office building could be built with so few parking places. They ran out even before the building was completely leased.

Kimberly went promptly to the tenth floor. When she got off the elevator, she immediately lost her orientation. There were signs of construction everywhere, with cardboard boxes on the floor and no directing signs. Kimberly took off down one of the corridors. Pipes and electrical wiring were hanging limp from the ceiling and miscellaneous clutter lined both sides of the hall so that there was only a narrow space in which to walk. No office had a door on it, so knowing the correct office number didn't help. Kimberly finally stopped and asked some people she saw sitting at desks. They told her Popstein had moved temporarily to another building, across the street.

Back into the heat! By the time Kimberly found Popstein's office she was both relieved and exhausted. Popstein greeted her apologetically by saying, "I hope you didn't have too much trouble finding the place."

He then introduced Kimberly to one of the senior people on his staff, Jack Klaus, and asked Jack to go over Hero's records with her.

As Popstein excused himself, Jack turned to Kimberly. "I want to cover the types of records that are used for Hero and for other types of companies. Rather than have you ask questions, I would just like to go over it all and discuss the accounting records that I show you. Okay?"

"That's fine with me." After the frustrating experience she had been through Kimberly didn't feel much like talking anyway.

Jack began.

ORIGINAL TRANSACTION DOCUMENTS

The first step for an accountant is to analyze original transaction documents. The documents are: sales slips, cash register receipts, checks, shipping documents, invoices, petty cash slips, and deposit slips. They represent the first recording of a business transaction at the point of exchange.

The documents can be grouped as follows:

- Sales documents (cash register receipts, sales slips, daily cash summary, and invoices)
- Bank documents (check, check register, deposit slips)
- Petty cash
- Purchasing documents
- Shipping and invoice documents
- Travel and entertainment records
- Payroll records

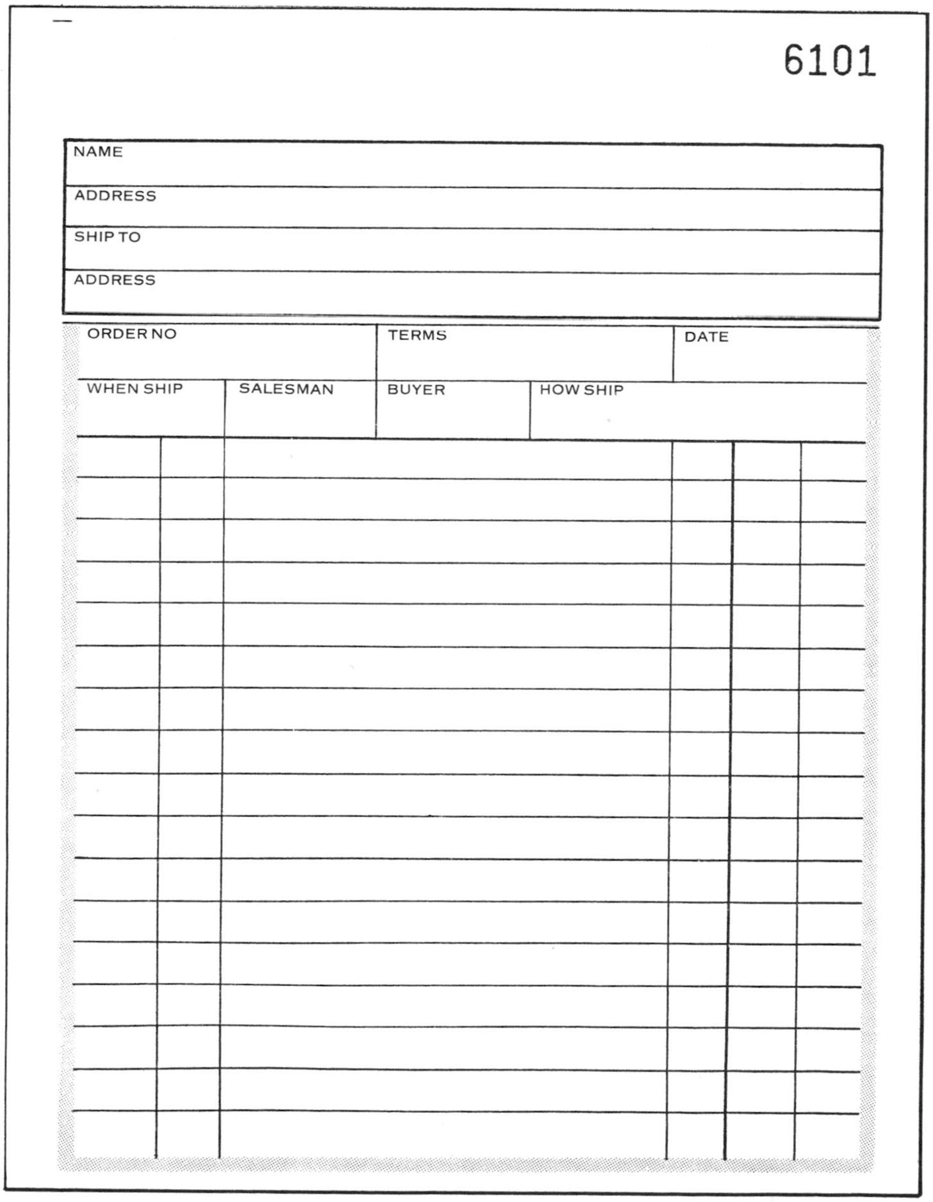
6101

NAME

ADDRESS

SHIP TO

ADDRESS

ORDER NO | TERMS | DATE

WHEN SHIP | SALESMAN | BUYER | HOW SHIP

Figure 10.1 Sample sales slip.

Sales Documents

Examples of sales documents include: a cash register receipt (tape), credit card receipts, and sales slips.

Most retail firms use a cash register for handling transactions where cash sales are involved. A cash register usually has two paper printouts of the transactions, one for the customer and one for the records of the business. This paper tape is called either a *cash register receipt* or a *detailed audit strip*. Some businesses have terminals that are linked to computers or some computer storage device. These cash registers not only have the paper tape, but also relay this information directly to a computer.

Sales slips are another method for recording sales, one usually reserved for larger sales, such as those of Hero Manufacturing. Here is a copy of a sales slip (see Figure 10.1).

The first line of the sales slip usually contains the department and/or salesperson number and an indication of whether it is a cash or credit sale ('terms'). Credit sales are almost always recorded on a sales slip. The sales slip has a place for the name and address of the customer, followed by a space for any delivery instructions. Further spaces are allowed for a description of the item including quantity, name, unit price, total price, and sometimes the inventory number.

The salesperson gives the customer a copy of the sales slip and retains a copy for the business (Hero has four copies because shipping or special orders are sometimes required).

Today many sales are not made for cash, but are instead charged on a credit card in retail sales and charged to a receivable account for other types of industries. These sales are called *charge sales* or *credit sales*.

The documents for a charge account would include an application record, a charge card slip, and a sales invoice or sales slip.

The first step in opening a credit line with a customer is to obtain certain application information from them. The application requires information such as address and name, past credit information, income (either company or personal), expected monthly orders, and so on.

Here is an example of a credit application for a business customer:

BUSINESS:	Zlapps Tulip Works 34 Flower Street Weed, Calif. 90000
SALESMAN:	Charles Smit
LAST YEAR SALES:	$3,000,000
D&B RATING:	3A-2
TYPE:	Tulip Fabricator
MERCHANDISE MOST FREQUENTLY ORDERED:	F-719 Tulip Stems
PURCHASING MAN:	Fred Zlapps
LAST YEAR PROFIT:	$48,000
CREDIT LIMIT:	$100,000

Credit cards are often used by retail customers. Credit card sales slips have specific forms, such as this bankcard sales slip (Figure 10.2). It can be used for either Visa® or for Mastercard®. The information required is a description of the item purchased and the cost, the customer's signature and (sometimes) telephone number, driver's license number, or some other form of identification.

Figure 10.2   Bankcard credit slip.

At the end of the business day, a retailer totals the cash in the cash register and compares it to the cash register tape (or detailed audit strip). This form (Figure 10.3) is a typical daily *cash summary form*.

The daily report may be in the form of an envelope on which sales and payments on account can be checked against cash in the register. The day's total cash register receipts are usually put into the envelope.

Bank Documents

The most commonly used bank documents are the *check* and the *deposit slip*. Here (Figures 10.4 and 10.5) are a business check and sample deposit slip. The checks and deposit slips are usually coded at the bottom of the slip or check with the account number of the business so that it can be read by automated equipment. The name of the business and the address are usually printed in the top left-hand corner.

Whenever a check is written by a company, it is recorded on a *check stub* or *check register*. In the check register (Figure 10.6) the amount of each check, date, check number, payee, and account number or explanation are recorded each time a check is written. The check register may also have a space for entering deposits. Deposits are recorded by date, payer, reason, and total.

Note: When checks are deposited there are two types of endorsements that can be used. One endorsement is just the signature of the *payee* (the person to whom the check is made out to). The other type of endorsement is the *restrictive endorsement*. This indicates that the check is for deposit only. The back of the check in Figure 10.4 shows a restrictive endorsement.

Other bank documents include *savings account deposit slips* and *withdrawal slips* (a deposit slip is illustrated in Figure 10.7). Savings account slips require the name of the depositor, account number, date, and the total deposited or withdrawn.

Petty Cash

Most businesses set aside a small sum of cash for the payment of minor business expenses. This sum of cash is called the *petty cash fund* and it is kept in either a cash box or an envelope. Items that are usually paid out of petty cash include postage, transportation, telegrams, incidental office supplies, and sometimes parking, duplicating, and entertainment expenses (for lunches, etc.).

Figure 10.8 is an example of a petty cash envelope or *office fund voucher* as it is called in the illustration. When money is paid out of petty cash the receipt is placed in

DAILY REPORT

Date FEB. 15   19 80

CASH RECEIPTS

Sales	$ 2,018.16	
MISC. - VENDING MACH. . $	20.00	
. $		
. $	2,038.16	$ 2,038.16

RECEIVED ON ACCOUNT

TABADDA TRINKETS . $	346.18	
. $		
. $		
. $		
. $		
TOTAL RECEIPTS . . . . $	346.18	$ 2,384.34

CASH PAID OUT

PETTY CASH . $	100.00	
. $		
. $		
. $		
. $		
. $		$
. $		$
TOTAL PAID OUT . . . . $	100.00	$ 100.00

NET RECEIPTS . . . . . $		$ 2,284.34

CASH IN REGISTER . . . . . . $	2,464.34
Less Change Fund . . . . . . $	200.00
NET CASH . . . . $	2,264.34
CASH OVER OR (SHORT) . . . . . $	20.00
DEPOSITED IN BANK . . . . . . $	2,264.34 $ 2,264.34

Figure 10.3   Daily cash summary form.

the envelope and a notation is made indicating the date, the receipt number (if any), to whom it was paid, to what expense category it belongs, the account number, and the amount. At the bottom of the envelope in this particular illustration, there are columns for recording the distribution of the expenses to the different accounts. The first entry in the example is for a postage expense of $3.50 paid to the U.S. Post Office on January 5, 1980. A notation is made that the postage account number is 510. At the bottom of the envelope the two entries recorded for postage are placed under account 510 in a column.

The usual procedure is to issue a check for "petty cash" for some dollar amount, usually $100, and to keep the cash in the envelope, a cash box, or a cash register. The money is spent for the various cash expenses and recorded accordingly. When $100 (or whatever the fund amount) is spent, another check is written for that amount and another envelope is started. The envelope that has been completed is entered in the

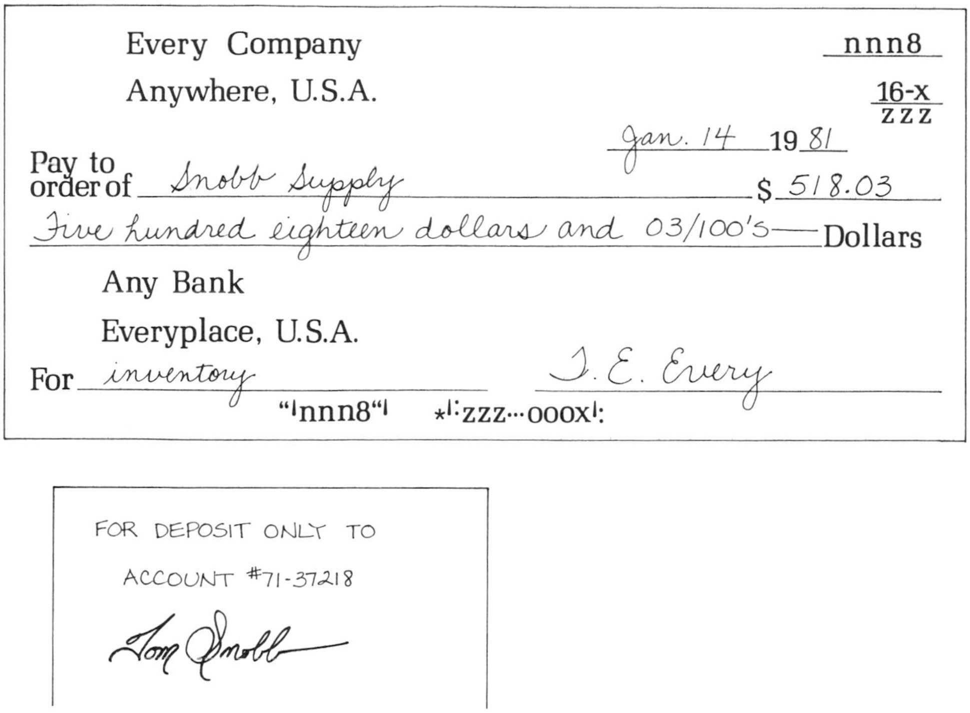

Every Company   nnn8

Anywhere, U.S.A. $\dfrac{16\text{-}x}{zzz}$

                                         Jan. 14 19 81

Pay to
order of ___Snobb Supply_____ $ 518.03

_Five hundred eighteen dollars and 03/100's___—Dollars

Any Bank

Everyplace, U.S.A.

For __inventory_____   J. E. Every_____

                    "innn8"   *I:zzz···ooox!:

FOR DEPOSIT ONLY TO

ACCOUNT #71-37218

Tom Snobb

Figure 10.4 Sample check with sample endorsement (appearing on reverse side of the check).

general journal, and the amount of each expense is posted to the proper account (postage, parking entertainment, etc.) in the ledger.

Purchasing Documents

Sometimes a business can simply order inventory by telephone, but many suppliers require that a firm request merchandise by written order. The form for requesting goods is called a *purchase order*. The purchase order is a form sent by the purchaser to another company to order goods from that company. Purchase orders are usually in triplicate, with each sheet a different color. One copy is sent to the vendor (supplier), the second copy is usually retained for the purchasing company's files, and the third copy is furnished to the receiving department where the goods are to be delivered.

The purchase order usually contains this information:

- Number of the purchase order
- Name and address of the vendor
- Name and address of where the goods are to be shipped
- Special shipping instructions
- Date
- Quantity, description, and price of the items ordered

When the goods are shipped, the vendor prepares an invoice, or bill, that he sends to the buyer (illustrated in Figure 10.9).

These invoices may be packaged with the shipment, in which case they are then

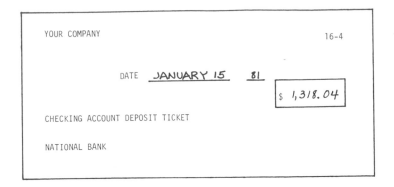

CHECKS	DOLLARS	CENTS
1 16-20	412	01
2 4-18	310	73
3 6-71	242	12
35		
CHECKS	964	86
CURRENCY	321	00
COIN	32	18
TOTAL	1,318	04

Figure 10.5 Sample bank deposit slip. "Checks, dollars, and cents" catagories are on the reverse side of the deposit slip.

CHECK NO.	DATE	CHECK ISSUED TO	IN PAYMENT OF	AMOUNT OF CHECK	√	DATE OF DEPOSIT	AMOUNT OF DEPOSIT	BALANCE
	1981					BALANCE BROUGHT FORWARD →		1,016 72
1198	1/14	SNOBB SUPPLY	INVENTORY-601	518 03				498 69
1199	1/14	ATOMIC EDISON	UTILITIES-640	112 18				386 51
1200	1/14	WORLD TELEPHONE	TELEPHONE-640	150 12				236 39
	1/15	DEPOSIT REGISTER				1/15	1,318 04	1,554 43

DESCRIPTION OF DEPOSITS				
DATE OF DEP.	SOURCE OF ITEM	NATURE OF ITEM	AMOUNT OF ITEM	TOTAL AMOUNT OF DEPOSIT
1/15/81	ED SINALL (ACCT. #173)	PMT. ON ACCT.	412 01	
	JOHN BIG (ACCT. 195)	√	310 73	
	S.W. FOX (ACCT. 100)	√	242 12	
	CASH SALES		353 18	
				1,318 04

Figure 10.6 The amount of each check, date, check number, payee, account number, and explanation are recorded in the check register.

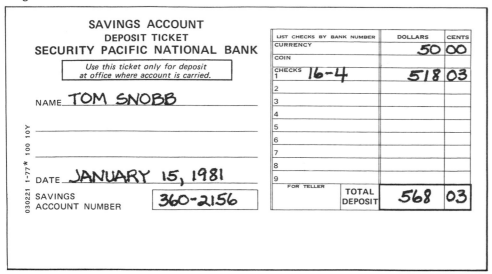

Figure 10.7   Sample savings account withdrawal and deposit slips.

referred to as *packing slips*. Or, the vendor may simply mail the invoice directly to the buyer. This invoice transfers rights to property (providing the property is paid for) to the buyer.

Travel and Entertainment Records

The Security and Exchange Commission (SEC) requires that businesses disclose *perks* (perquisites) given to employees that were previously considered company-paid entertainment and travel expense. This, plus pending IRS regulations, has caused confusion as to just what are travel and entertainment expenses.

Figure 10.10 illustrates an expense report for travel and entertainment. It breaks down the cost for 11 separate items, one of which is not tax deductible as an expense. The items recorded are:

1. *Transportation* includes airfare, trainfare, busfare, or transportation by automobile compensated at some rate per mile. Note that farther down the page this item is broken down into destination and departure points. If the amount of this transportation cost is over $25.00, then receipts should be included, but it is wisest to include receipts no matter what the cost.

2. *Taxi-limousine-carfare* represents the cost of transportation by private or public transport at the destination or departure points. This is also broken down by departure and destination.

3. *Hotel* includes the cost of room at a hotel. Receipts are always required.

4. *Meals–personal* are *not* tax deductible.

5. *Telephone–telegraph* expenses are business-related communication costs. Whenever possible receipts should be kept for this item also.

6. *Laundry–valet service* is for laundry costs required by business necessities.

7. *Other auto* includes the cost of tools, parking, service, repairs, etc. Receipts should be kept. These are itemized in a section at the bottom of the report.

8. *Tips* may be recorded here.

9. *Postage* for business correspondence is an expense.

OFFICE FUND VOUCHER   No. _____1_____

From ___JAN. 1___ 19 _80_ to _____ 19___ Paid by Check No. _____

AUDITED BY		APPROVED BY			

DATE	RECEIPT NO.	TO WHOM PAID	FOR WHAT	ACCOUNT	AMOUNT
1/5/80		U.S. POST OFFICE	POSTAGE	510	3|50
1/8/80		COPY CROP	DUPLICATING	511	20|16
1/10/80		DOWNTOWN PARKING	PARKING	512	2|50
1/15/80		COPY CROP	DUPLICATING	511	7|40
1/20/80		U.S. POST OFFICE	POSTAGE	510	7|50
1/22/80		GREEN ONION	DINNER - G. ZAP	520	14|80
			TOTAL DISBURSED		
			CASH ON HAND		
			AMOUNT OF FUND		

DISTRIBUTION

510	511	512	520								
3|50	20|16	2|50	14|80								
7|50	7|40										

Figure 10.8 When money is paid out of petty cash, the receipt is placed in an envelope like this one and a notation is made as shown.

10. *Miscellaneous and gifts* should be carefully itemized as to name of recipient, cost, and purpose. Gifts cannot be for more than $25 per person per year.

11. *Entertainment expense* requires careful attention in reporting details. In addition to the breakdown at the bottom of the report, we suggest that you attach receipts and give particulars as to customer's name and title, place of business, amount, and what was discussed. We would suggest that the reporter

```
PARKENSON PRETZEL MANUFACTURING
2000 Gold Avenue
Stick, Texas 08960
```

SOLD TO	SHIPPED TO	CUSTOMER'S ORDER	INVOICE NO.	DATE
Street Corner Grocery	Same	211	0950	2/18/81
STREET & NO.	STREET & NO.	SALESMAN	TERMS	F.O.B.
41635 W. Van Gogh Avenue		Ed. S.	30 Days	
CITY STATE ZIP	CITY STATE ZIP	WHEN SHIP	VIA	
Hell, Texas 08720		10th	UPS	

QUANTITY				DESCRIPTION	UNIT	AMOUNT		TOTAL	
ORDERED	BACK ORDERED	SHIPPED							
2			cases	#3 pretzels	2	50	00	100	00
3			cases	#1 pretzels	3	55	00	165	00
								$265	00

Figure 10.9 Sample invoice that is usually mailed or shipped with merchandise to the customer.

go as far as maintaining at least one-paragraph summaries of what was discussed at the meeting. If there are further tax restrictions on expenses, entertainment expense is the area where it will most likely occur. But as long as the entertainment expense was conducted for business purposes and this is carefully documented, the businessperson has little reason to worry.

Payroll Records

When you have employees in your business, you have certain obligations to the federal government for payment of payroll taxes and withholding of income taxes. You have similar obligations for payroll and/or withholding taxes to the state and to local jurisdictions.

Federal regulations do not prescribe the form in which your payroll records must be kept, but the records should include the following information and documents:

1. The amounts and dates of all wage payments subject to withholding taxes and the amounts withheld.
2. The names, addresses, and occupations of employees receiving payments.
3. The periods of their employment.
4. The periods for which they are paid by you while they are absent because of sickness or personal injuries, and the amount and weekly rate of payments.
5. Their social security account number if they are subject to social security tax.
6. Their income tax withholding exemption certificates.
7. Your employer identification number.

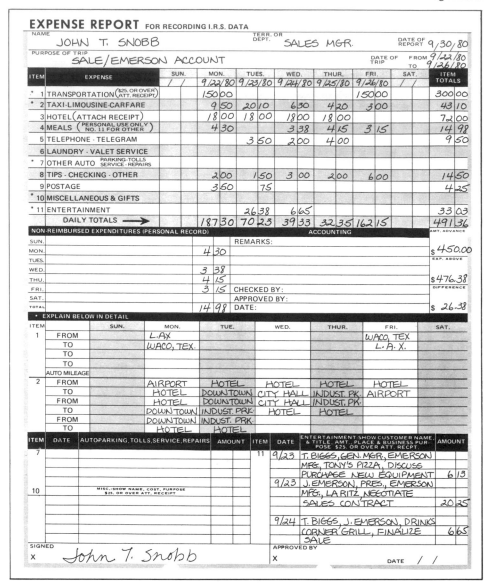

Figure 10.10   Sample expense report for travel and entertainment.

8. Duplicate copies of returns filed.
9. Dates and amounts of deposits made with government.

Usually, an employee's earnings card is set up for each employee. Every wage payment to the employee is recorded on this card: all the information needed for meeting federal, state, and city requirements relating to payroll and withholding taxes, and all other amounts deducted from the employee's wages.

There are three types of federal payroll taxes: (1) income taxes withheld, (2) social security taxes, and (3) federal unemployment taxes. IRS *Publication 15*, "Employer's Tax Guide," should be consulted for additional information about employer–employee relationships, what constitutes taxable wages, the treatment of special types of employment and payments, and similar matters.

Income taxes are withheld on all wages paid to an employee above a certain minimum. The minimum is governed by the number of exemptions claimed by an employee.

Social security taxes (in 1980) apply to the first $25,900 of wages paid an employee during a year. A percentage deduction (presently 6.13%) from the employee's wages is matched by an *equal amount* in taxes *paid by the employer*.

In addition to taxes withheld from employees' salaries and also paid by the employer, there is also a tax that is paid by the employer *only*. This is the FUTA tax. Federal unemployment taxes (FUTA) are required only of employers who have:

1. paid wages of $1,500 or more in any calendar quarter, or
2. employed one or more persons for some portion of at least one day during each of 20 different calendar weeks. The 20 weeks do not have to be consecutive. Individuals on vacation or sick leave are counted as employees in determining the business's status.

The FUTA tax is paid by you as the employer (no deduction is made from the employee's wages). The rate is 3.4% on the first $6,000 of wages paid to each employee.

Using the example of Jo Anne Topps from Figure 10.11, a full accounting for the

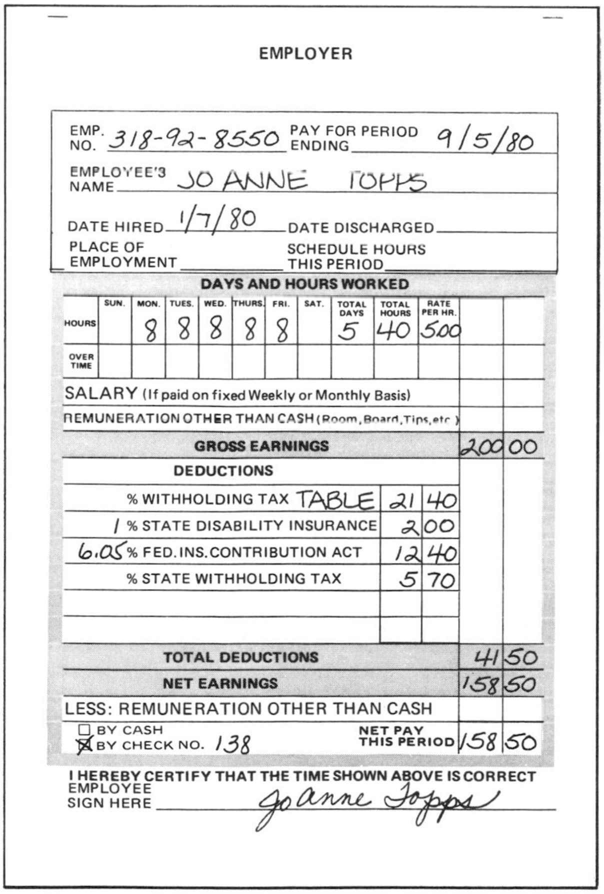

EMPLOYER

EMP. NO. 318-92-8550 PAY FOR PERIOD ENDING 9/5/80

EMPLOYEE'S NAME JO ANNE TOPPS

DATE HIRED 1/7/80 DATE DISCHARGED

PLACE OF EMPLOYMENT SCHEDULE HOURS THIS PERIOD

DAYS AND HOURS WORKED

	SUN.	MON.	TUES.	WED.	THURS.	FRI.	SAT.	TOTAL DAYS	TOTAL HOURS	RATE PER HR.
HOURS		8	8	8	8	8		5	40	5.00
OVER TIME										

SALARY (If paid on fixed Weekly or Monthly Basis)		
REMUNERATION OTHER THAN CASH (Room, Board, Tips, etc.)		
GROSS EARNINGS		200 00
DEDUCTIONS		
% WITHHOLDING TAX TABLE	21 40	
1 % STATE DISABILITY INSURANCE	2 00	
6.05 % FED. INS. CONTRIBUTION ACT	12 40	
% STATE WITHHOLDING TAX	5 70	
TOTAL DEDUCTIONS		41 50
NET EARNINGS		158 50
LESS: REMUNERATION OTHER THAN CASH		
☐ BY CASH ☒ BY CHECK NO. 138 — NET PAY THIS PERIOD		158 50

I HEREBY CERTIFY THAT THE TIME SHOWN ABOVE IS CORRECT

EMPLOYEE SIGN HERE Jo Anne Topps

Figure 10.11 Sample payroll record form.

employee's taxes and the employer's taxes and payments would be made a general journal entry, which I will discuss later.

For the employer-paid items (social security, FUTA, and state unemployment), the employer does not pay them in cash every week, but charges them to a payable account that is usually paid quarterly in cash. The employee items (except the net wage amount of $158.50) are made payable to be disbursed in cash quarterly.

If you are liable for social security taxes in excess of $200 quarterly, you must file a quarterly return, Form 941. Form 941 combines the social security taxes (including hospital insurance) and income tax withholding. Form 941E is used for reporting income tax withheld from wages, tips, annuities, and supplemental unemployment compensation benefits when no Federal Insurance Contribution Act (FICA) coverage is required.

Due dates for the Forms 941 or 941E and the full payment of tax are as follows:

Quarter	Due Dates
January-February-March	April 30
April-May-June	July 31
July-August-September	October 31
October-November-December	January 31, next year

If you make timely deposits in full payment of the taxes due, you may file your quarterly return on or before the tenth day of the second month following the period for which it is made. In this case the due dates are as follows:

Quarter	Due Dates
January-February-March	May 10
April-May-June	August 10
July-August-September	November 10
October-November-December	February 10, next year

Deposits are made by sending a filled-in Form 501 (Federal Tax Deposit) together with a single remittance covering the taxes to be deposited to an authorized commercial bank or federal reserve bank in accordance with instructions on the back of Form 501. Names of authorized commercial bank depositories are at your local bank.

Jack Klaus stopped and looked at Kimberly. "Do you understand the original transaction documents and what they mean?"

"Yes, I understand. I've done some work with these things before. Let me review the documents that Hero uses:

- Sales documents are the sales slips or purchase orders that are maintained on customers by Hero.
- Purchasing documents, such as packing slips, are the orders from suppliers (vendors) and the subsequent billings that they send Hero.
- Hero has records of their shipments and also inventory records (something that you didn't mention).
- Payroll records are the time and tax records that Hero keeps on each employee. They pay the bank to perform these services.
- Travel and entertainment records are maintained to verify these expenses for tax purposes.

"Okay," Jack said. "Maybe I'm going too slow for you. The next thing that I want to discuss is the books themselves—the journals and the ledgers. Are you ready for that?"

"Yes, I am," Kimberly replied.

Jack continued. To make sense of all the thousands of transactions that the average business has during the year, these transactions are entered daily into a book called a *journal*. It allows the business to keep track of every daily transaction in one place. Transactions are recorded sequentially, as they happen.

However, if a business wants to know how much was paid for office supplies in the last two months, they would still have a problem. Even with the journal, they would have to look through every transaction in the last two months to pick out the supplies they bought in order to obtain a total. To solve this problem, another book that categorizes everything under specific topics, or accounts, is needed. This book has one page called Office supplies that has every office supply expense listed. This summary book has come to be known as a *ledger*.

Looking at Figure 10.12 gives you an idea of the flow of documents when a simple act such as the purchase of office supplies is initiated. When the office supplies are purchased, this immediately produces two original transaction documents (a check and a sales slip) and one recorded document (an entry in the check register showing amount, date, and to whom paid). The next entry is in the journal summarizing the transaction (debit office expense, credit cash). At the end of the accounting period two

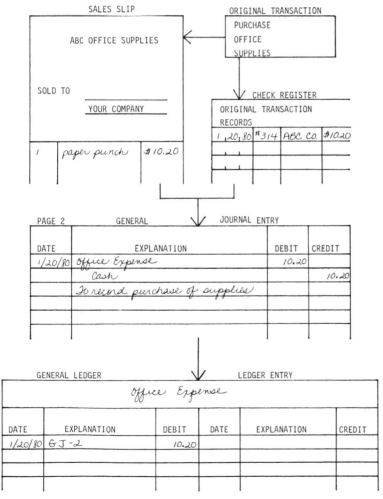

Figure 10.12 Transaction and recording documents used by a company and their relationships.

more entries are made, both in the ledger. A debit entry is made in the office expense ledger, and a credit entry is made in the cash ledger account.

Chart of Accounts

A common practice for most businesses is to assign various accounts a number in addition to a name. For instance, the Cash account could have the number '101' so that when entries are made the number may be used instead of writing out the name. Using numbers instead of, or in addition to, names of accounts is not only easier, but it also lends itself readily to computerization.

When you assign numbers to all of the accounts, the list of account names and numbers is called a *chart of accounts*.

Here is a list of assets, liabilities, and expenses that are generally considered to be common account names:

Assets
Cash
Inventory
Accounts receivable (sales that have not been collected)
Notes receivable (short-term money owed to your company)
Prepaid expenses (money advanced for services or goods not yet received)
Short-term investments
Equipment (for business use)
Land and buildings (for business use)
Leasehold improvements
Goodwill paid when the business was acquired
Long-term investments
Certain development costs

Liabilities
(money or goods not paid for but used for business purposes)
Accounts and notes payable
Provisions for pensions and taxes
Accrued items
Mortgages
Bonds and debentures
Long-term debt
Deferred taxes

Expenses
(including cost of sales)
Rent or leases (for equipment or real property)
Outside services (accounting, consulting, janitorial, trash pickup, security, etc.)
Personal salareis
Payroll taxes and benefit plans for employees
Travel required for business purposes
Material purchased
Supplies purchased
Inventory purchased
Freight
Utilities
Business license and local taxes

Equipment or tools with a life of one year or less
Repairs and maintenance
Certain clothing and laundry expenses

Income is revenue from sales of merchandise, fees, or royalties. Separate accounts may be assigned to the different sources of income.

Equity accounts represent money put into or retained by the business. Equity includes stock in the company (preferred, common, or treasury); paid-in, surplus, and retained earnings; and interest in subsidiaries.

When you arrange all of these accounts under the basic groups—assets, liabilities, equity, income, expenses, and cost of sales—to simplify identification, you have a *chart of accounts*.

Since there are likely to be many different accounts in business records, it is necessary to establish a plan for identifying each account and locating it quickly. If, besides listing all the accounts under the above groups, you also assign numbers to them, identification becomes that much easier. In developing an index or chart of accounts, blocks of numbers are assigned to each group of accounts. For example, assets are assigned the block of numbers from 100 to 199 (or 1000 to 1999 for large companies with many accounts); liabilities have the numbers 200 to 299 (2000 to 2999); and so on. Here is an example of a chart of accounts:

Chart of Accounts

Account #	Account Name
100–199	ASSETS
101	Cash
110	Accounts receivable
115	Notes receivable
120	Prepaid expense
120.1	Prepaid rent
150	Equipment
150.18	1970 Dodge pickup truck
200–299	LIABILITIES
201	Accounts payable
201.29	Accounts payable— Associated Wagontongues
211	Notes payable
211.2	Notes payable Bank of Suez
221	Taxes payable
. . .	Etc.
300–399	OWNERS' EQUITY
301	Capital stock
310	Preferred stock
330	Retailed earnings
. . .	Etc.
400–499	INCOME
401	Income from operations
401.3	Income from Model B solid- state mousetrap
401.5	Income from mousetrap accessories
410	Interest income
450	Income from extraordinary items
. . .	Etc.

500–599	OPERATING EXPENSE
501	Salary expense
501.7	Officer's salary
505	Payroll taxes
505.2	Administrative employees payroll tax
508	Rent' expense
572	Small tool expense
. . .	Etc.
600–699	COST OF SALES EXPENSE
601	Material purchases
601.62	Purchases of steel whatchets
610	Factory salaries
610.3	Factory salaries, plant #3
. . .	Etc.

JOURNALS (THE DAILY BOOKS)

General Journal

The general journal is the original journal developed to cover all types of entries. The general journal (Figure 10.13) is a form that has a space for the date, a description of the entry, the account number (from the chart of accounts), a check space to check off the entry when it is transferred to the ledger, and spaces for debit or credit entries.

Every accounting transaction can be recorded in the general journal, and for the very small one-person operation or for service businesses, this general journal is all that is needed. For larger operations with lots of special transactions, such as credit sales and purchases and many cash transactions, it is advisable to have special journals such as the cash disbursements journal, the cash receipts journal, the sales journal, and the purchases journal. In the case of Hero Manufacturing where special journals are used, the general journal is only used to record transactions that do not fit into the special journals. For instance, such transactions as recording salaries and taxes or closing out the books at the end of the year would be recorded in the general journal because they have no place in the special journals (cash disbursements, receipts, sales, or purchases).

Cash Disbursements Journal

The cash disbursements journal is a specialized journal designed to record all cash disbursements—usually checks written. The cash disbursements journal is comparable to the check register because it records all the checks written and what accounts they represent. The cash disbursements journal differs from the check register in that it has special columns for accounts for which many checks are written. For instance, payments of accounts payable and purchases of inventory for cash might require a large number of checks to be written monthly, so the cash disbursements journal has special columns for these items.

The cash disbursements journal allows you to show on one line both the debit (to the account the check is made out to) and the credit (cash) in each transaction. Figure 10.14 presents an example of a cash disbursement journal page. The cash disbursement journal also has a check (✔) column to show when the accounts have been posted to a ledger.

Date	Description	Acct. No.	Debit	Credit

Figure 10.13   A general journal, where the figures from the original transaction documents are entered. Date, description, account number, and debit or credit give the journal its form.

Cash Receipts Journal

For sales recording, it is a better idea to use a cash receipts journal than the general journal. The cash receipts journal records your cash sales and can record sales from different categories in separate columns. For management reasons, you want to know the sources of your sales. An example of a cash disbursements journal is Figure 10.15.

For miscellaneous income the cash receipts journal has a sundry credits column.

CASH DISBURSEMENTS JOURNAL

For the Month of _____ 19___

DATE	CK. NO.	EXPLANATION	ACCT NO.	SUNDRY DR AMOUNT	ACCTS PAY DR. 201	SUB-CONT CR.600-610	CASH CR. 101

Figure 10.14   The cash disbursements journal records all cash expenditures including cash and checks.

Since Hero has more than one source of income, it is necessary to use the (sundry) credits column.

Sales Journal

Because most of Hero's customers buy on credit, it is a good idea to have a special journal that will record this. Each time a credit sale is made, and only when a credit

CASH RECEIPTS JOURNAL for the month of _____ 19____

DATE	EXPLANATION	ACCT	SUNDRY CR AMOUNT	ACCTS REC CR. 111	SALES CR. 410	MISC SALE CR. 420	CASH DR. 101	

Figure 10.15 The cash receipts journal records receipt of cash only. It does not record sales other than sales for cash and receipts from accounts receivable.

sale is made, this journal is used. A sample sales journal is shown as Figure 10.16.

The purpose of the sales journal is to record all accounts receivable as they are created by the customer and to record these sales on credit as part of the gross sales of the company.

Remember, the sales journal does not record all sales, *only those on credit*.

The particular format that Hero Manufacturing uses has two separate columns for sales as well as a column for debits to accounts receivable.

Purchases Journal

The last commonly used special journal is the purchases journal. The purchases journal is for recording purchases made on *credit only*. An example of the purchases journal form is given as Figure 10.17.

Hero needs a purchases journal to record goods bought from suppliers on credit. This is sometimes called *trade credit*. The purchases journal is for recording Hero's accounts

SALES JOURNAL

For Month of_____19_____   Page_____

Date	Sales Slip No.	Customer's Name	Accts. Rec. DR. 111	Sales CR. 410	Misc. Sales CR. 420

Figure 10.16   The sales journal does not record all sales. It records only sales on credit (accounts receivable).

payable as they are incurred. The purchases journal only has entries for goods purchased on credit; it never records the cash payments to the suppliers. When the money is paid to the suppliers, the entry will appear in the cash disbursements journal.

The purchases journal has a column for the date, the name of the supplier, the number of the supplier's invoice, the date of that invoice, the terms, and a column for credits to accounts payable and debits to inventory purchases.

PURCHASES JOURNAL

DATE	PURCHASED FROM	INV. NO.	INV. DATE	TERMS	ACCOUNTS PAYABLE CR. 201	INVENTORY PURCHASES DR. 601

Figure 10.17 The purchases journal records only purchases on credit (accounts payable).

LEDGERS (THE SUMMARY BOOKS)

Now you have seen how all your accounting transactions are recorded chronologically under the special journals. If you want to review the checks you have written in a given period, you check the cash disbursements journal. You can track Hero's purchases, cash receipts, credit sales, and other transactions in total, and in chronological order, without viewing the original checks.

But what if Hero wants to know the total of last month's expenditures for merchandise from Richland Company? What if you want to find out what John Kitt bought from Hero during the last year? How much did Hero spend on utilities (telephone plus gas plus water)?

One way to find these totals is to go back through the journals during the entire period and take the separate items and total them. Another way would be to write or call the supplier, custimer, or utility company and ask them for the total. The best way, however, is to keep a summary book during the period, transferring each entry to a particular category. In other words, if you could have a book that lists each account separately (a page for utilities, a page for Richland Company, etc.) you could tell at a glance how much you owe, who owes you, or how much you've already paid. Such a book that lists each account under a separate category is called a *ledger*.

Weekly, monthly, or quarterly all the journals are totaled and "posted" into ledgers. Ledgers are summaries of activities under each account in the chart of accounts. Ledgers are divided into two groups: the general ledger and the subsidiary ledgers.

Historically, there was only the *general ledger*. In the general ledger, all the accounts were posted after a given period from their respective journal or journals. Entries in the journal indicate to the accountant what is to be debited and what is to be credited. With the journals as a guide, the information is entered into the respective individual accounts. The accountant uses printed forms for his account records, as shown in the illustration in Figure 10.18. Each account is kept on a separate form called a *ledger sheet*. All the accounts taken together constitute a *ledger* or *book of final entry*. Generally the ledger is posted from the journals, and eventually a "trial balance" is made. This is put into the form of a balance sheet and income statement (profit and loss statement). The ledger is the master reference book of the accounting system and provides a permanent and classified record of every element involved in the business operation.

The general ledger is divided into separate accounts (e.g., "Cash 101") with a debit and credit column for each account. A look at the ledger account record will reveal a complete history of the increases and decreases of the items involved. Ledgers may be kept in book or card form in a ledger tray. Or, of course, these records may be kept on computer records.

Ledger Format

Figure 10.18 shows a general ledger format. Note that the format has a column for the date. The date used here may be either the date entry was made in a journal or the date that the entry was transferred from the journal to the ledger. The former is preferable, but either is acceptable as long as the bookkeeper is consistent.

There are two columns for explanation and two for posting reference. This allows a separate explanation and a posting reference for a debit and for a credit entry. The explanation is usually something like 'total 1/15/80' or the name the check was made payable to, such as 'Titian Telephone' for a telephone deposit entry.

The posting reference (the "folio" column in Figure 10.18) refers to the journal that is the source of the entry. Generally the post reference consists of the type of journal and the page number. However, in the case of the general journal, the journal entry number is used. For instance, if a total for cash disbursed (credit to cash) is taken from the cash disbursements journal at the end of the month, the post reference would be "CDJ-1," which means the entry comes from the cash disbursements. journal, page 1. General journal summaries would have a post reference like "GJ-1-5," meaning general journal, entry 1-5, which is the fifth entry (5) for the month of January (1). To repeat:

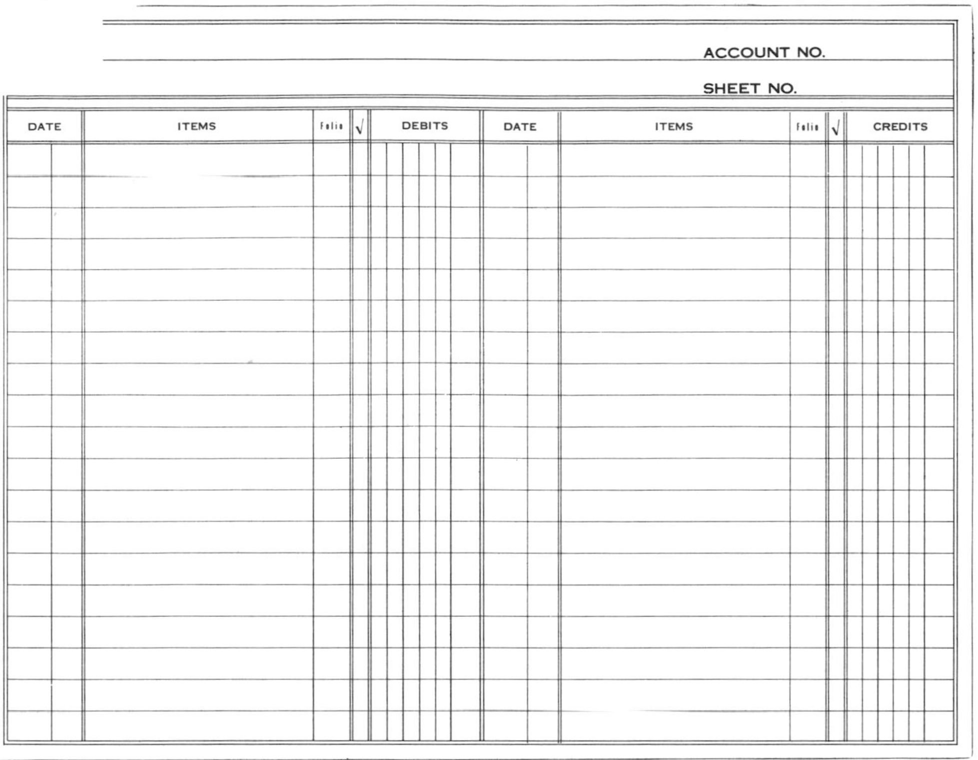

DATE	ITEMS	folio	√	DEBITS	DATE	ITEMS	folio	√	CREDITS

ACCOUNT NO.

SHEET NO.

Figure 10.18 Sample General Ledger form. Note that it is divided into two parts, one side only for debits, the other only for credits.

POST REFERENCE

CDJ	1
GJ	1-5

(Abbreviation for the type of journal from which the entry comes.)

(Page number of the journal from which the entry originates; or, in the case of the General Journal, the number of the entry.)

The appreviations that are commonly used for the post reference are shown in Figure 10.19.

The ledger format is divided into a debit and a credit side. If the entry is a credit, it is entered on the credit side; if it is a debit it is entered on the debit side.

Note that in Figure 10.18 the format has a line at the top and a space for the number of the account. The line should be filled in with the name of the account, and the

Name of Journal	Abbreviations Used
General Journal	GJ
Cash Disbursements Journal	CDJ
Cash Receipts Journal	CRJ
Purchases Journal	PJ
Sales Journal	SJ

Figure 10.19 Abbreviations for journals commonly used in accounting.

number space should be filled in with the number of the account from the chart of accounts. The accounts are usually in the general journal in order of their chart of accounts numbers. The first account entered is usually cash or cash in bank or cash in bank (Amerigold), plus the account number (such as 101)."

Special Ledgers (Accounts Receivable and Accounts Payable Ledgers)

It is important for a company to keep careful track of who owes them what for product sales. You also want to know how much your customer owes you and for how long; and when he bought and how much he bought. The total in the sales journal will tell you the total you have for sales on credit, and if you trace through it and separate out the customers, you can find the individual statistics. Most people, however, find that it is much smarter to keep an account for each customer apart from the sales journal. The ledger that keeps track of what each customer purchases and later pays for under the customer's name is called the *accounts receivable ledger*.

The ledger that keeps track of what *you owe* to your suppliers under the suppliers' name is called the *accounts payable ledger*. The reasons for keeping the accounts payable ledger are the same as the reasons for keeping the accounts receivable ledger, although perhaps not as compelling. Since you are continually ordering and paying for merchandise it becomes difficult to keep track of the exact balance you owe each supplier and how much you typically buy from them. This is especially true of a company that has several suppliers. Although your suppliers will be glad to tell you how much you owe at any given time, it is a mistake to depend on their honesty and accuracy. There is not a company in the world that has not billed the wrong amount at one time or another.

Figure 10.20 is a sample of the special ledger format. The same format is used for both the accounts receivable ledger and the accounts payable ledger.

The format has a place for the name of the account. This would be the customer's name in the case of an accounts receivable ledger and the supplier's name for the accounts payable ledger. It also includes a space for the terms such as net 30 days, 2/10 net 30, and so on. It has a column for the date of the transactions, which is the date the order was shipped as per the sales journal or the purchases journal, or the date the payment was recorded in the cash receipts or the cash disbursements journal.

The special ledger also has a column for the description which is generally used for pertinent information such as the invoice number.

The post reference column could be used for the name and page number of the special journals or the entry number for the general journal. This is the same column used before in the general ledger. An example would be "PJ-1," which means that the entry is from the purchases journal page 1.

The debit column in the accounts receivable ledger would be for all credit sales to customers recorded in the sales journal. The credit column in the accounts receivable ledger would be used to record payments from the cash receipts journal. In the accounts payable ledger the debit column is for payments made to suppliers from the cash disbursements journal, and the credit column is for recording any trade credit that you receive from the suppliers recorded in the purchases journal.

The balance column is the amount now owed the supplier in the case of the accounts payable ledger, or the amount the customer owes you in the case of the accounts receivable ledger.

DATE	DESCRIPTION	POST REF.	DEBIT	CREDIT	BALANCE

Figure 10.20 Sample of a ledger including its format: date, description, post reference, debit, credit balance, and name of the account. This format is used for accounts receivable and accounts payable only.

**Special Note on Accounts Receivable and
Accounts Payable Ledgers**

The *accounts receivable ledger* generally has a *debit* balance because it is an asset account. All debit entries will come either from the sales journal or the general journal. Credit entries are made when the receivables are paid by your customer. Credit entries will always originate from the cash receipts journal or the general journal.

The *accounts payable ledger* will generally have a *credit* balance because it is a liability account. All credit entries will come from the purchases journal or the general journal. Debit entries are made when the trade credit is paid by Hero, and they are recorded either in the cash disbursements journal or in the general journal.

SUMMARY

Jack Klaus leaned back in his chair. "Well, that's the story with original documents, journals, and ledgers. Besides, it's lunch time. Any questions?"

"Yes," Kimberly asked, "what is the biggest concern of an accountant when considering journals and ledgers?"

"The biggest difficulty has always been inaccurate entries through human error. The most important rule when making entries is to always double check. One way that has traditionally been used to spot errors is the *trial balance*. Do you understand about the trial balance?" Jack Klaus asked.

"Of course. And I'm going to a class tonight at University Extension and that just happens to be the topic they will cover," Kimberly answered.

"Good." Klaus continued: "The best thing for me to do now, then, is to summarize . . . if you don't have any more questions."

Kimberly shook her head now indicating that she couldn't think of any more questions.

Jack summarized, "Recordkeeping starts with the original documents. The original documents are recorded in a book of original entry—the journal. Once every week Hero takes these journal entries and enters them in a ledger under the title of the account (i.e., cash and rent expense). It's as simple as that."

Kimberly left for her office so she could apply some of what she had learned to her program writing. The only unpleasantness she encountered for the rest of the day was the parking tab. She felt like telling the parking cashier, "I could rent a luxury flat for what it costs me to park here," but she knew that it was not the cashier who made the rules.

Chapter Eleven
Closing the Books and the Business Financial Statements

Kimberly Rogers was puzzling over the Earthapple accounting software that she was intending to use. There were no less than four subroutines required to close the books. The whole section just seemed too muddled and cryptic to Kimberly. She was sure that there was some way to make all this simpler.

As she was mulling over all of this a smile crept across her face. She remembered something one of her computer benefactors used to tell her. He said, "It's best to keep programs simple. But you can't rewrite everything you have to use that isn't simple. If it works, leave it alone. The biggest problems with computers are not long, complicated programs, but the fact that any idiot can wreck havoc with a magnet or spill coffee down the back of the terminal."

Kimberly looked at her watch. She had to leave immediately or she might be late for Udjat Her's last class. And he'd really be hurt if she didn't make it. Besides, tonight he was going to have a close friend talk to his class about closing the books and the corresponding financial statements that are produced.

The guest lecturer was just being introduced as Kimberly entered the classroom winded from running the last block.

"I would like to introduce a friend of mine who is a practicing bookkeeper and has been for 20 years. She is going to talk to us about closing out the books and the financial statements. Ms. Penny Lane." A precisely attired gray-haired woman thanked Udjat and began to speak.

"I'd like to thank you for having me here tonight. I'll start my discussion by talking about accounting periods and some assumptions of accounting. . . ."

An accounting period can be a maximum of one year and usually not less than one month. Large corporations traded in the public market usually end their accounting period every three months and then obtain final totals at the end of a year. Smaller businesses and closely held corporations usually end their accounting period at the end of a year.

At the end of a period, all of the accounts that a business has (assets, liabilities, equity, income, expenses, and cost of sales) have to be totaled and summarized. The summarizing process performed on a business's books is called *closing the books*. You simply transfer all the totals of all the accounts for one year to a summary sheet.

The Assumptions of Accounting for Business

To understand the process of closing the books you must understand the primary assumptions of accounting. These assumptions are:

1. Businesses are ongoing entities with unlimited life.

2. Although businesses have unlimited lifetimes, they require "an accounting" of their actions at least once per year.

3. There is a part of a business's accounts that live forever and another part that "dies" each time an accounting is made. That is, acounting has *permanent* and *temporary* or *cyclical* accounts.

First, let's discuss the propositions that a business's life is unlimited. In the early days of accounting there usually wasn't any reason for closing the books. The accountant just kept track of the transactions as they happened. Few people were interested in what the cumulative total was until the business was dissolved.

Every business is expected to continue until the owner sells or retires, and it is in this spirit that the accounting period records are kept.

A business may in fact exist on a moment-to-moment basis with an unpredictable future. But this line of thinking is not in accord with a logical system. And accounting is *above all* a logical system.

For instance, an accountant, to prepare a depreciation schedule for the business and for tax purposes, must assume that the business will last long enough for the business equipment (cash register or forklift) to lose its value. The equipment will be part of the business long enough for the equipment to become completely depreciated.

The second assumption, that businesses require periodic accountings, is fairly recent. In the early days, there was really no reason to summarize the accounts at the end of a period because transactions were relatively few and simple. As the number of accounts grew, periodic summarizing of the transactions became important for two reasons:

1. Summarizing provides milestones to compare how the business did in the past with how it is doing now. The periodic accountings (closing of the books) of a business are a measure of the business's past performance against its present performance.

2. In most countries (including the United States), a periodic accounting is required by law.

Governments that tax businesses require that every business prepare a summary of its performance (sales, expenses, profit, etc.). The businesses are then taxed on the basis of these summaries. The summaries that the U.S. government requires of business are called *income* or *profit and loss statements* and, in some cases, a *statement of financial condition (balance sheet)*. If the company is publicly traded it must provide annual reports and financial statements quarterly. These summaries that businesses provide to the government cover, by law, a period no longer than one year.°

The third assumption, that there are some business accounts that have only a limited (cyclical) life and others that are permanent, is a result of the periodic accounting assumption. Some account information is only needed for one period. For the next period summary, the information from the first period is not needed. For example, sales for last year are not needed to calculate this year's sales. Expenses and cost of sales that you incurred last year should not be added to this year's expense and cost of sales. Sales, expenses, and cost of sales records need only exist for the one period that they are used to calculate profit or loss. These are *temporary* or *cyclical* accounts.

Some accounts continue as the business does. These accounts are never closed, but are summarized and brought forward each year. These *permanent* accounts are assets, liabilities, and equity. Obviously, if you owe someone money at the end of one period

---

°There are some exceptions to this one year rule in the tax codes. The exception would be when a company can show that its business cycle requires that the period be longer (up to 13 months).

(liabilities) that obligation will continue into the next period. If someone owes you money (accounts receivable—an asset), this obligation will also continue into the next year. The equipment your company possesses—buildings, cash, inventory, and other assets—also has a permanent nature. These assets are not lost at the end of the period. They retain their value from one period to the next.

THE TRIAL BALANCE AND THE ACCOUNTING WORKSHEET

Format of the Trial Balance

This (Figure 11.1) is the format of a trial balance sheet and company worksheet. Notice that the form has one column for the account number (usually taken in numerical order) and another column for the name of the account. The third and fourth columns are for recording the totals from each account in the general ledger.

Making Entries: X Company Examples

The *trial balance* is made as a test to see if the accounts properly balance. The total debits should equal the total credits. The equality of debits and credits is determined by:

• the total balance in each account in the general ledger, and
• adding debit and credit balances separately to see if the totals are equal.

The balance of an account is computed by (1) adding the figures on each side and then (2) subtracting the smaller total from the larger total to obtain the difference.

Let's use the Cash account (account number 101) of X Company (Figure 11.2) as an example. First the debit side is added, and then the credit side. The total of each column is usually entered in pencil at the bottom of the column. These totals are called *footings*.

You see from adding the debit column that the total cash taken in by X Company is $30,429. The total cash spent by the company (total cash credits) is $41,520. They spent more than they took in. Subtracting the smaller total (cash received—the debit total) from the larger total (cash spent—credit total), you get $11,091. Since the credit total is larger than the debit total by $11,091, the cash account is said to have a credit balance of $11,091. When we total the account columns, we write the amount of the totals and the balance ($11,091 in this case) in pencil. Since the balance is a credit balance, we write "Balance $11,091" on the credit side.

No footings are required if the account has only one entry on one side or one entry on each side.

When you find the balances in the various accounts you list them in numerical order on the trial balance (Figure 11.3). The totals from the accounts are placed in the proper column: debit balances are shown in the left column and credit balances are shown in the right column.

Since we don't have time today to go through all the accounts for every month, we'll just use the January X Company accounts and complete the trial balance with them.

Notice that the 100 (with the exception of cash), 500, and 600 accounts (assets, expenses, and cost of sales) are all entered in the debit column because they all have debit balances. The 200, 300, and 400 accounts (liabilities, equity, and sales), are all entered in the credit columns because they all have credit balances.

the total of the debit column is $52,220. The total of the credit column is also

XCOMPANY WORKSHEET

ACCT.	ACCOUNT NAME		TRIAL BALANCE	
			DEBIT	CREDIT

Figure 11.1   **Sample format for a trial balance calling for the totals from each account ledger.**

$52,220, and thus the columns are in balance. This shows that the original journal entries were made correctly.

If the debit and credit columns do not equal each other an error has been made. Some of the common errors are:

1. Errors in addition.
2. Recording only half an entry (the credit without the debit, or vice versa).

CASH							ACCOUNT NO.	101	
							SHEET NO.	1	

DATE	ITEMS	folio	√	DEBITS	DATE	ITEMS	folio	√	CREDITS
1980					1980				
1/2	BANK LOAN	GJ1-1		25000 —	1/3	TEST EQUIP.	GJ1-2		5000 —
1/12	TOTAL 1/1 - 1/12	CRJ-1		5429 —	1/4	INVENTORY - PRTS.	GJ1-3		15000 —
					1/5	ACCTS. PAY.	GJ1-4		13500 —
					1/5	RENT EXPENSE	GJ1-5		1200 —
					1/7	TOTAL 1/1 - 1/7	CDJ-1		6820 —
				30429					41520
						BALANCE $11,091			

Figure 11.2 Sample cash ledger account at the end of a period with the balances calculated.

3. Recording both halves of the entry on the same side (two debit or two credit entries rather than one debit and one credit).
4. Recording one or more accounts incorrectly.
5. Arithmetic errors in a journal entry.
6. Arithmetic errors in balancing the accounts.
7. Errors made by putting an entry in the wrong account.

One technique used by experienced bookkeepers to find errors is to divide the difference between the debit side and the credit side by nine (9). If the amount of the difference is evenly divisible by 9, the discrepancy may either be a transposition ($432 for $423) or a slide ($423 for $42.30). Dividing the difference by two (2) may suggest that a credit was posted as a debit or vice versa.

Trial Income Statement and Balance Sheet: Workpaper Format

After you have posted the trial balance and it is accurate, you can then change the trial balance summary into the more usable form of an income statement and a balance sheet.

The trial balance extended for four more columns becomes the total workpaper. Notice (Figure 11.4) that a debit and credit column are added for the balance sheet.

The columns marked "Income Statement" and "Balance Sheet" are used to organize the figures needed for these financial reports.

Accounts 100, 200, and 300 (the asset, liability, and equity accounts) are carried over to the balance sheet columns. Accounts 400, 500, and 600 (the income, expense, and

ACCT.	ACCOUNT NAME	TRIAL DEBIT	BALANCE CREDIT
101	CASH		11091
111	ACCOUNTS RECEIVABLE	1980	
120	DEPOSITS	130	
130	PARTS INVENTORY	30000	
150.1	TEST EQUIPMENT	10000	
201	ACCOUNTS PAYABLE		3720
211.1	NOTES PAYABLE - BANK OF AMERIGOLD		25000
211.2	NOTES PAYABLE - ZARKOFF EQUIPMENT		5000
410	SYSTEM INCOME		3280
420	COMPONENT SALES		3429
430	RENTAL		700
508	RENTAL EXPENSE	1200	
510	TELEPHONE EXPENSE	300	
560	OFFICE SUPPLIES	150	
591	BUSINESS LICENSE	40	
601	INVENTORY PURCHASE	7220	
610	SUB-CONTRACT	1200	
	TOTALS	52220	52220

Figure 11.3   Completed trial balance with all the active accounts listed. Before proceeding further, the accountant must make sure that this balances.

cost of sales accoutns) are carried over to the income statement columns. Accounts that had *debit* amounts in the trial balance will continue to be recorded as *debits* when transferred to the income statement or balance sheet columns. Accounts that are listed as *credits* in the trial balance will continue to be listed as credits in either the balance sheet or the income statement columns.

ACCT.	ACCOUNT NAME	TRIAL DEBIT	BALANCE CREDIT	INCOME STATEMENT DEBIT	CREDIT	BALANCE DEBIT	SHEET CREDIT

Figure 11.4   Trial balance extended to include an income statement and a balance sheet set of columns.

X Company Balance Sheet and Income Statement Example

Figure 11.5 shows the trial balance from Figure 11.3 expanded into the balance sheet and income statement columns.

Income Statement.   The three income accounts system sales (410), component sales (420), and rental income (430) are moved to the credit side of the income statement. All

XCOMPANY WORKSHEET

ACCT.	ACCOUNT NAME	TRIAL DEBIT	BALANCE CREDIT	INCOME STATEMENT DEBIT	CREDIT	BALANCE DEBIT	SHEET CREDIT
101	CASH		11091			⟨11091⟩	
111	ACCTS. REC.	1980				1980	
120	DEPOSITS	130				130	
130	PARTS INVENTORY	30000				30000	
150.1	TEST EQUIP.	10000				10000	
201	ACCTS. PAY.		3720				3720
211.1	NOTES PAY.-B.A.		25000				25000
211.2	NOTES PAY.-Z.E.		5000				5000
410	SYSTEM INCOME		3280		3280		
420	COMPONENT SALES		3429		3429		
430	RENTAL INCOME		700		700		
508	RENTAL EXPENSE	1200		1200			
510	TELEPHONE	300		300			
560	OFFICE SUPPLIES	150		150			
591	BUS. LICENSE	40		40			
601	INVENTORY	7220		7220			
610	SUB-CONTRACT	1200		1200			
	TOTALS	52220	52220	10110	7409	31019	33720
					2701		⟨2701⟩
				10110	10110	31019	31019

Figure 11.5 Trial balance carried over from Figure 11.3 to include income statement and balance sheet grouping of accounts.

the expense accounts are moved to the debit side of the income statement. This includes rental expense, telephone expense, office supplies, and business licenses. Both of the cost of sales accounts—inventory purchases (601) and sub-contract work (610)—are moved to the debit side of the income statement.

Next you total both columns (debit and credit). You will notice from the example that the income statement totals do *not* balance. The total of the credit column (which is only the total of sales) is $7,409, which is $2,701 less than the debit total. The debit side total of the income statement is $10,110. This means that the expenses and cost of sales exceeded the sales. That is, the company has a net operating loss. Since expenses and cost of sales (the debit side) exceed sales (the credit side), the company has a net loss equal to the difference (a $2,701 loss).

This is somewhat misleading because X Company may have some of the inventory they purchased left over, total expenses do not include depreciation, and no allowance was made for bad debt. These are "adjustments" that I will discuss later.

Balance Sheet. All assets from the trial balance debit column are transfered to the balance sheet debit column. These assets include: cash (101), accounts receivable (111), deposits (122), parts inventory (130), and test equipment (150.1). All liabilities and equity accounts are transferred from the credit column of the trial balance to the credit column of the balance sheet. The liabilities that are transferred are accounts payable (201), notes payable—Bank of Amerigold (211.1), and notes payable—Zarkoff Equipment (211.2).

It is important to note that the cash balance of minus $11,091 (credit) is placed in the debit column as a negative entry. The reason for this is that it tells you your assets total more accurately than if you put the cash balance as a credit.

If you add up the debit column and the credit column of the balance sheet workpaper, you see that the liability and equity column (credit) exceeds the asset (debit) column. this is because there is a net loss of $2,701 which will be deducted from the company equity to make the balance sheet in balance. If the company had a profit, the two columns would also have different totals, but the asset column would be a larger number. Equity would have to be increased by the amount of the net profit to bring the totals into balance.

The balance sheet debit (asset) total is $31,019, and the credit column (liabilities and equity) total is $33,720. Subtract the amount of the net loss carried from the income statement ($2,701) from the credit side, and the totals come into balance at $31,019 each.

Again, this is not totally accurate. The ending inventory might be higher or lower than the beginning inventory (the $30,000 that X Company started with), and equipment should be depreciated.

ADJUSTMENTS TO ACCOUNTS

Before you add up the accounts and summarize them, there are some expenses that have to be calculated that only occur at the end of an accounting period. Depreciation and Bad debt expense must be calculated. Furthermore, in all businesses which do not have a "perpetual" inventory system, a physical count of inventory must be made.

At the end of the period, the following is usually true:

1. Equipment and fixtures are carried in their accounts at their original cost without regard for the usual wear and tear during the period or for what their salvage value will be if they are sold after a number of years.
2. The amount in the accounts receivable account might include some money that will not be collected by you in the future.
3. There is no recognition of merchandise you have in inventory that has not been sold by the end of the period.

Depreciation

Note the adjustments format (Figure 11.6). Two adjustments columns are added to the trial balance format.

The general ledger of X Company shows that the company has $10,000 worth of test equipment (account 150.1). In reality, of course, this test equipment experiences wear and tear. Accounting logic and the tax authorities allow this wear and tear to be taken into consideration and listed as an expense. This expense is called *depreciation*. Depreciation is unusual in that it is not a cash expense. It is an allowance for the decline in value of the equipment.

Because most equipment does not lose all of its value in one period, the loss in value is apportioned over a longer period—the useful life of the asset. The *useful life* of an asset (equipment) is a period of years after which the asset will be useless to the company and will, therefore, be sold. The IRS gives certain guidelines for depreciating different types of equipment and other assets in *Publication 534*. Generally, equipment averages about five to seven years of useful life.

In addition to a life of five years, X Company's test equipment will also have a value at the end of that time. This is the value that the equipment will bring if it is sold. Sale value is called the *salvage value*. Assume that in five years the test equipment will be worthless except for the sale value of the parts. This salvage value is about $500.

The depreciation is calculated as follows:

$$\text{equipment} - \text{salvage value} = \text{depreciable value}$$
$$\$10,000 - \$500 = \$9,500$$

$$\frac{\text{depreciable value}}{\text{useful life in years}} = \text{depreciation expense each year}$$
$$\frac{\$9,500}{5} = \$1,900$$

When the period for which the books are being closed is less than one year, the depreciation expense must be adjusted to reflect depreciation for a period of less than a year. In the X Company example the books are being closed for a one-month period. Therefore, the amount of depreciation for the year ($1,900) must be divided by 12 because the depreciation is for only one month. The general formula would be as follows:

$$\frac{\text{total depreciation for year}}{\text{number of periods in the year}} = \text{depreciation for that period}$$
$$\frac{\$1,900}{12} = \$158.33$$

If the period were three months (one quarter) the total depreciation would be divided by four (the number of three-month periods in a year).

When depreciation is calculated, it is entered in the adjustments column (see Figure 11.7) as a debit to Depreciation expense (595) and a credit to Allowance for depreciation (150.1A). Note that in my example both entries are labeled "(A)" so that they can be easily identified for future reference.

Bad Debt Expense

In any business there is always the probability that some accounts receivable will not be collected.

ACCT	ACCOUNT NAME	TRIAL BALANCE		ADJUSTMENTS	
		DEBIT	CREDIT	DEBIT	CREDIT

Figure 11.6   Adjustments must be made to the trial balance. Therefore this form illustrates the format of a trial balance with an adjustments column.

There are two methods for determining such *bad debt* loss. One method is to wait until the company is sure that the account of a specific customer is uncollectable, and then record the expense. An entry is made debiting the expense account, bad debt, and crediting the asset account, accounts receivable.

Another way to allow for this expense is to anticipate the losses and provide for them ahead of time. This is called an *allowance for bad debt*.

XCOMPANY WORKSHEET

ACCT.	ACCOUNT NAME	TRIAL BALANCE		ADJUSTMENTS			
		DEBIT	CREDIT	DEBIT		CREDIT	
101	CASH		11091				
111	ACCOUNTS RECEIVABLE	1980					
120	DEPOSITS	130					
130	PARTS INVENTORY	30000					
150.1	TEST EQUIPMENT	10000					
150.1A	ALLOWANCE FOR DEPRECIATION					(A)	15833
201	ACCOUNTS PAYABLE		3720				
211.1	NOTES PAYABLE – B.A.		25000				
211.2	NOTES PAYABLE – ZARKOFF		5000				
410	SYSTEM INCOME		3280				
420	COMPONENT SALES		3429				
430	RENTAL INCOME		700				
508	RENTAL EXPENSE	1200					
510	TELEPHONE	300					
560	OFFICE SUPPLIES	150					
591	BUSINESS LICENSE	40					
595	DEPRECIATION			(A)	15833		
601	INVENTORY	7220					
610	SUB-CONTRACT	1200					
	TOTALS	52220	52220				

Figure 11.7 Partially completed adjustments column using information from Figure 11.3.

Bad debt losses are estimated as a percentage of total credit sales. In some industries bad debt loss might be 10% and in others only 1% of credit sales. By using the industry experience or your own past experience you can create a bad debt account.

X Company's industry generally experiences a 3% loss on credit sales. We will use that figure:

Credit sales for the month	$2,055
Less: Sales returns and allowances	–0–
Net credit sales	$2,055
Times: Estimated percentage bad debt loss	×0.03
Estimated bad debts on January sales	$61.65

X Company's expected bad debt loss for January sales is $61.65, 3% of total credit sales ($2,055).

In Figure 11.8 the bad debt allowance and expense are added to the adjustments column. The amount of bad debt for the month is debited to bad debt expense (599) and credited to allowance for bad debt (111A). The allowance for bad debt (111A) is a reduction in accounts receivable.

Note that the two entries are marked with a (B) for later identification.

At this point, all the entries for the adjustments column have been made. We can now total the columns. Next we add three more sets of columns: the adjusted trial balance, income statement, and balance sheet (see Figure 11.9). The adjusted trial balance columns can now be completed by adding the debit and credit columns of the trial balance to the adjustments. All the entries of the trial balance are now combined with the entries from adjustments. See Figure 11.9.

There is still one more adjustment to be made to the working papers, but this will be made when the worksheet is extended to an income statement and balance sheet. The remaining adjustment is in the inventory asset and the cost of sales figure.

Inventory and Cost of Sales Adjustments

Before finishing the worksheet, you must recognize that some of the purchased merchandise has not yet been sold and is still on hand. For this reason the following steps must be taken:

1. The value of the merchandise that is unsold at the end of the period must be recorded as an addition to the asset inventory.
2. *Only* the cost of the merchandise sold should be recorded as part of the cost of sales.

Before any recording can be done, you must first determine how much inventory is on hand at the end of the period. That is, you must take inventory. This almost always require a physical count of the inventory. The result of this count is recorded on an *inventory sheet* that shows the type of item (description), the amount of that item (quantity), the unit cost, and the total. Luckily, X Company took a physical inventory last January. Figure 11.10 shows the result of the physical inventory that was taken at the end of January 1980.

Before we can go any further, we have to look at X Company's ending inventory for the end of year before last (1979). In order to get an accurate picture of the inventory at the end of January 1980, you need to know what it was at the beginning of January 1980. This information is on X Company's income tax for 1979. The income tax shows a closing inventory of $5,000.

The amount of inventory used during January is calculated as follows:

X COMPANY   WORKSHEET

ACCT.	ACCOUNT NAME	TRIAL BALANCE DEBIT	TRIAL BALANCE CREDIT	ADJUSTMENTS DEBIT	ADJUSTMENTS CREDIT
101	CASH		11091		
111	ACCOUNTS RECEIVABLE	1980			
111A	ALLOWANCE FOR BAD DEBT				(B) 6165
120	DEPOSITS	130			
130	PARTS INVENTORY	30000			
150.1	TEST EQUIPMENT	10000			
150.1A	ALLOWANCE FOR DEPRECIATION				(A) 15833
201	ACCOUNTS PAYABLE		3720		
211.1	NOTES PAYABLE – B.A.		25000		
211.2	NOTES PAYABLE – ZARKOFF		5000		
410	SYSTEM INCOME		3280		
420	COMPONENT SALES		3429		
430	RENTAL INCOME		700		
508	RENTAL EXPENSE	1200			
510	TELEPHONE	300			
560	OFFICE SUPPLIES	150			
591	BUSINESS LICENSE	40			
595	DEPRECIATION			(A) 15833	
599	BAD DEBT			(B) 6165	
601	INVENTORY	7220			
610	SUB-CONTRACT	1200			
	TOTALS	52220	52220	21998	21998

Figure 11.8   Worksheet showing completed adjustments and trial balance column.

Total Merchandise purchases (601)	$ 7,220
Plus: Subcontract work (610)	1,200
Plus: Parts inventory purchased (130)	30,000
Plus: Beginning inventory	5,000
Subtotal	43,420
Less: Ending inventory	39,620
	$ 3,800

XCOMPANY WORKSHEET — MONTH ENDING JANUARY 1980

ACCT.	ACCOUNT NAME	TRIAL BALANCE DEBIT	TRIAL BALANCE CREDIT	ADJUSTMENTS DEBIT	ADJUSTMENTS CREDIT	ADJUST. TRIAL BAL. DEBIT	ADJUST. TRIAL BAL. CREDIT	INCOME STATEMENT DEBIT	INCOME STATEMENT CREDIT	BALANCE SHEET DEBIT	BALANCE SHEET CREDIT
		1	2	3	4	5	6	7	8	9	10
101	CASH		11091				11091				
111	ACCTS. RECEIVABLE	1980				1980					
111A	ALLOW. BAD DEBT				(B) 6165		6165				
120	DEPOSITS	130				130					
130	PARTS INVENTORY	30000				30000					
150.1	TEST EQUIPMENT	10000				10000				(c) 39620	
150.1A	ALLOW. DEPRECIATION				(A) 15833		15833		(c) 39620		
1201	ACCTS. PAYABLE		3720				3720				
2161	NOTES PAY - B.A.		25000				25000				
2162	NOTES PAY - ZARKOFF		5000				5000				
410	SYSTEM INCOME		3280				3280				
420	COMPONENT SALES		3429				3429				
430	RENTAL INCOME		700				700				
508	RENTAL EXPENSE	1200				1200					
510	TELEPHONE	300				300					
560	OFFICE SUPPLIES	150				150					
591	BUSINESS LICENSE	40				40					
595	DEPRECIATION			(A) 15833		15833					
599	BAD DEBT			(B) 6165		6165					
601	INVENTORY	7220				7220					
610	SUB-CONTRACT	1200				1200					
	TOTALS	52220	52220	21998	21998	5243998	5243998				

Figure 11.9 Entire trial balance, income statement, balance sheet, and adjustments.

	X COMPANY		
	INVENTORY SHEET		
	JANUARY 31, 1980		
QUANTITY	DESCRIPTION	UNIT COST	TOTAL
100	Z-90 chips	$100/ea.	$10,000
200	breadboards	$3/ea	600
89	misc. I.C.'s	$25/ea	2,225
70 boxes	screws	.50/ea	35
60 cases	X-198 I.C.'s	$30/ea	18,000
510	V-196-X12 assemblies	$26.66/ea	8,760
			$39,620
COUNTED BY: Harris		CHECKED BY: O.S.	

Figure 11.10 Sample inventory sheet showing inventory as counted at the end of the period.

Recording Inventory Adjustments on the Worksheet

The adjustments to inventory are recorded directly on the income statement and balance sheet areas of the worksheet (see Figure 11.11). The value of the closing inventory ($39,620) is recorded on the Parts inventory line in the *debit* column of the balance sheet. The entry is marked "(C)" for identification.

The other part of the entry is a little more difficult to see. The other entry will be a *credit* entry of $39,620 (the amount of the ending inventory) to the income statement. Also the beginning inventory of $35,000 (the $30,000 purchase plus beginning inventory of $5,000) is entered but as a *debit* to the income statement. These entries will have the effect of reducing the cost of sales° by the amount of inventory that was not sold. There is already an entry of $7,200 for the amount of inventory purchased (inventory purchases, 601). The credit entry of $39,620 and the debit entry of $30,000 will reduce the effective cost of merchandise sold.

The entry of the inventory purchased but not sold in the credit column is like the cost of goods sold calculation:

°Cost of sales is the cost of the merchandise sold during the period.

XCOMPANY   WORKSHEET - MONTH ENDING JANUARY 1980

ACCT.	ACCOUNT NAME	TRIAL BALANCE DEBIT	TRIAL BALANCE CREDIT	ADJUSTMENTS DEBIT	ADJUSTMENTS CREDIT	ADJUST. TRIAL BAL. DEBIT	ADJUST. TRIAL BAL. CREDIT	INCOME STATEMENT DEBIT	INCOME STATEMENT CREDIT	BALANCE SHEET DEBIT	BALANCE SHEET CREDIT
101	CASH	1980				1980				1980	
111	ACCTS. RECEIVABLE		11091				11091				11091
111A	ALLOW. BAD DEBT				(B) 6165		6165				6165
120	DEPOSITS	130				130				130	
130	PARTS INVENTORY	30000				30000		35000	(c) 39620	(c) 39620	
150.1	TEST EQUIPMENT	10000				10000				10000	
150.1A	ALLOW. DEPRECIATION				(A) 15833		15833				15833
201	ACCTS. PAYABLE		3720				3720				3720
211.1	NOTES PAY. - B.A.		25000				25000				25000
211.2	NOTES PAY-ZARKOFF		5000				5000				5000
300	EQUITY		5000				5000				5000
410	SYSTEM INCOME		3280				3280		3280		
420	COMPONENT SALES		3429				3429		3429		
430	RENTAL INCOME		700				700		700		
508	RENTAL EXPENSE	1200				1200		1200			
510	TELEPHONE	300				300		300			
560	OFFICE SUPPLIES	150				150		150			
591	BUSINESS LICENSE	40				40		40			
595	DEPRECIATION			(A) 15833		15833		15833			
599	BAD DEBT			(B) 6165		6165		6165			
601	INVENTORY	7220				7220		7220			
610	SUB-CONTRACT	1200				1200		1200			
	TOTALS	52220	52220	21998	21998	5243998	5243998	4532998	47029	51730	5003098
	NET PROFIT FOR MONTH							169902			169922
	TOTAL							47029	47029	51730	51730

Figure 11.11   The completed worksheet.

Merchandise purchases (601)	$ 7,220
Plus: Subcontract (610)	1,200
Plus: Inventory purchases (130)	30,000
Plus: Beginning inventory	5,000
Less: Ending inventory	39,620
Cost of goods sold	$ 3,800

Completing the Worksheet

The following steps are now taken to complete the worksheet (see Figure 11.11).

1. Carry over the balances from assets, liabilities, and equity (100, 200, and 300 accounts) to the balance sheet.
2. Carry over the balances from income, expenses, and cost of sales (accounts 400, 500, and 600) to the income statement.
3. Total all the columns. The Income Statement and the Balance Sheet will both have different amounts in the debit and credit columns. This difference represents X Company's net profit. On the income statement the debit column expenses and cost of sales totals to $45,329.98 and the credit column (income and inventory adjustments to cost of sales) equals $47,029. The difference between $47,029 (the credit total) and $45,329.98 (the debit total) is $1,699.02. This amount represents the *net profit* and is added to the debit side to bring the columns in balance. Similarly, the balance sheet debit and credit columns do not balance when they are first totaled. If the $1,699.02 net profit from the income statement is carried over and entered in the balance sheet's credit column, the totals will both equal $51,730. This is because net profit is actually an addition to Owner's Equity.

"You may notice that the $5,000 beginning X Company inventory is listed as Owner's equity. This is because X Company had this much at the beginning of the year.

Flow Diagram of Closing Procedures

Closing the books is not difficult, but it does require several steps. This diagram (Figure 11.12) summarizes the procedure step by step.

Step 1 is to determine the debit or credit balances in each of the ledger accounts. This is done by adding both columns in each account and calculating the difference (subtracting one from the other). The column that has the higher total will have this difference written in the explanation space (see Figure 11.2).

Step 2 requires that the balance in each account be entered in either the debit or credit column of a trial balance of the ledger accounts (see Figure 11.3).

Step 3 is to adjust for depreciation and bad debt in the adjusted trial balance columns in the worksheet (see Figures 11.7 and 11.8).

Step 4 is to extend the trial balance figures over to the adjusted trial balance (see Figure 11.9).

Step 5 is to make the inventory adjustments to the income statement and balance sheet columns of the worksheet (see Figure 11.11).

Step 6 extends all the totals from the adjusted trial balance to the income statement and balance sheet columns (see Figure 11.11).

Step 7 is to make all the closing entries in the general journal and the ledgers.

Figure 11.13 is an example of an end-of-the-period journal entry, closing various income and expense accounts to the Income and expense summary, an equity account.

Step	Action
1	Total debit and credit balances in all accounts
2	Enter account balances in trial balances
3	Adjust for depreciation and bad debt on adjusted trial balances
4	Extend trial balance figures to adjusted trial balance
5	Make inventory adjustments to income statement and balance sheet columns of worksheet
6	Extend totals from adjusted trial balance columns to income statement and balance sheet columns
7	Make all closing entries in general journal and ledgers

Figure 11.12   Steps to closing the books. Note comments in text.

Date		Debit	Credit
12/31/79	Income	$150,000	
	Income and expense summary		$150,000
	Income and expense summary	142,000	
	Merchandise purchases		120,000
	Salary expense		10,000
	Rental expense		4,000
	Utilities		2,000
	Supplies		1,000
	Taxes		500
	Accounting		1,200
	Entertainment		2,300
	Transportation and travel		1,000
	To record transfer of accounts to income and expense summary.		

Figure 11.13   An end-of-the-period closing journal entry.

For a sole proprietorship, the closing entries in the general ledger are as follows:

1. If you have a profit, the amount of the profit is entered as a debit in the profit and loss summary account and as a credit in the proprietor's capital account

2. If you have a loss, the profit and loss summary account is credited and the proprietor's capital account is debited.

3. The total of the proprietor's drawings account is then credited to that account and debited to the proprietor's capital account.

These entries reduce the profit and loss summary and proprietor's drawings account to zero.

1. For a net profit:
       Profit and loss summary
           Proprietor's capital

2. For a net loss:
       Proprietor's capital
           Profit and loss summary

3. To close the account:
       Proprietor's capital
           Proprietor's drawings

Ms. Lane was about to ask the students if there were any questions, but Udjat stopped her. "Before you answer any questions, Ms. Lane, why don't we all go on a break?" Udjat had noticed that the students were starting to become restless, and his perceptions were accurate. By the time he finished his sentence, two students were already out the door.

"Thank you for coming, Penny," Udjat said to Ms. Lane when most of the students had left the room.

"I'm not being boring, am I?" she asked.

"Not at all," Udjat replied. "As always, you have good, practical information to pass on to the students. Can I get you a cup of coffee or something to munch on from the snack bar?"

"Oh, no thank you," Ms. Lane replied. "I brought my own tea." Ms. Lane was eager to go on by the time the students all returned. She cleared her throat and began.

BUSINESS FINANCIAL STATEMENTS

Business financial statements include:
* The income statement (profit and loss statement)
* The statement of financial condition (balance sheet)
* statement of retained earnings and funds flow statement.

The financial statements are the culmination of the accounting process. They are also the beginnings for finance. These statements are the summary of all the activity that has happened in the business during the period.

The most used of the financial statements is the income statement—the IRS requires an income statement for all businesses. The income statement is a summary of money that came into the business (revenue or income), money that was spent (cost of sales and expenses), and money that remained after costs were paid (net profit).

The next most widely used financial statement is the balance sheet. The IRS does not require that partnerships and proprietorships file a balance sheet with their income tax returns. Due to the lack of IRS-required balance sheets, many small businesses do not understand or use the balance sheet. The balance sheet is a summary of how much the business owns (assets), how much it owes (liabilities), and how much of the owner's money is invested (equity).

Let's assume that there are two photograhers assigned to document the last trip of the Wabash Cannonball. One photographer chooses to use a 35-mm still camera. The other will use a movie camera.

The Wabash Cannonball heads through the countryside and the still photographer waits at the Copper Canyon Bridge. When the Wabash arrives at the bridge, the still photographer takes a snapshot of the train. This is a picture of the Wabash at one moment in time.

The movie photographer, on the other hand, travels alongside the train and takes a movie of it from the time it leaves the station until it arrives at the Copper Canyon Bridge. This is a picture of the train over a period of time.

The still photo is similar to a balance sheet. The photo is a picture of the Wabash at one moment in time. The balance sheet is a picture of a business at one moment in time—at the end of a period. It shows how many assets the business has, how much it owes, and how much the owner(s) have at a certain date.

The movie of the Wabash Cannonball from the station to the Copper Canyon Bridge is like the income statement. The income statement measures costs and expenses against sales revenues over a period of time. The income statement shows the operation of the business and the profit over an *entire period*.

Since the balance sheet is a statement of one moment in time, it is headed with the date. For example:

X Company
Statement of Financial Condition
January 31, 1980

The income statement, on the other hand, is for a continuous period ending on the date of the financial statement. Therefore, the income statement date is prefaced with the words 'for the period ending. . . .' For example:

X Company
Income Statement
For the One-Month Period Ending January 31, 1980

The *statement of retained earnings* and the *funds flow statement* are not used as frequently as the balance sheet and income statement. The IRS does *not* require the statement of retained earnings or funds flow statement to be included in any business's income tax. However, for an audited statement generally accepted accounting principles require that these financial statements be included.

Retained earnings is the amount of money that is *retained* from net profit to be reinvested in the business. Retained earnings are what remains of the net profit after tax, dividends, owner's draw, principal loan repayment, and other items are deducted. *Funds* are defined as either the amount of working capital (current assets minus current liabilities) or cash.

By stretching the Wabash Cannonball example, you can see what the statement of retained earnings and the funds flow statement measure in a business. Assume that the Wabash has a certain amount of coal to fire the engine when it starts and along the track it occasionally picks up more coal as it gets low. The coal is constantly consumed and must be replaced. Besides using the coal for the engine, the engineer may use it to heat the train or he may carve statues from it for the tourist trade.

At the beginning of the train trip, the Wabash has a certain amount of coal and en route it obtains more. During the trip it uses a certain amount and at the end it will have some coal left over. The engineer keeps an account book summarizing all the sources and uses of coal.

The statement of retained earnings and the funds flow statement are like the engineer's account book. Instead of coal, a business uses cash, working capital, and long-term capital. The statements are a summary of the sources and uses of cash, working capital, and long-term capital.

The Income Statement

An income statement, commonly called a *profit and loss statement*, consists of income, cost of sales, and expense accounts. Gross profit (gross margin) is the difference between income and cost of sales. The gross profit is the difference between income and cost of sales. The net profit is the difference between gross profit and operating expenses. Gross profit and net profit are income statement amounts that are calculated.

Here is a graphic presentation of an income statement (Figure 11.14). The account groups used (income, cost of sales, and operating expense) have amounts that come directly from the company's general ledger. By subtracting cost of sales from income, the result is the gross margin (gross profit). If you subtract the operating expense from the gross margin the result is net profit. An income statement is usually presented in the following format:

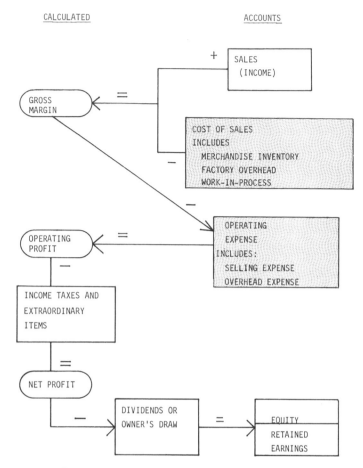

Figure 11.14   **A graphic presentation of the income statement dividing into accounts on which journals are kept and calculated numbers. For example, sales minus cost of sales equals gross margin. Gross margin minus expenses equals net profit. Net operating profit minus income tax, etc. equals net profit after tax. Dividends are paid out of net profit and the balance goes to the equity section of the balance sheet (retained earnings.)**

	Income
Less:	Cost of sales
Equals:	Gross margin
Less:	Operating expense
Equals:	Net profit

Example.   Zip Tips Company has $100,000 in sales for the year. Zip has $60,000 in costs of sales and $30,000 in operating expense. Their income statement would be calculated as follows:

Sales	$100,000
Cost of sales	60,000
Gross margin	40,000
Operating expense	30,000
Net profit	$10,000

You can also see (Figure 11.14) that some costs, such as taxes, principal loan repayment, and owner's salary or dividends, come out of net profit. Whatever remains after these costs are deducted from net profit becomes *retained earnings*, which is part of the owner's equity on the balance sheet.

Figures 11.15, 11.16, 11.17, and 11.18 show a cross section of income statements from various industries. Notice that the Monar Company income statement (Figure 11.15) is for a retail store which has only one figure for cost of sales. The Wald Wholesale Company (a wholeseller) (Figure 11.16) has a more complex statement of cost of goods sold. They include beginning inventory, purchases, freight, and ending

The MONAR Company
Profit and Loss Statement
For the Year Ended December 31, 19—

Sales		$120,000
Cost of goods sold		70,000
Gross margin		$ 50,000
Selling expenses:		
Salaries	$15,000	
Commission	5,000	
Advertising	5,000	
Total selling expenses		25,000
Selling margin		$ 25,000
Administrative expenses		10,000
Net profit		$ 15,000

Figure 11.15   Income statement (profit and loss) on a simplified basis.

Wald Wholesale Company
Profit and Loss Statement
For the Year Ended December 31, 19—

Net sales			$666,720
Cost of goods sold			
Beginning inventory, January 1, 19—		$184,350	
Merchandise purchases	$454,920		
Freight and drayage	30,210	485,130	
Cost of goods available for sale		$669,480	
Less ending inventory, December 31, 19—		193,710	
Cost of goods sold			475,770
Gross margin			$190,950
Selling, administrative, and general expenses			
Salaries and wages		$ 88,170	
Rent		24,390	
Light, heat, and power		8,840	
Other expenses		21,300	
State and local taxes and licenses		5,130	
Depreciation and amortization on leasehold improvements		4,140	
Repairs		2,110	
Total selling, administrative, and general expenses			154,080
Profit from operations			$ 36,870
Other income		$ 7,550	
Other expense		1,740	5,810
Net profit before taxes			$ 42,680
Provision for income tax			15,120
			$ 27,560
Net profit after income tax			127,560

Figure 11.16   A more detailed income statement from a wholesaler.

Hayes Manufacturing Company
Profit and Loss Statement
For the Year Ended December 31, 19—

Net sales			$669,100
Cost of goods sold			
Finished goods inventory, January 1, 19—		$ 69,200	
Cost of goods manufactured (exhibit 6)		569,700	
Total cost of goods available for sale		$638,900	
Less finished goods inventory, December 31, 19—		66,400	
Cost of goods sold			572,500
Gross margin			$ 96,600
Selling and administrative expenses:			
Selling expenses			
Sales salaries and commissions	$26,700		
Advertising expense	12,900		
Miscellaneous selling expense	2,100		
Total selling expenses		$ 41,700	
Administrative expenses			
Salaries	$27,400		
Miscellaneous administrative expense	4,800		
Total administrative expenses		32,200	
Total selling and administrative expenses			73,900
Net operating profit			$ 22,700
Other revenue			15,300
Net profit before taxes			$ 38,000
Estimated income tax			12,640
Net profit after income tax			$ 25,350

Figure 11.17 Sample income statement of a manufacturer.

Hayes Manufacturing Company
Statement of Cost of Goods Manufactured
For the Year Ended December 31, 19—

Work in process inventory, January 1, 19—			$ 18,800
Raw materials			
Inventory, January 1, 19—		$154,300	
Purchases		263,520	
Freight in		9,400	
Cost of materials available for use		$427,220	
Less inventory, December 31, 19—		163,120	
Cost of materials used		$264,100	
Direct labor		150,650	
Manufacturing overhead			
Indirect labor	$23,750		
Factory heat, light, and power	89,500		
Factory supplies used	22,100		
Insurance and taxes	8,100		
Depreciation of plant and equipment	35,300		
Total manufacturing overhead		178,750	
Total manufacturing cost			593,500
Total work in process during period			$612,300
Less work in process inventory, December 31, 19—			42,600
Cost of goods manufactured			569,700

Figure 11.18 Manufacturing company (Hayes) showing detail of cost of sales figures on figure 11.17.

inventory in their cost of sales. The Hayes Manufacturing Company (Figure 11.17) has a cost of sales that is even more complex. For this reason, they included a separate cost of goods schedule (Figure 11.18).

Income statements of various industries differ primarily in their reporting of cost of sales. Service industries generally have *no* cost of sales, whereas retail, wholesale, and manufacturing have cost of sales.

The Balance Sheet

A balance sheet (statement of Financial Condition) is a summary of what a business owns (assets) and what claims there are against those assets (liabilities = creditors' claims, and equity = the owner's claim). The balance sheet is the financial summary in the form of the basic accounting equation:

ASSETS = LIABILITIES + EQUITY

The balance sheet is based on historical costs. Assets are stated on the balance sheet at their original cost less any depreciation. Common and preferred stock recorded at the original amount received for the stock. Liabilities are recorded at the amount presently (at the end of that accounting period) owed. Historical costs are used because they reduce to a minimum the extent to which the accounts are affected by the personal opinions of the owners.

Balance Sheet Examples. Figure 11.19 shows the three account groups that make up the balance sheet: Assets, liabilities, and equity. Notice that there is no computation required for a balance sheet as there is for an income statement. The statement is fully represented by the accounts on the books. Notice also from the illustration that "retained earnings" from the income statement is incorporated into the equity position.

Figure 11.20 presents a sample balance sheet for Fatcat, Inc. This illustration shows

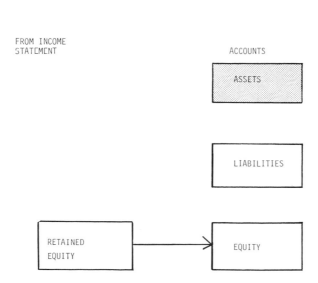

Figure 11.19 Three account groups that make up a balance sheet.

Balance Sheet of
Fatcat, Inc.
December 31, 19—

Assets:

Current assets

Cash	$ 12,000	
Accounts receivable	119,000	
Notes receivable	7,800	
Inventories at cost (LIFO)	235,200	
Prepaid assets	26,000	
Total current assets		$ 400,000

Fixed assets

Land	45,000	
Buildings and improvements	230,000	
Equipment and vehicles	497,000	
Furniture and fixtures	31,456	
Less: Accumulated deprec.	(212,456)	
Total fixed assets		$ 591,000

Other assets

Investment in subsidiaries	49,000	
Goodwill	76,000	
Research and development	82,000	
Less: R&D amortization	(51,000)	
Total other assets		$ 156,000
Total assets		$1,147,000

Liabilities

Current liabilities

Accounts payable	$ 98,500	
Notes payable	7,340	
Accrued taxes	103,182	
Accrued salaries	10,340	
Provision for pensions	56,300	
Total current liabilities		$ 275,662

Long-term liabilities:

Notes payable	28,503	
Bonds (8½% due 1985)	310,635	
Total long-term liabilities		$ 339,138
Total liabilities		$ 611,800

Equity

Capital stock	100,000	
Paid-in surplus	120,000	
Retained earnings	315,200	
Total equity		$ 535,200
Total liabilities and equity		$1,147,000

Figure 11.20   Sample balance sheet.

the typical categories and items of a balance sheet. Assets are on the left (or are presented first), and liabilities and equity are on the right (or are presented last). The first items of assets are the current assets. The first items presented in liabilities are the current liabilities. Current assets are assets that can be converted to cash within one year. Current liabilities also reflect a one-year period, but they are debts which must be repaid within the next year.

Current assets are followed by a group of assets called fixed assets and by another group called other assets. Fixed assets are assets which will remain for more than one year and generally (with the exception of land) are depreciable or amortizable assets.

Other assets are not owned by every company. They are assets that cannot be converted to cash within one year and are usually not depreciable or amortizable. Other assets include such assets as patents and intangibles which are amortized.

Following current liabilities are long-term liabilities. Long-term liabilities are debts that will take more than one year to repay. In accounting, more than one year is considered long-term.

The equity (or capital) portion of the balance sheet shows the basic components of the owners' investment and retention of capital in the business: stock, paid-in surplus, and retained earnings. In proprietorships and partnerships, this section may just contain the owners' cumulative equity in the business (owners' equity) and the retained earnings for that period (sometimes just stated as net profit).

Statement of Retained Earnings and Funds Flow Statement

The major difference between a statement of retained earnings and a funds flow statement is that the first is only concerned with determining retained earnings at the *end of a period*. The funds flow statement includes the results of the statement of retained earnings, but it *also* goes further by tracking down every movement of cash *during* the period.

The statement of retained earnings shows the retained earnings at the beginning of a period, the adjustments to retained earnings during the period, and the retained earnings calculated for the end of the period.

The purpose of the funds flow statement is to trace the flow of working capital during the accounting period.

Neither the statement of retained earnings nor the funds flow statement is required for income tax purposes, but one or the other or both are required by the generally accepted accounting principles set down by the American Institute of Certified Public Accountants (AICPA), the rule-making body of American CPAs.

Statement of Retained Earnings

Most corporations are required to show their retained earnings in a statement of retained earnings. This financial statement shows the retained earnings at the beginning of the period (the end of the *last* period), adjustments made during the accounting period, and what the retained earnings are at the end of the present period.

Adjustment made during the period include:

1. Profit or loss from period after taxes.
2. Dividends or owner's draw.
3. Principal loan repayment.
4. Adjustments or charges or credits resulting from transactions in the company's own capital stock (buying treasury stock or selling stock).
5. Transfers to and from accounts properly designated as appropriated retained earnings, such as contingency reserves or provisions for replacement costs of fixed assets.
6. Adjustments made pursuant to a quasi reorganization.

Statement of Retained Earnings Design and Examples

Figure 11.21 shows the general design of the statement of retained earnings. The illustration is divided into three parts labeled from income statement, cash costs (-) or inflow (+), and from balance sheet. From the balance sheet comes the (1) retained

STATEMENT OF RETAINED EARNINGS

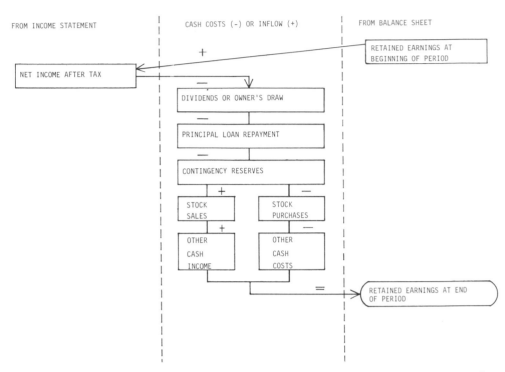

Figure 11.21   Sample design of statement of retained earnings. This statement ties together activity from the income statement through cash flow to the balance sheet.

earnings for the last period (the beginning of this period) and (2) the calculated retained earnings from this period (circled in the illustration). All adjustments to retained earnings except "net income after tax" are from cash funds and do not appear either on the income statement or on the balance sheet (except as a decrease or increase to the cash asset). In the illustration, a plus sign (+) indicates that that item is added to retained earnings from the beginning of the period, and a minus sign (−) indicates that items are subtracted.

| | For the Year Ending | |
	Dec. 31, 1979	Dec. 31, 1980
Retained earnings at beginning of the period	$100,320	$212,431
Net income for period	112,111	157,900
Common stock divided—5% (4,320 shares and $435 cash for partial shares)	-0-	$ 43,645
Retained earnings at end of period	$212,431	$326,696

Figure 11.22   Example of statement of retained earnings.

The Funds Flow Statement

Publicly held companies are now required to have a funds flow statement along with their income statement and balance sheet. The funds flow statement traces the flow of working capital during the accounting period. *Working capital* is the excess of current assets over current liabilities.

The funds flow statement answers some of the following questions.

1. Where did profits go?
2. Why were dividends not larger in view of the profits made?
3. How was it possible to distribute dividends when the company has a net operating loss?
4. How was the expansion in plant and equipment financed?
5. What happened to the sale of additional stock and the proceeds from the sale of fixed assets?
6. How was the retirement of debt accomplished?
7. What brought the increase or decrease in working capital?

Figure 11.23 shows how the funds flow statement can be divided into sources of funds (working capital) and application (uses) of funds. Notice that working capital is a *source* of funds when there is: (1) an *increase* in liabilities or owner's equity or (2) a *decrease* in fixed assets. Funds are used *(applied)* when there is: (1) a *decrease* in liabilities or owner's equity or (2) an *increase* in fixed assets.

Examples of sources of funds are loans and mortgages, injection of ownership cash into the business (stock or owners' injection), or an increase in retained earnings from the previous year (from statement of retained earnings). Funds sources also include a decrease in fixed assets, such as sales of equipment and other fixed assets, and the ongoing depreciation expense.

Funds are used (applied) by paying off loans and mortgages (decreasing liabilities), withdrawals by owners through dividends or owners' draw, or by decreases in retained earnings resulting from net losses or large nonoperating cash expenditures. Funds are

---

FUNDS FLOW STATEMENT

Sources of Funds	Application of Funds
Increase in liabilities	*Decrease* in Liabilities
Loans	Pay-off loans
Mortgages	Pay-off mortgages
Increase in owner's equity:	*Decrease* in owner's equity
Owner cash injection	Withdrawals by owners
Stock sales	Decrease in retained earnings
Increase in retained earnings	Net loss
Decrease in fixed assets	*Increase* in fixed assets
Sale of fixed assets	Purchase equipment, furniture
Depreciation	and fixtures, land and buildings,
	and leasehold improvements

Figure 11.23 Sources of funds and uses of funds and their causes.

ACME Mousetraps, Inc.
Funds Statement
For the Period Ending Dec. 31, 19—

Sources of Funds

Operations

Net income	$25,316	
Add depreciation	5,720	$31,036
Sale of stock		10,000
Total sources		$41,036

Use of Funds

Purchase of fixed assets	$ 4,750	
Cash dividends paid	10,000	
Retirement of long-term debt	17,812	$32,562
Net increase in working capital		$ 8,474

Figure 11.24   Example of a funds flow statement.

also used by increasing fixed assets through purchase of equipment, building and so on.

SUMMARY

"I would like to summarize." Ms. Lane took a sip of tea. "At the end of an accounting period all the accounts (assets, liabilities, equity, income, expenses, and cost of sales) have to be totaled and summarized. The summarizing process performed on a business's book is called 'closing the book.'

"The basic assumptions of accounting are: (1) businesses are ongoing entities with unlimited life, (2) businesses require an accounting of their ventures at least once per year, and (3) a business has some accounts (cyclical or temporary) that are closed each year and others (permanant) that are never closed.

"All the account totals are transferred to accounting working papers called the trial balance. It is called a trial balance because you want to test to see if the total of all the debit balance accounts (assets, expense, and cost of sales) equals the total of the credit accounts (liabilities, equity, and income), that is they balance. If the total debits do not equal the total credits, all accounts must be reexamined to determine where the error was made.

"Once the total debits equal the total credits, the accounts are divided between the balance sheet (assets, liabilities, and equity) and the income statement accounts (income, cost of sales, and expenses). When this is done, adjustments are made to the income statement and the balance sheet. The adjustments are made with regard to depreciation, bad debt losses, and inventory/cost of sales.

"The closing process has these steps: (1) total all accounts, (2) enter account balances on the trial balance and check for accuracy, (3) adjust for depreciation and bad debt, (4) extend trial balance to adjusted trial balance, (5) make inventory adjustment to come statement and balance sheet, (6) extend totals from adjusted trial balance to income statement and balance sheet columns, and (7) make all closing entries in the general journal and ledgers.

"Financial statements include the income statement, the statement of financial condition (balance sheet), and the statement of retained earnings. These financial statements are the culmination of accounting, the beginnings of finance. The income statement measures total costs and expenses against sales revenues over a period of time. The balance sheet is for one moment in time. Retained earnings is the amount of money that is retained after all the costs (including taxes and owner payments) are deduced from profit.

Ms. Lane paused and slowly looked at the classroom full of bright faces—all accountants and computer people. "You are all in professions requiring that a great deal of information be learned and used every day. Outsiders hear you talk in computerese or accounting metaphors and don't understand what you are saying. So naturally they think that you are wise. 'He's a computer genius,' they say; 'She is a tax whiz.' But don't delude yourselves. Information is not wisdom. This information must be synthesized and made useful.

"People who need information always suppose they need wisdom. If they really possess information, they will see that they next need wisdom. When you are possessed of wisdom, only then are you free from the need for information."

Appendix
Account Interaction

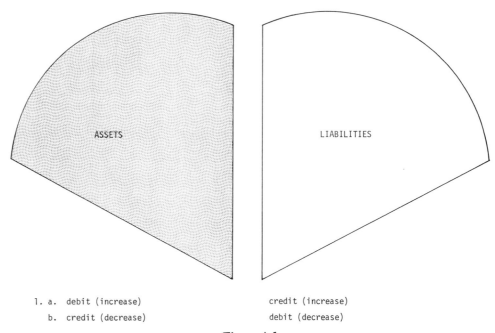

1. a. debit (increase)   credit (increase)
   b. credit (decrease)   debit (decrease)

Figure A.1

2. Transactions between Equity and Assets

3. Transactions between Equity and Liabilities

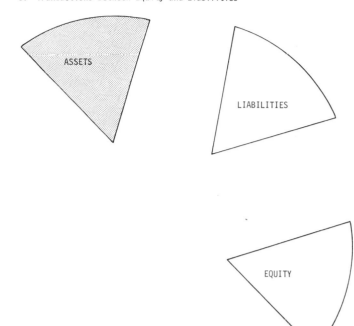

2. a. debit (increase)   credit (increase)

   b. credit (decrease)   debit (decrease)

3. No transactions

Figure A.2

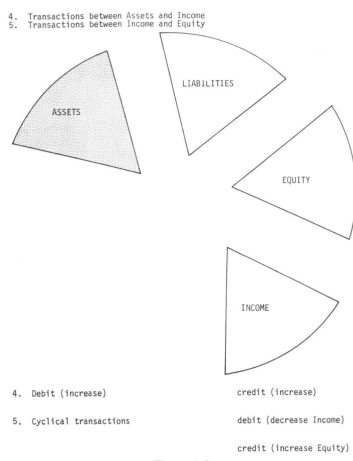

4. Transactions between Assets and Income
5. Transactions between Income and Equity

4. Debit (increase)   credit (increase)

5. Cyclical transactions   debit (decrease Income)

                                       credit (increase Equity)

Figure A.3

6. Transactions between Cost of Sales and Assets
7. Transactions between Cost of Sales and Equity
8. Transactions between Cost of Sales and Liabilities

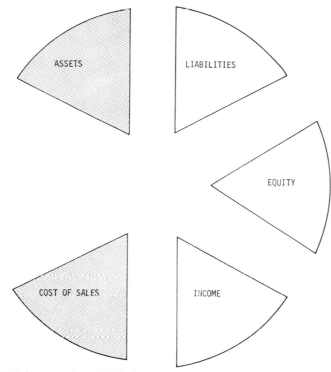

6. a. debit (increase Cost of Sales)
        credit (decrease Assets)
    b. cyclical transaction

7. cyclical - credit (decrease)   debit (decrease)

8. debit (increase)   credit (increase)

Figure A.4

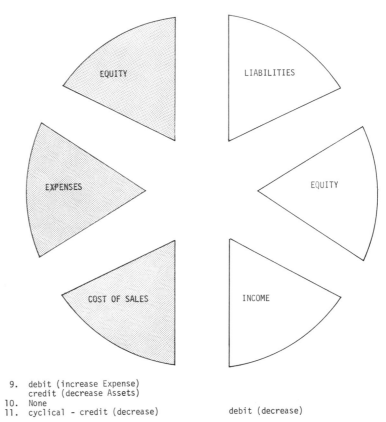

9. debit (increase Expense)
   credit (decrease Assets)
10. None
11. cyclical - credit (decrease)   debit (decrease)

Figure A.5

Index